John B. Jones

The War-Path

A narrative of adventures in the wilderness: withminute details of the captivity of sundry persons, amusing and perilous incients during their abode in the wild woods, fearful battles with the indians

John B. Jones

The War-Path
A narrative of adventures in the wilderness: withminute details of the captivity of sundry persons, amusing and perilous incients during their abode in the wild woods, fearful battles with the indians

ISBN/EAN: 9783337084523

Printed in Europe, USA, Canada, Australia, Japan

Cover: Foto ©Andreas Hilbeck / pixelio.de

More available books at **www.hansebooks.com**

THE DEATH OF CHARLES.—P. 329.

WILD WESTERN SCENES.—SECOND SERIES.

THE
WAR-PATH:

A NARRATIVE
OF
ADVENTURES IN THE WILDERNESS:

WITH MINUTE DETAILS OF THE CAPTIVITY OF SUNDRY PERSONS;

AMUSING AND PERILOUS INCIDENTS DURING THEIR ABODE IN THE WILD WOODS;

FEARFUL BATTLES WITH THE INDIANS;

Ceremony of Adoption into an Indian Family;

ENCOUNTERS WITH WILD BEASTS AND RATTLESNAKES, &c.

> Ye who love a nation's legends,
> Love the ballads of a people,
> That like voices from afar off
> Call to us to pause and listen,—
> * * * * * *
> Listen to this Indian Legend!
> *Song of Hiawatha.*

By J. B. JONES,
AUTHOR OF "WILD WESTERN SCENES," FIRST SERIES—"THE WINKLES," ETC.

Illustrated with Engravings from Original Designs.

PHILADELPHIA:
J. B. LIPPINCOTT & CO.
1870.

Entered according to the Act of Congress, in the year 1856, by
J. B. JONES,
in the Clerk's Office of the District Court of the United States for the Eastern District of Pennsylvania.

PRINCIPAL CHARACTERS OF THE NARRATIVE.

WILLIAM FRANKLIN, *Governor.*
OLD MR. CAMERON, *the Exile.*
CHARLES, *his son.*
THOMAS SCHOOLEY, *Quaker.*
RICHARD, *his son.*
DAVID JONES, *Baptist missionary.*
SAMUEL GREEN, *surveyor.*
DANIEL BOONE, *the Pioneer.*
SIMON KENTON, *the Scout.*
HUGH MCSWINE, *a bloody Indian-fighter.*
SKIPPIE, *a Scotch messenger.*
BONNEL MOODY, *a Tory.*
JOHN BROWN, *innkeeper.*
WILL VAN WIGGENS, *a blacksmith.*
PETER SHAVER, *an overseer.*
PADDY PENCE, *coachman and gardener.*
SIMON GIRTY, *a renegade.*
THAYENDANEGEA, *a Mohawk sachem.*
WILTED GRASS, *a Delaware youth.*
ST. TAMMANY, *aged Delaware chief.*
GROUND-HOG,   } *Warriors.*
BLUE PIGEON, etc., }
MARY SCHOOLEY, *Thomas's wife.*
JULIA LANE, *Thomas's ward.*
KATE LIVINGSTON, *Julia's friend.*
JOAN, *Van Wiggens's wife.*
MARY BOONE,   } *Kentucky girls.*
SUE CALLOWAY,   }
ESTHER, *Queen of the Senecas.*
GENTLE MOONLIGHT, *Brandt's aunt.*
BROWN THRUSH, *Bandt's sister.*
DIVING DUCK, *an old squaw.*
ROSE, *Julia's old nurse.*
SOLO, *Julia's Newfoundland dog.*
WATCH, *Van Wiggens's mongrel cur.*
A JACKASS.

SCENES IN NEW JERSEY, NEW YORK, PENNSYLVANIA, OHIO, AND KENTUCKY.

WILD WESTERN SCENES:

SECOND SERIES.

CHAPTER I.

BEGINNING OF THE JOURNEY.

A DENSE fog hung over the placid surface of the Delaware River, and enveloped in its folds many of the ancient buildings of Burlington, then the capital of the colony of New Jersey. The stately mansion of the British governor, William Franklin, situated on the beautiful green bank so much admired at the present day, was wrapped in the vapour, and, as was often said of its occupant, seemed lost in a mist. Even the haunted tree in front of the governor's residence—the witches' sycamore—was reported by fearful pedestrians to have vanished, or at least to have become invisible.

Yet, notwithstanding the gloom which oppressed the atmosphere, a most extraordinary sound of hilarity burst from the hall of one of the dwellings on the principal street running at right angles with the river. The house from which the sound proceeded was the habitation of a solemn Quaker. The hall-door was open, and within, erect as a young man of thirty-five, stood Thomas Schooley, in his sixtieth year, surrounded by several of his friends, of about the same age and stature, all being tall and athletic, and habited alike, as they were all Quakers.

Friend Schooley was receiving the parting adieus of the last of his society brethren in Burlington, before departing on what was then termed the long and perilous journey to the northwestern counties of the colony. And the mirthful sound, so unusual on such occasions, and so extraordinary at any time among that class of people, had been produced by the following remark:—"Thee will save thy property, Thomas, and also thy neck, by fleeing to the mountains." The old men laughed quite heartily for a brief interval; while a youthful auditor in the parlour seemed to yield to uncontrollable merriment. She had beheld the sudden relaxation of the countenances of the aged men; and their long sharp noses, singularly alike, reaching beyond their sunken lips almost down to their peaked chins, had caused her cachinnation.

Beside the young lady sat the wife of Thomas, erect and tall, and plainly habited in a costly hooded salmon-coloured cloak and scooped bonnet. Her bloodless lips experienced no contraction; but her pallid brow, with a quiver slightly perceptible, was turned toward her youthful companion.

"Julia, thee dost not seem to be cast down at the moment of departing."

"Indeed, I could not help laughing, Mrs. Schooley, when I saw the faces of the old men."

"I fear they will suffer many agonies in the wrathful storm soon to burst upon this devoted country," said she, with a deep sigh; "and I trust the Lord will so sustain them that they may not find their laughter turned to groans under affliction. But thee must call me Mary, Julia, and not Mrs. Schooley, as is the wont of those with whom Thomas, thy guardian, has permitted thee to dwell."

"Pardon me, Mary; I will strive to obey thee in future. And in truth it should be a very melancholy moment; for from among the savages and the wild beasts of the wilderness, whither we are going, there can be no certainty we shall ever return. Thy son Richard, whom I see endeavouring to wash away his tears at the pump, must be sorely distressed at the idea of the hardships and dangers to be encountered."

"No, Julia. He merely grieves at the wickedness of mankind and the abominations of rebellions. He is a dutiful child, and strong, too. He is quite as tall as his father, and can perform as much labour as the stoutest slave we possess. He is industrious and careful, and will not see diminished the estate he is to inherit. But here is Thomas," she continued, rising.

"Sit still, Mary," said Thomas. "Let us tarry until I can utter the words which I am prompted to speak to Julia, my ward. Julia, dost thou think thy mind is quite decided upon making this journey?"

"Oh, quite, Mr. Schooley—Thomas, I should have said. I am delighted at the idea of dwelling in the wilderness, and am very impatient to be gone."

"Thee shall be gratified. But thee must be prepared to endure a great many inconveniences:—rude and often uncomfortable houses; but few companions of any sort, and none of the like frivolity and gayety of thy friends in East Jersey, or even here, in this once quiet and sedate seat of piety; no shops where are vended the playthings of silly fashion; no harpsichords and lutes, the instruments of idle sounds——"

"Pray, Thomas, do not call them idle sounds! But are there not birds? Will I not hear my precious woodrobins, the thrushes, the bluebirds, and even the daring catbirds?"

"I do not know; but thee may expect to find them."

"Oh, yes! And fie upon thee, Thomas, for deeming idle the glorious songs the Creator puts in the throats of those tiny beings for our enjoyment!"

"I would warn thee of the privations of a forest life, and then, and for the last time, leave it optional with thee to go or remain. I am thy guardian, and might exert my authority; but bad motives would be attributed if any mischance should follow. Thou art the sole descendant of one of the proprietors under William Berkeley, who derived by James——"

"James, Duke of York, brother of the King—Sir William Berkeley, Earl of Stratton; and my ancestor was a knight—Sir Thomas Lane. But pardon me—I did not intend to interrupt thee."

"Thee knows I regard titles as merely frivolous appendages, although I practise submission to those in authority. Well! thou art the heiress of all the lands held by thy father at his death, as I am the heir of my father, whose first ancestor was landed in this town from the "Willing Mind" in 1677, some twenty years before thy titled ancestor was appointed governor."

"Yes, he was governor; I forgot that."

"He was a better officer and man than his successor Edward, called Lord Cornbury, the presumptuous and dissipated cousin of Ann, denominated the Queen. But, as I was saying to thee, thou art the heiress of many large tracts of which we know but little. Some are in Hunterdon and Sussex counties, and some lie in East Jersey, in Bergen, Morris, and Essex, which may be valuable at a future period, if not confiscated."

"Confiscated?"

"Listen, and thee will learn my meaning. As I was saying to thee, I have likewise many tracts, of more or less fertility, besides the mountain, which I have been told will perpetuate my name—truly a useless distinction,—and all of which might be lost if we were to become identified with the people about to engage in this rebellion. George will surely pour out his wrath upon his enemies; and many who remain upon the scene of strife, although they may not participate in its heinousness, may nevertheless be involved in the doom of the guilty. Burlington is sadly demoralized since our forefathers landed upon its soil; and there may be those among us who would not hesitate to bear false-witness against their neighbours."

"Do you really think there will be war, Thomas?"

"Dost thee not hear the firing of that swivel at the Ferry Tavern?"

"Richard told me those engaged in it were boys."

"He told thee truly. But they are celebrating the battle of Lexington, and the burning of a cargo of tea from a ship in Cohansey Creek, about which I will inform thee on our journey—if thee resolves to go. But, if thee decides at the last moment to remain, William Franklin is ready to receive thee."

"I will go with thee. And, if I did not, I would not stay at the governor's house."

"Thee is positive, Julia," said Mary.

"I mean, with my guardian's permission, I would prefer to live at the house of———"

"William Livingston, thee would say," added Thomas.

"True, and be with my old schoolmate, Kate."

"William Livingston will join the rebels. And wouldst thou prefer to dwell with him for that reason?"

"No, Thomas—that is—I know not what to say. But do not frown upon me. Indeed, it was not on that account I preferred to dwell in his mansion. But if the rebels should succeed, and if I were to live with Governor Franklin, might we not lose our lands?"

"Thee must not suppose the rebels can succeed. And I hope thee has not formed an *attachment* for any one but thy friend Kate at Elizabethtown?"

"Indeed, *indeed*, I have not!"

"Then do not blush, Julia," said Mary, smiling.

"Nor at Princeton," continued Thomas, while poor Julia continued to blush, "where I learnt thy Elizabethtown friends used to visit, and that thou hadst danced with the young man who won the first honour in college."

"If I do blush, Thomas, it is not the blush of shame. You are my guardian, to whom I promised my dying father to render all reasonable obedience. I danced with Charles Cameron. Kate Livingston and myself danced with him an equal number of times. But I deny having formed any *attachment* such as you allude to." As Julia uttered these words, a sudden pallour chased away her blushes.

"I believe thee, Julia. Thou didst never yet fear to tell the truth, and I honour thy candour. This Charles, I am told, is a young man of talent. He was taken, Mary, when an infant, by the Indians, and lived among them some fifteen years. When restored to his father, who had long mourned his loss in solitude, living a hermit's life on the Delaware, near the Gap——"

"Does he live there still?" asked Julia, quickly.

"He does, and on thy land, or on a tract adjoining thine."

"Poor child!" said Mary.

"Thee must not decide too hastily," continued Thomas. "It does not appear that he is poor, or an object of pity. At all events, his father, it seems, had money to bestow upon him an expensive education; and thee has heard the young man achieved the first honour. Nevertheless, his father was not present."

"He was not? How strange!" said Julia, abstractedly.

"I have seen this youth at the governor's, and I assure thee, Mary, he made a good appearance; seemed affable and polished, and was treated with courtesy by William. But let us not linger. The sun breaks forth through the mist, and we shall have a fine day. The coach waits at the door. Come, Richard. We leave an open house in the keeping of thy old nurse. Thou wilt go, Julia?"

"Oh, yes, freely, eagerly," said she, rising and taking his arm.

"Thee will meet him, perhaps, at his father's house," said Richard, who had been listening, half archly and half reproachfully.

"When didst thou see him at the governor's, Thomas?" asked Julia, not heeding Richard.

"This very morning. He was William's guest last night."

"You see, Mary, and you too, Richard, that he did not visit me," said Julia.

"He arrived late in the night," resumed Thomas, while Julia seemed to lean somewhat heavily on his arm. "He had been sent for by William, who has perhaps employed him in the service of George, since he is familiar with the dialects of the Indians."

"I am sure he would not assume any such—that is—I mean—I am quite certain he would not use his influence to incite the Indians to hostility—to make war upon the innocent inhabitants——"

"No, child, thee need not fear it. But it would be no trifling service to ascertain, through the instrumentality of this young man, the sentiments of the various chiefs in regard to the unhappy quarrel with the mother country, and to persuade them to remain neutral during the contest. I know not whether the lad agreed to the proposals of the governor; but I saw him set out in company with another college-bred Indian youth, named Bartholomew Calvin—in the Delaware language *Shawuskukhkung*, meaning *Wilted Grass*. They were mounted on fine horses, and quickly disappeared on the road we will soon be traversing."

By the time the last speech was ended, the party of four were seated in the carriage; and Paddy Pence, the Irish coachman, flourished his long whip over the horses' ears as they bounded forward on the Trenton Road.

Julia Lane, who had not smiled at Mr. Schooley's expression of "*another* college-bred Indian youth," now sat silently and thoughtfully beside her female companion seemingly unconscious of the subject of the conversation maintained between her guardian and his son Richard, who occupied the front seat of the vehicle.

Julia was just in her blissful seventeenth year. Though slight and fragile, her stature was sufficiently tall, and her form of beautiful proportions. She had an exquisite complexion, wavering between the fair and the dark, sometimes the one and sometimes the other; and features not susceptible of classification, but ever varying with her emotions and fully expressing them

Julia sat in silence, leaning her delicate chin upon her small hand, listlessly oblivious of the appraisements of the farms and tenements they passed uttered by her guardian and his son Richard. She was not even startled by the remark that a certain broad domain in view belonged to a handsome young widow.

Her thoughts were divided between the past and the unknown future. Hitherto her life had been an unbroken dream of pleasure, with the exception of the agony of the loss of her beloved father. But, death being one of the inevitable incidents of nature, nature itself provides a solace for the pang. It is natural to die, and it is natural to mourn the departed; but nature enables us to bear the loss, and provides other objects to occupy our affection, so that in turn we shall be loved and lost, mourned and forgotten.

Julia's guardian had been the agent and then the partner of her father; and many vast tracts of land were held in common between them, and remained undivided at the demise of Mr. Lane. The estate of Mr. Lane was left to the sole use of the heiress upon attaining a certain age. She was to be permitted to attend the church of her fathers, having been baptized by the Rev. Dr. Jonathan Odell, rector of St. Mary's, Burlington; but she was not to marry during her minority without the permission of her guardian. Nevertheless, relying upon the rectitude of the Quakers, among whom he had dwelt the greater portion of his life, the dying parent had besought his daughter to heed the counsels of his friend, and be governed by his advice in matters wherein her own mind might need instruction or be involved in doubt; and she had promised to conform to his injunction. Having completed her education, Julia supposed that but few exigencies could arise wherein her action would require the guidance of an adviser. She was permitted to associate with the acquaintances she had formed before her father's death, and, among the rest, Kate Livingston—the daughter of an able lawyer living at Elizabethtown, near Staten Island Sound, with whom Mr. Lane had much legal business, and who was destined subsequently to act an important part in the affairs of his country.

It was at the mansion of Mr. Livingston, where Julia sojourned the greater portion of her time, that she became acquainted with Charles Cameron and Bartholomew S. Calvin,—the latter being the nephew and heir of the king of that portion of the Delaware nation which remained upon the seaboard; a lad of mournful spirit and great meekness, upon whom Dr. Witherspoon, of the College at Princeton, had resolved to bestow a classical education. These youths had attracted the notice of Mr. Livingston; and, foreseeing the benefits which might be derived from their knowledge of Indian character during the approaching struggle with the mother country, he had prevailed on them to spend their vacations at his house, and from whom both himself and his daughter Kate, as well as Julia, learned many of the remarkable characteristics of the tribes of the forest. And Kate and Julia listened to accounts of—

"Rough quarries, rocks, and hills whose heads touch heaven;"

And doubtless they thought the tale was

'Strange, 'twas passing strange;
'Twas pitiful, 'twas wondrous pitiful;

But, unlike the Venetian beauty, they did not dream of love. It was merely friendship and romance.

So much for the past. We have said that Julia, in her obliviousness of the present, only strove to penetrate the future. For hours she mused in silence. Would she see the young graduates upon the margin of one of the bright lakes embowered in the wilderness? Would they lead her to the wild summit of the mountain, whence the eye might distinguish objects dimly in the distance? Would they not resume their savage dispositions in the solitudes of the forest? Would she see Charles's father? Who could he be? Such were some of the conjectures of the tender maiden as she journeyed toward the wilderness.

CHAPTER II.

A FIRESIDE STORY—THAYENDANEGEA—PADDY'S BLUNDER.

The fog of the morning having been dispelled by the glorious sun in a cloudless sky, and the road leading mostly through a level country until it passed the northern limits of the present Mercer county, our travellers accomplished what was deemed a good day's journey long before the approach of darkness. Paddy Pence had not spared his horses, nor had Thomas Schooley restrained his hand, until they came in view of the beautiful valley in Hunterdon county, in which the famous log tavern of John Ringo was situated, and where it had been determined to rest the first night.

Paddy was now ordered to permit the horses to fall into a gentler pace, for they exhibited symptoms of weariness, and one of them had loosened a shoe.

The travellers gazed with delight at the beautiful aspect of the country as they descended into the valley, which, however, became wilder in its features as they progressed. The settlements were perceptibly farther apart, and the forest was but slightly variegated by cultivated fields. Majestic oaks, and tall pines, and budding chestnuts, from which the squirrel's joyous cry and the songs of happy birds were heard incessantly, almost constantly surrounded them. In the dim distance on the left Thomas pointed to the blue outline of the Musconetcong Mountain; and on either hand they had occasional glimpses of mills situated on the crystal streams flowing toward the Delaware River, some ten miles distant.

"Plase yer honour," said Paddy, drawing the reins suddenly and causing the horses to stand perfectly still, "what sort of a baste is that?"

"Baste, Patrick? Oh, you mean beast!"

"Yis, yer honour, I mane baste, and it's as ugly a crather as my eyes iver beheld. One end is under the stone, and the other swags backwards and forwards, and jangles like wee sleigh-bells wid their clappers broken."

"Patrick," said Thomas, descending from the carriage, "that is a snake—a rattlesnake!"

"Och, the baste!" cried Paddy, who had likewise descended from his seat; but he ran back hastily, and leaped upon the box, where he sat shivering with terror.

"Drive on, Patrick, and let Mary and Julia see him. He is nearly dead. Some one has cast a stone on his head," continued Thomas, who had been joined by Richard.

"Och, murther!" cried Paddy, making an involuntary movement, as if to turn the horses in the opposite direction. "Plase yer honour, let's go back agin! That baste will be the death of poor Paddy Pence! They tould me I'd find sich divils of blackguard bastes in the same country with the nagers, and that they'd ate me up in the garden, and swaller me down on horseback."

Mr. Schooley chided his coachman for using such language; and, being joined by Julia, whose curiosity overcame her fears, he made Richard stand upon the stone, and, stooping down, dispossessed the snake, which was a pretty large one, of his rattles. He likewise explained to his ward the very natural affright of Paddy, who was a recent importation, and had never beheld a serpent before.

"Be the powers, if yer honour aint afraid to take hould of the baste with your naked hands, Paddy Pence is not the boy to hould back on his high box." And so Paddy urged his horses—which pricked up their ears and snorted repeatedly—beyond the snake.

"Patrick, my friend," said Mr. Schooley, with much gravity, "thee must not swear. Thee must read the third chapter of James."

"Och, yer honour, I'm a thrue Jacobite, and there's niver a bit of danger that I'll take the oath against the rightful—"

"Ha! ha! He will never understand thee," said Julia, laughing heartily.

"Och, but I will, my beautiful young mistress," continued Paddy; "and I'll die, but I'll sarve him faithfully, for, of all the masters it's iver been my lot to own, niver a divil of 'em called me friend before."

"Patrick, thee misunderstands me. I am a loyal subject of George. But I meant thy profane swearing."

"Be my sowl, I wouldn't be guilty of such a thing in yer prisence."

"Thou hast done it twice already, Patrick."

"Then I beg yer honour's and the ladies' pardons; for, be my life, I didn't know it, and I hope yer honour will tache me betther manners."

"I will strive to do so, Patrick. And thee must remember to swear not at all. But thee must read the New Testament."

"I thank yer honour, and I'll try and remimber not to forgit what you say; but, yer honour, I darsn't rade the Tistament widout permission of the praist."

"It is a great pity, Patrick, that thou hast been bred in such ignorance of thy rights; but, if thou wilt read, thou wilt learn all about the precious privilege which is the birthright of every one.

"If yer honour advises it, I will larn what Saint James ses about swearing, which is a foul-mouthed practice. But there is one difficulty, yer honour."

"I tell thee there can be none where there is a will."

"I mane, yer honour, that divil a bit was I iver taught to rade! There agin! I see yer honour is offinded at the mintion of the blackguard! But, pardon me, yer honour, till I larn betther the nixt time."

The horses crept along slowly, and Mr. Schooley remained on foot, declining to re-enter the carriage.

Julia and Richard, proceeding more briskly, were soon several hundred paces in advance, and appeared to be much interested with the objects which met their view.

"I am glad to see thee joyful, Julia," said the young man, when he perceived a smile upon the fair face of his companion, as she stooped ever and anon to observe a severed wild-flower, to which she evidently attached a signification incomprehensible to Richard.

"There is a freshness in the air, Richard, a perfume in the wild-flowers, a grandeur and sublimity in the woods and hills, never known in cities or densely-peopled districts, and irresistibly productive of an exhilaration of spirits."

"I wish I could feel it!" said he, sighing. "Even the hieroglyphics on the tree by the snake—the Indian marks—seemed to be interesting to thee, while to me they were without meaning. I wish some one would teach me to enjoy the things which afford thee pleasure, and also the way to please thee."

"Oh, don't sigh, Richard! The things which please my fancy would be considered frivolous by thy father, and no doubt he has long since taught thee to regard them as he does."

"No, no, Julia; if any thing I could do might appear pleasing in thy sight, I would not deem it frivolous."

"I thank thee, Richard. You were ever kind to me. I am sensible of your goodness, and of your father's indulgence to a wayward orphan. I am striving to conform to his rules. I have learned his manner of speech——"

"And it sounds like music from thy lips."

"Why, Richard, thou hast been learning to compliment a poor maiden after the fashion of the world!"

"Nay, Julia, it was the untutored impulse of my heart!"

"Then nature was the model for poets! And, truly, thy father never encouraged thee to be enraptured of sweet sounds. Nevertheless, I am the more thankful for the compliment as it cannot be a vain and empty one. Thou didst ask me what would give me pleasure. Flowers and birds. Gather the first on the hills, and Paddy Pence will cultivate them for me; and entice the birds into the garden, rather than frighten them away, as thy father did in Burlington. But how can I repay thee? What meanest thou by such incessant sighing?"

"How repay me? One smile is enough—but I—I declare to thee I do not know what I do! I will strive to correct the fault of sighing."

"Do, Richard. I would like to see thee cheerful. Stay! don't trample upon them!" she added, quickly, as her companion's foot was suspended over a collection of blossoms of various hues.

"They were plucked, Julia, by some one unknown to us. Thee seems to study them as if thou wert superstitious."

"I am a little superstitious, Richard," said she, smiling, as she collected the blossoms and enjoyed their perfume. The next moment they were joined by Mr. Schooley and overtaken by the carriage. They were in front of Ringo's log tavern, where they were welcomed heartily.

The shades of evening, and the descending dew, even in May, made the blazing logs in the broad fireplace productive both of a cheerful aspect and a congenial temperature.

Our travellers, therefore, after a hearty repast, collected in front of the broad, glowing hearth.

"Come in, Patrick," said Mr. Schooley, seeing his man at the door, "and eat thy supper. I suppose thee has fed the horses?"

"Plase yer honour, not yit. I was in a quandary."

"My man Jake's got the ager," said Mr. Ringo, the host, "or he'd a' done it."

"I told thee, Patrick," said Mr. Schooley, "to give them corn in the ear.* In that way they are not likely to eat too fast and become foundered. Do you not understand me, Patrick?"

"Yes, yer honour," said Paddy, bowing and withdrawing. But in a few moments he reappeared with a bewildered look.

"Well," said Mr. Schooley, "thee has fed them?"

"Plase yer honour, the horses have good enough tathe in their mouths, but divil the one could I find in their ears. And how could I fade 'em, as yer honour tould me, when they wouldn't ate wid their ears, but snatched it wid their tathe."

In the laughter which followed this blunder of Paddy's even the staid Mary and the melancholy Richard participated. Paddy, as we have said, was a recent importation, and had never seen any corn in the ear.

Later in the evening, when the moon shone brightly, and the sinking embers threw up a crimson glow which illuminated the recesses of the loft above, a howling in the woods attracted notice.

---

* This occurrence has been recently going the rounds in the papers, an editorial friend of the author being permitted to transcribe it.

"What is that?" asked Julia.

"That," said John Ringo, "is either a wolf or an Indian."

"Murther! Did you say Indian, Mr. Rango?" exclaimed Paddy, rising from the table, and, unbidden, occupying a stool near the corner of the capacious fireplace.

"Or a wolf, Paddy," replied Mr. Ringo. "But take a dram, and I will tell you what took place here one night when I was a boy."

"John," said Mr. Schooley, "thee must not tempt Patrick to drink. We still have a long road before us. But thou mayest tell him some of the anecdotes of early times. And I see Julia is impatient to hear thee. But thy listeners must not forget that thy adventures happened many years ago."

"But, father," said Richard, "thee heard William Franklin say——"

"Richard! thee forgets that thou art not permitted to repeat what the governor said."

Richard was dumb.

"I believe the governor* intends to take sides against his father," said Ringo, between the puffs of his replenished pipe, the smoke from which, although it seemed to ascend the chimney, nevertheless perfumed the apartment.

"Pray go on now, Mr. Ringo," said Julia, in an attitude of attention.

"It was about this time o' night," said Ringo, "and at this season of the year, the moon shining brightly, as it is now,—when I was a boy, Paddy,"—he added, seeing Paddy stretching his neck, and with open mouth looking toward the window,—"that we heard an uncommon howling. The wolves seemed to be all around the house, and a great deal nearer than the one we now hear."

"John, dost thee hear it now?" asked Mrs. Schooley, who was likewise an attentive listener; for she had never before accompanied her husband to his western estates.

"No; he is silent, now," said John, between two prolonged puffs; "and it's likely he's eating one of my pigs. On the night I am speaking of, there was an old man by the name of Jobes with us. He came down from Sussex

---

* He was a natural son of Benjamin Franklin.

county, where he had lived several years, and had often been chased by the Indians; and once, while he was absent, two of his sons were killed. He and my father were making a bargain for the piece of land you saw on the left, with the girdled trees on it, when the old man stopped talking, and said they were not wolves, but Indians, howling around the house. And soon they stopped howling, and began to hoot like owls."

"Dost thee not hear an owl now, John?" asked Mrs. Schooley.

"I do," replied Ringo, after expelling a long whiff of smoke.

"Murther!" cried Paddy, starting up.

"Who's killing you, Paddy?" asked Ringo.

"Thee must not forget it was twenty or thirty years ago, Patrick," said Mr. Schooley.

"I will try not, yer honour," replied Paddy.

"We looked into the yard," continued Mr. Ringo, "and saw a large party of Indians aiming their French muskets at us. We dodged down. You can see the bullet-marks on that side now."

"Murther!" said Paddy, drawing closer to the corner.

"Recollect it was before you were born," said Julia, amused at Paddy's evidences of affright.

"Then," resumed Mr. Ringo, "we rose and fired, and when the smoke cleared away there was not an Indian to be seen."

"They were handsomely defated," said Paddy.

"They were not gone far," said Ringo. "For, when Jobes peeped out, a bullet came in and cut off his ear."

"The blackguard savage!" said Paddy.

"From that time both parties were more cautious. But we were besieged till morning, when we heard the joyful sound of fire-arms a short distance from the house, which we knew to be the signal of relief, and the Indians instantly disappeared. Our deliverers were from the block-house on the river, and had been following the trail of the enemy. Since that night we have never been molested.

"Wilt thou not be made fearful, Patrick," asked Mr. Schooley, "listening to such stories?"

"Niver a bit, yer honour, if the young mistress won't be frightened. Bless yer life, sir, all these botherations happened before I was born, and surely before the young lady iver dramed of such a thing. Yer honour, I'll show you I'm not afraid! I'll go to the stable be meself, and see if the horses are comfortable; and airly in the morning I'll have the shoe faxed at the shop down at the mill."

Paddy walked bravely out into the yard, and on to the gate, upon which his hand was resting, when he espied a solitary horseman coming slowly down the road. He stood undecided whether to advance or retire, until the stranger was sufficiently near for him to perceive that he wore a blanket thrown gracefully over his shoulders, that his head was surmounted with a crest of feathers, and that he held a gun in his hand. Then Paddy was undecided no longer. Starting back, he ran into the house, his face as pale as death and his limbs trembling at every joint.

"Why, what hast thou seen?" demanded Mrs. Schooley.

"Tell me, Paddy, what it is!" cried Julia, with a smile.

But Paddy was almost speechless, and could barely articulate the word "Indian!"

Ringo went out immediately, followed by Mr. Schooley and Julia. The stranger had dismounted, tied his horse to a tree, and was standing near the front entrance of the house.

"Who are you?" demanded Ringo.

"Thayendanegea," replied the Indian, with a lofty brow and erect stature.

"That means Brandt, in English," said Ringo, advancing. "How do you do, Brandt? I'm glad to see you. How you have grown since I saw you last! Why, you are a large man, now!"

"Ay, and a sachem," said the young chief, smiling, (for he could speak our language very well.) "But, tell me, how high was the moon when the White Eagle departed toward the Kittaning?"

"White Eagle?"

"Ay:—my white brother."

"You mean the young Cameron?"

"Ay."

"It was before the middle of the afternoon."

"And who was with him? By the trail I see there were two, and one was of the Lenni Lenappé family, of which I too am descended. His totem is on the tree at the crossing, a tortoise, like mine. His name?"

"We call him Bart Calvin," said Ringo.

"His name is Shawuskukhkung," said Brandt, without other emotion than a slight sneer of contempt. "It is the right name," he continued, "meaning, in your language, *Wilted Grass*. The wild-flower perishes in the hothouses of the pale-face, and, when cooped, the eagle becomes a dunghill-fowl. The once mighty Algonquin droops like wilted grass! Its shrivelled branches should be bathed in blood."

"Blood!" said Julia, who could not avoid admiring the form and poetry of the speaker, but was startled at the mention of the sanguinary remedy for the resuscitation of a decaying race.

"And thou art the fair Antelope which charmed the eye of the young eagle? Thayendanegea, too, can write with the quill, as well as his brother, and we have corresponded."

"I have often heard him speak of thee," said Julia, from habit using the terms employed in the family of her guardian; "and he loves thee as a brother."

"I hope so," was Brandt's laconic reply.

"Come in," said Ringo. "Forgive me, Brandt, for my forgetfulness."

"John," said Mr. Schooley, as the party entered the house, "thee ought never to forget that hospitality is one of the chief virtues in the estimation of the Indian."

Mrs. Ringo did not forget it; and the table was soon spread, and honey and other luxuries, which had been hitherto withheld, were placed before the young chief, who partook of them without hesitation.

"And would not your horse like to have a bite?" asked Ringo.

"A little," said Brandt. "Not much, like the horses of the pale-faces."

"Paddy," continued Ringo, "you know my hostler has the ager, and I can't leave my guest. Won't you bait* the gentleman's horse for me? You needn't be afraid of his taking your scalp."

"Is it a bating you would have me give him?"

"Yes, Paddy," said Ringo.

---

* This, too, was inserted in the journal of the author's friend.

"I'll do it!" said Paddy, quite reassured upon seeing the Indian eating like other people, and somewhat enraged at the twinkle of Brandt's eye when he recognised him as the one who fled from the gate.

"Thee did expect to meet the White Eagle and Wilted Grass at this place?" interrogated Mr. Schooley.

"White Eagle—not Wilted Grass. His speech, left at the crossing, says the Antelope and her pale friends must fill the wigwam here, and he will light a camp-fire some miles distant on the path, which will guide me to his couch."

"And thou didst call him brother?"

"I did. He was a pappoose when brought to our wigwam, and lived with us until he began to pluck hairs from his chin. We swam, and fished, and hunted together among the cool lakes. I had lost my brother, and he supplied his place. But the White Head came and removed him to the college of the pale-faces. I will see him once more. If he loves the pale-faces better than his brother, he will desert the paths of the forest. Ha!" he exclaimed, rising, his eyes glowing with a sudden fierceness as he heard the peculiar snort of his horse. He strode to the window, and in amazement beheld Paddy belabouring his steed with a stout branch of an apple-tree, which he had wrested off at the corner of the orchard. Every time the bough descended the heels of the animal flew up, and Paddy had to exercise some skill in dodging.

Brandt rushed forth into the road, and, seizing the halter and the bough at the same time, after bestowing the latter upon the shoulders of the astonished Paddy, mounted his steed and galloped away.

"Murther!" cried Paddy, running into the house; "he's been bating me—the wild savage blackguard! If I had thought of my shelalah, I'd 'ave broken his punkin-head for him!"

"Patrick," said Mr. Schooley,—while Julia was irresistibly diverted,—"why didst thou beat his horse?"

"Bate his horse? And sure Misther Rango tould me to bate him."

"I meant a snack—a lunch—a bite of corn; but a stupid Irishman never knows any thing in this country," said Ringo. "And the Indian," he continued, evincing much vexation, "dashed off without getting an explanation, and it may cost some of us our scalps if we have war with them again."

"And it's a stupid Irishman, is it, Mr. Rango?" cried Paddy, who had been touched in a tender place. "Be the powers, if you'll walk out on the grane wid me, we'll see whose head is the softest!"

"Patrick," said Mr. Schooley, "be silent! Thee must never have any strife in my service."

"I ax yer honour's pardon," responded Paddy, who could not abide the idea of being discharged in such a country as that.

"Heigho!" sighed Mrs. Schooley, and then, rising in all her native stateliness, suggested that it was time to be reposing after the fatigues of the journey.

"And Richard must have thought so a long time ago," added Julia, who perceived that her ungallant beau had succumbed to slumber in his chair.

After a somewhat lengthy prayer from Mr. Ringo, who was a Presbyterian,—the stoical Quakers remaining steadfastly in their chairs,—the ladies were conducted into an opposite room, while the male portion of the company remained. It was thus they lodged in early times. Two rooms, twenty feet square, sufficed for twenty lodgers.

The authentic traditions, which we follow without material deviation, do not dwell upon the mere dreams of Julia Lane, as she reposed upon her couch that night, with the stars blinking upon her through the uncurtained window. But doubtless the flowers she had found, and the interpretation of the hieroglyphics she had seen, and which she had been taught by Charles to render into good English, were reproduced in her slumbers.

CHAPTER III.

THE MIDNIGHT CAMP-FIRE — MEETING OF THE FOREST CHIEFS.

WHILE our travellers are slumbering at "The Old Ringo Tavern," we will accompany Thayendanegea to the camp of the White Eagle and Wilted Grass.

Having had many interviews with General Gage and Sir William Johnston, Brandt had already resolved upon the course he would pursue in the impending conflict. And, whatever else may be said of the renowned chief by poets and historians, it can never be truthfully alleged that he was prompted in his action by either a mercenary motive or a cruel disposition.

A frown contracted the young chieftain's brow as he swept past the cultivated fields, and ever and anon the new foundations laid for the future residences of the encroaching white man. The hills and valleys, where his fathers had chased the deer from remotest ages, were to be torn asunder by the ploughshare; the gurgling streams, which had furnished them the delicious trout, were to be dammed by the millwright; and the majestic trees, which had sheltered them in the solitudes of the forest, were to be laid low, and the familiar haunts of the spirits of the great departed were to be desecrated by the active cupidity of European mercenaries. Such were the thoughts which animated the young chief, as he pursued his solitary way, and stimulated the resolve to be amply revenged.

It was near the hour of midnight when Brandt perceived the glimmer of a light on an eminence to his left. It was upon a knoll surrounded by ancient oaks, through the interstices of which the sinking embers could be seen at intervals. It had been one of the favourite camping-grounds from time immemorial. Brandt had not revisited it since the days of his early youth, and then Charles was with him.

MEETING OF CHARLES AND BRANDT.—P. 26

The young chief dismounted and drew near the sinking fire. In peace or war, the Indians do not generally have sentinels at night. Brandt found the two young men steeped in slumber; but the light was not sufficient to distinguish their faces. Their forms merely were discernible as they lay together wrapped in their blankets. They had made use of the decayed forks of the old camp, by placing poles across and forming a shelter of bark. The rear of the camp was protected by the fallen trunk of a gigantic tree, and next to this were their heads, while their feet reached nearly to the fire.

Brandt stood with folded arms, gazing intently. Had he been an enemy, how easily he might have dispatched them both! But such was not his mission. He was in quest of friends and coadjutors. He made a single step forward, as if to rouse them, but paused abruptly. In the dusky gloom their features might not be distinctly recognised. He turned away and noiselessly replenished the fire. He then approached the open end of the camp, and stood again with folded arms and a thoughtful brow.

Charles turned uneasily on his couch, and muttered in his dream the following words:—"I am no Indian; I have no savage blood in my veins."

Brandt started forward with a horrible scowl, snatched the tomahawk from his belt, and flourished it menacingly over Charles's head. But the next moment the shining weapon was replaced, and the young Mohawk resumed his meditative attitude.

The dry wood was now crackling and blazing brightly, and the whole scene became distinctly apparent. At length a smile illuminated the handsome features of Brandt, and, taking a reed from his bosom, played one of the tunes familiar to the ears of Charles when gliding over the smooth surface of the Ontario or floating in the canoe on the waters of the gentle Wyalusing. At the conclusion of the strain Charles rushed forth, and, with the words, "Brother!" "My brother!" the young men were locked in each other's arms. It had been five years since they parted. Before that event, and for many years previously, they had been inseparable. Charles had been loved and treated quite as well as the lost son and brother whose place he had been chosen to fill. No word of lamentation for the dead had been uttered in the family after the first month of his adoption.

After a prolonged silence, they sat down and smoked the pipe which Brandt had filled, gazing with delight and affection at each other.

Wilted Grass came forth and sat down beside them.

"Shawuskukhkung," said Brandt, extending his hand. "we, too, are brothers. We flow from the same parent stream,—the Algonquin,—and come from the same Lenni Lenappé family. Why should we widen the tract which separates us?"

"Thayendanegea speaks the truth," replied the Delaware chief. "But streams never more run together when parted by mountains. I will die where my fathers died."

"But not live as they did. Your hunting-grounds are turned into pig-pens."

"There is a land beyond the grave—forests where the axe never sounds. Such are the peaceful hunting-grounds of my fathers, and thither I will join them."

"True. But the same Great Spirit bestowed upon us this beautiful land. Will it please him if we meanly surrender it to the trafficking stranger, from whom the game flies in horror and disgust? Can a coward enter the hunting-grounds of the spirit-land?"

"Thayendanegea, I am no coward," said the Delaware.

"Tschichohocki (Burlington) was once the village of a thousand braves. But the Mantas came from the slimy creeks, and licked them into another shape, and blew their own breath down their throats, and swam away with their squaws to Matinicunk, where their children became frogs."

"Frogs!"

"They still croak upon the banks of the Delaware River; but when danger approaches they close their eyes and dive down to the bottom."

"And do you mean to call me a frog and a coward?" demanded the young Delaware, rising indignantly, with his hand on his tomahawk.

"I do not raise my hand against the Wilted Grass," said Brandt, with imperturbable composure. "When the Great Council was held at the Forks of the Delaware, your people were all women. Teedyuscung, your head chief, spake without rising, like a squaw, until Tagashata removed the petticoat which had once been worn at a treaty. Then he was a great chief again."

"He was always a great chief," said the Delaware, resuming his seat with a sigh. "At that council he removed the French hatchets from the heads of the English. You and I and White Eagle were present. We were too young to listen; but we were told afterward by our fathers what had been done. The nations listened to Teedyuscung, and made solemn pledges of peace. The Delawares forget not their pledges."

"The Mohawks do not violate their treaties," said Brandt. "The Five Nations then signed a treaty of friendship with their Great Father over the broad water. They will keep their promise."

"You forget what the Senecas have since done, instigated by their chief Tagashata. Five years after the meeting of the Great Council they murdered Teedyuscung, and falsely said the English had perpetrated the foul deed."

"Not the English, but the Yankees, who were seizing the Susquehanna valleys. And they say so still."

"But they say falsely. The Minisinks loved Teedyuscung, and it was known they would be revenged."

"Let us not discuss those things, my brother," said Charles.

"No!" cried Brandt, springing to his feet. "The past is gone forever. We who were boys are men, and our fathers have gone to the hunting-grounds of the spirit-land unarmed and in fetters. Let us follow them with our rifles, that they may eat. It was you, my brother, I wished to go with us. The Wilted Grass will bend over the graves of his kindred. But the nations of the West will come in multitudes, like the leaves and the stars. The blood of our enemies will run into the sea, like the rushing streams after a mighty storm. Let your face not be white."

"The Great Spirit made it white," said Charles.

"But that was when you dwelt beyond the broad water. It was the Great Spirit also that made Thayendanegea call the White Eagle his brother."

"But who are the enemies you speak of?"

"They who brought the small-pox and the fire-water;

who stop our running streams and hack down our trees The elk and deer have fled to the mountains, the buffalo to the plains near the setting sun. Our homes are desolate. The wolf and the owl and the rattlesnake only remain. We, the lords of the wilderness, to whom the Great Spirit gave the whole country, now flit like dusky bats in the shadows of the evening. My brother, scalding tears roll down my cheeks. It is the last time. The Great Spirit calls upon us once more to hurl the invaders from our shores. It is the last call. Look up through the weeping leaves at the stars. During many thousands of moons they smiled on our happy people. The song of joy echoed through the valleys around. The merry dance was prolonged till morning beneath the boughs of these spreading oaks. All is silent and desolate now; and the last chief of a mighty race stands by a solitary camp-fire and mourns in tears. My brother, I dash these woman's tears into the ashes at my feet. The spirits of my fathers shall not grieve for the bondage of their son. I will break the chains the white man has drawn around me. I will die with the tomahawk in one hand and a scalping-knife in the other. I hurl away the pipe of peace. War is declared!"

"War against whom, my brother?" asked Charles.

"Against whom? Alas! I fear, against my brother, if he will not fight at my side. Against the white man! First, against those who fell our trees and dig our grounds; next against the army of King George. The royalists and the rebels shall slaughter each other, and we will slay the survivors."

"Ha! ha! Brandt, you are mad!"

"I am. And there is no time for idle delay. Will the White Eagle return with his brother to the lakes?"

"No; not if my brother intends to come back and tomahawk my father. But I will go with him if he will remain at peace."

"Peace! My brother does not seem to know that the Five—or rather the Six—Nations have already sounded the warwhoop. Only a few trembling Cayugas and Oneidas remain with their women. And the great tribes of the West are echoing the scalp-halloo from the war-paths of the mountains. The royal governors of Pennsylvania, New Jersey, and New York, have sent us arms and money."

"I feared so," said Charles, despondingly.

"Feared, brother?"

"Not for myself."

"Who, then?"

"*You*, and thy devoted race. My brother, our Great Father over the broad water is a bad man. His armies will be beaten. The Americans will triumph, and the poor Indian be the last victim."

"Farewell, my brother. The day is dawning. I go alone, unless Shawuskukhkung will accompany me."

"I will die in peace by the graves of my fathers on the sea-shore," said Wilted Grass, his head drooping on his breast.

Just then a hailing halloo was heard in the valley below, where the path diverged from the main road, and the party in the camp became singularly excited at so unexpected a salutation. It proceeded evidently from a party of Indians or from men familiarly conversant with their mode of shouting. Brandt answered it; and a few minutes after three men—two Indians and a tall white man—came trotting up to the encampment. The white man was the famous Simon Girty, who had been dwelling among the Western Indians since the French war, and had been taken prisoner about the time of Braddock's defeat. The others were the chiefs of the Shawnees and the Ottoways,—Cornstalk and Pontiac.

"And you will join your brother, I suppose?" said Girty, in the English language, to young Cameron.

"I shall remain at home in peace, if possible," said Charles.

"It will not be possible. You must be with us or against us. And you will have to decide without delay. Already preparations are being made in every direction. I am now returning by night marches from a conference with Lord Dunmore, the Governor of Virginia, and with messages for the Western tribes. A secret treaty has been concluded with the Ottoways and Shawnees, and we are authorized to engage the Creeks, Cherokees, Potowottomies, Wyandots, and all the other powerful tribes, to fall upon the rebels. And the rebels are about to appoint George Washington their general. There will be stirring times———"

"*I* will not stir, if I can help it. I will not take up arms against the colonists, who have demanded nothing but justice from their oppressor. And, Girty," he continued, in a low tone, "beware what you do. You know, I, too, was a prisoner, and have had an opportunity to learn something of the intention of the Indians."

"I know what you mean. They propose assisting the British to destroy the Americans, and then exterminating their ally. You and I are aware of the impossibility of such a thing. But, if it were practicable, it would be our best policy to become red men."

"Once more, my brother," said Brandt, approaching Charles, "I ask you to go with us."

"No!" said Charles.

"Then, farewell! But, if we should meet again in bloody strife, still, let us remember we were brothers."

"I would have it so, Thayendanegea. But I have no desire to spill any man's blood, and I hope this war may be smothered in its birth. I go to see my gray-haired father; after that, I know not what I shall do. I did hope to fish and hunt with my brother on the head-waters of the Susquehanna. But such may not be if the scalp-halloo reverberates through the valleys. Give this to the Brown Thrush, my sister. Tell her the White Eagle will dream of her, although he may not see her."

Brandt opened the casket which had been placed in his hand, and glanced at the jewels that were to adorn his sister's brow and wrists; and then, gazing silently and long at his white brother, turned slowly away and joined the departing guests, who had completed the scanty meal which had been placed before them.

And Charles and his Delaware companion followed soon after. They had not proceeded more than a mile, however, when they beheld Brandt returning at a brisk pace.

"My brother," said Brandt, "when the Brown Thrush shall look upon these presents, she will wish to know how long the White Eagle means to stay away. She will ask me if thou art betrothed to the lovely Antelope of whom thou hast written more than once. What shall Thayendanegea say?"

"Say I am not betrothed to the fair maiden: only that she was as kind to me as a sister, when I had no other friend. I will see the Brown Thrush again; I know not when. You can speak for me.'

"The Antelope is very beautiful. I have seen her."
"When?"
"Last night. And I saw thy tokens. But I will not tell my sister. She would be broken-hearted, and sing no more. Farewell—if thou wilt not go with me."

"Farewell!" said Charles, and the chief rode furiously away.

CHAPTER IV.

THE FOREST HOME—NIGHT SCENE.

The sun was descending in the azure west, when the carriage suddenly paused. It had reached the summit of the Jenny Jump Mountain, in the southern part of Sussex county.

"Why hast thou stopped, Patrick?" asked Mr. Schooley, as he thrust his head out of the window, and to do which it was necessary for him to remove the broad-brimmed hat from his head.

"Plase yer honour, the horses had a dazziness in their heads, and I was afraid they'd fall off the mountain. It's so high, yer honour, it almost takes my breath."

Mr. Schooley descended to the ground, and stood for several moments gazing at the scene. There were no precipices near, and the surface was almost level on the eminence where the horses stood. But the surrounding scenery was sublime, gilded by the golden tints of the declining sun. Behind was the Musconetcong Mountain, which they had passed several hours previously, and before them rose the Blue Mountain, enclosing the intermediate space, like the walls of an impregnable fortress. Far to the left, but distinctly perceptible, a depression in the range indicated the locality of the Delaware Gap, and seemed to be the only outlet from the vast enclosure—the stupendous battlements on either hand being some two thousand feet in height.

Not many settlements now met the view. Some five or

six primitive farm-houses were all that could be discovered in a diameter of several miles. But near the base of the hill called the Jenny Jump Mountain, which attained an elevation of some six or eight hundred feet, was a massive stone structure, being the church edifice of a small colony of Moravians, founded by the good Count Zinzendorf.

Even the stoicism of Thomas Schooley yielded for a moment to the enthusiastic admiration inspired by the landscape; and he turned to the carriage-door and beckoned Julia, who had just awakened from a short slumber, to join him. She did so with alacrity, and stood enraptured, gazing at the spectacle. Then she uttered incessant exclamations of delight, while the staid Mrs. Schooley and the sober Richard listened with imperturbable gravity.

"Thee seems to be pleased with the features of the country," remarked Mr. Schooley, his rigid lips relaxing almost into a smile.

"Oh, enchanted!"

"But if there were fewer hills and rocks, and more acres of arable land, both thee and I would be the richer," said Mr. Schooley.

"And yet Mr. Green wrote us that there were many arable slopes and valleys," said Julia.

"True; Samuel did say so, and he is a good judge of land. No doubt he made good selections for himself. That is his house on the hill near the church."

"Can we not see the house we are to occupy?"

"Thee can see it, but indistinctly, to the left of the village."

"Where there is a forest of dead trees?"

"Yea; they stand in the largest field, and were girdled by William Van Wiggens, our overseer."

"Girdled? And did that kill the trees?"

"Thee must not think he belted them with gaudy ribbon, as thee sometimes does thy frail waist. What is meant by girdling is the cutting round the tree through the bark, which prevents the sap from ascending, and the tree dieth, just as the doctors say the habit of tightly belting the human chest produces disease and death."

"But, Thomas, why should William Van Wiggens kill the poor trees?"

"He did it by my direction. In the autumn the storms

and the axe will remove the trunks, and then we will have fields which may be cultivated with profit. To the right of the opening, if thee will look steadily, thee may see the roof of the house we are to dwell in."

"I see it! A long, double, two-story log-house! And I see the barn, and the orchard beyond, and cows grazing within it. Oh, I am so impatient to be there! I shall be delighted, Thomas, with our forest home. And it has a southern aspect, sloping gently down to the meandering ravine. Flowers will flourish there. And is there not a brook of crystal water flowing through the ravine?"

"Yea; a beautiful stream, that empties into the Paulinskill. It has many trout in it; but I have never taken any of them, and Richard has no taste for idle sports."

"Oh, let us be going! I am impatient to be at home in the wilderness, and to explore every grove and rock and cave and streamlet!"

When they resumed their seats, Paddy found no difficulty in proceeding, as the horses seemed to be recovered from their dizziness. And, as they descended from the summit of the Jenny Jump, Mr. Schooley endeavoured to describe to his family the condition of things they must be prepared to encounter at their new home. Nor had the far-seeing Quaker neglected to make the necessary preparations for his removal to a place of supposed security. The preceding year he had contracted with some of the numerous family of Stouts, and Mr. Green, to have him a dwelling and the usual out-houses completed by the ensuing spring; and he had sent up Van Wiggens with several slaves (the Quakers then were slaveholders) to girdle the trees for a new field and to raise a crop of corn.

The site had once been the abode of a squatter, without any title to the land, and the rude hut he had occupied was now the hen-house. But there remained more than a hundred noble fruit-trees of his planting, now in perfect maturity; and there were several acres of well-cleared land in the immediate vicinity, a portion of which had been enclosed for a garden, and was to be under the special superintendence of Paddy Pence, directed by the fair Julia.

Farming implements, articles of furniture, and other indispensable household goods, had been sent up from time to time in barges Van Wiggens had superintended every thing In his eyes the house was a palace and the lands a princely estate; for he was descended from one of the original Dutch families that lived and died on the broken hills of the highlands on the Hudson. And now he was to receive his reward. Fifty acres of good land at the foot of a hill in the vicinity were to be his own, to be conveyed to him and his heirs forever. Nor was this all. Thomas Schooley was to furnish him with the implements of a blacksmith-shop, William having learned the trade in a Dutch smithy. The anvil, the bellows, &c. were already on the way, and Van Wiggens ought to have been a happy man and his wife a happy woman, for they had been recently married.

At length the travellers were at the end of their journey, and William Van Wiggens and his wife Joan stood at the door to receive them. Julia bounded from the carriage, and was the first to receive their greetings.

"Why, William," said she, "you and Joan look as sedately as an old married couple." Joan was older than her husband; but girls were not so abundant in those days.

"Yes, miss, I'm dirty," said Van Wiggens, who could not easily pronounce the *th*, "and my vife is dirty-two."

"He means thirty-two," said Mrs. Van Wiggens.

Julia continued onward, laughing heartily, until she was arrested by Rose,—a very black rose,—who had nursed her when an infant, and who now attempted to lift her up in her arms.

"My sweet mistress—my baby dear—come to lib wid old Rose! I blesses de very arth you treads on! Why, Julie, you are a woman now. Gor bless your happy little heart!"

"I have a large heart, Rose, and it beats with true affection for my kind, faithful nurse. Release me now. I must see my room and gaze out of the window. There! That is my sweet wood-robin in the pear-tree. Listen! It is a song of welcome."

"Oh, Miss Julie," said Rose, following, "de trees are full of 'em. Dey sing from morning to night. In de night de owls come after 'em; but I knew you wouldn't have 'em eaten up, and so I made Sambo shoot de big-headed varmints."

"Thank you, Rose," said Julia, who had found her chamber, and was now standing before a plain bureau, upon which stood a small mirror, arranging her hair.

"Yes, Julie, and I made Sambo dig up all de pretty flowers in de woods and plant 'em for you in de garden."

"Thank you, thank you, Rose; but I hope he did not dig *quite* all, as I am also fond of seeing them wild in the forest."

"Lor' bless your sweet life, I don't mean ebery one! Goodness! dere's more flowers in de woods dan all de niggers in Jarsey could dig up in a lifetime. But, Julie, dere's some frightful-looking snakes in de woods, too."

"No rose without its thorn, Rose."

"Dat's edzactly what master used to say. But you can tie some bark on your legs like de Deckers did, and den dey can't hurt you."

"I don't understand you, Rose."

"Dey peel de bark off de young chestnut-trees and wrap it round der legs, and de snakes can't bite through it."

"Oh, I understand. But I will keep out of their reach. Is there any one, Rose, in the neighbourhood, who can tell long stories of winter evenings about the Indians and the wild beasts?"

"Lor' bless you, Mr. Green will set in de chimley-corner and talk all night if anybody'll listen. And he'll make your blood run cold wid his frightful tales. And de Indians does come sometimes; but dey're friendly. Den dere's bears, and painters, and catamounds!—I'm afraid your little heart'll be frightened out ob you."

"Not it! You know, Rose, I was never a fearful girl. I am sure I shall be charmed. I like the wild woods— though I would have no objection to a few neighbours of the right sort. I suppose there are some agreeable people living near—I mean within three or four miles,—besides the Stouts and Mr. Green?"

"Precious few, I tell you. Dere's one man living at de Jenny Jump cliff, in a kind ob crow's-nest ob a house. But I neber saw anybody who had been in it, 'cept Hugh MacSwine, his agent, and he's as sour as a green persimmon, and dey tink de master's as surly's de man.'

"What is his name, Rose?"

"Dey call him Cameron."

"That will do, Rose. You had better go to Mrs. Schooley now. She may require your services, and I can take care of myself."

Left alone, Julia pondered in silence over the discovery she had made. She was not really in love with Charles, but she admired him, and she had reason to believe the friendly feeling was reciprocal. She had heard much and read much of the magic influence of love; but she could not believe she was then in imminent danger of being swayed by its mysterious fascinations. She felt not the slightest alarm, and perhaps she could not have been made sensible of her peril.

During the first day after their arrival, the Burlington family were engaged in explorations within and without the house. The dwelling was quite spacious in dimensions, and, although neither plastered nor papered, the fireplaces seemed sufficiently ample to heat the apartments in winter, and there would certainly be no scarcity of fuel. And the rooms seemed to be furnished with every thing needful for the substantial comfort of the occupants. Indeed, but few articles of fancy were to be found in the parlours of the most wealthy city Quakers.

Mrs. Schooley was pleased—at least uncomplaining,—and Julia seemed really delighted. The climbers—Cocculus Carolinus and Vitus rotundifolia—which had been sent up were living where they had been planted, on each side of the main entrance. Then there was the garden,—an acre, at least,—and it had been enclosed with rude palings. There were rose-bushes (mainly the beautiful and fragrant damask) and lilacs at the corners of the borders. The fruit-trees were in blossom, and the birds in full song.

The lowing cows came up from the wild pasture to be milked, the pigs squealed in the pen for their food, and the fowls cackled in the barnyard. All was freshness and novelty, and Julia ran from one object of admiration to another like a gleesome school-girl. And Richard did his utmost to please her. He worked all day in the field with the slaves, and at eve brought in such blossoms as he could find among the bushes in the woods, mostly white and purple—the Cercis Canadensis and Cornus Florida.

Julia was thankful for every thing and to every one, and always happy. A large black Newfoundland dog on the place became attached to her, and was her inseparable companion whenever she emerged from the house. This was a great satisfaction, as it would not have been prudent for her to venture on the extensive rambles she meditated, without some sort of a protector. Richard was too industrious to lose any time in that way, and the corn was yet unplanted. But Solo was a sufficient guard and companion.

During the first week of her sojourn at her forest-home, Julia had been visited by Charles; and they laughed heartily over the subject of his picture and flower-writing, which had been so mysterious or unmeaning a thing to Richard and his unsophisticated parents.

But, if there were mysteries hidden from the old folks, they likewise possessed their secret, of which the young people had never dreamed. Charles and Julia had been aware of the frequent conferences held with Mr. Green, the surveyor, but could never have supposed the discussion referred to themselves or could in the slightest degree affect their interests.

They were not, however, to remain long in ignorance. The time appointed for the "shadows of coming events" to cross their path was at hand. A few hours more, and new subjects of meditation would be presented to them; but the short interval before the announcement was passed in almost perfect bliss, which is so often succeeded in this world by unhappiness.

Tea was just over. Richard had departed to the field, accompanied by the slaves, to labour for an hour in the night, and Mr. Green, as usual, had come to talk away the evening with the old people. Charles and Julia sallied forth, accompanied by the faithful Solo, to witness a spectacle which Richard had promised them,—an idea originated by Richard himself, and inspired, as he said, by the desire to exhibit something that would be magnificent in Julia's eyes. But it would be impossible for him to attend her during the evening. His time and labour would be required in the field. Charles, no doubt, would be willing to accompany her.

It was truly to be a spectacle of great grandeur and sublimity. For days the fallen boughs of the dead trees had been piled around the bases of the standing trunks;

and now, as the darkest hues of night were descending on the wild landscape, the heaps of dry wood were to be simultaneously ignited by the torches flitting between them.

Charles and Julia stood upon a knoll a few hundred yards distant from the scene, and Solo lay at their feet. During the hush that prevailed in the moment of expectation, a whippoorwill, frightened from the field, perched upon a rock in their immediate vicinity and uttered his monotonous wail. Ever and anon a panic-stricken hare bounded past, which Solo would pursue no farther than he could see it by starlight.

Ere long a deep red glare appeared on the dense woods which surrounded the field, and it was faintly visible on the faces of the young couple, while Solo's eyes resembled balls of fire. Some forty piles of dry boughs sent up their startling flames, roaring like an approaching hurricane.

"Beautiful! See the tall pines!" exclaimed Julia, releasing Charles's arm, and clapping her hands together. But, in the movement, the mantle which had enveloped her fell to the ground. Charles lifted it up and replaced it, gently encircling her form with his arm

The trunks of the gigantic trees, charged with inflammable resin, soon presented great columns of fire, rising high in the air. The illumination revealed the dusky forms of distant mountains, appearing like huge monsters reposing in the night; and, as the flames leaped upward, the whirling sparks seemed to mingle with the stars. Solo looked at the face of his mistress, and uttered a piteous whine.

"Poor Solo!" said she; "he seems to think we are in danger."

"And really, Julia," said Charles, gazing at her delicate features, "you are very pale."

"It is the contrast between the light and shade. The reflection on one side of your face makes the other seem like marble. I never felt less fear in my life. And, pray, what is there to frighten me?"

"Nothing, that I am aware of; and I am sure no injury can result from the magnificent conflagration before us. And yet, I confess, there is a singular weight oppressing me,—a sort of indescribable pain which is sometimes the premonition of a dreadful event."

"Dreadful event? And what could that be?"

"I know not, Julia, unless it be a separation from thee, and being forced into the scene of strife which may follow the unhappy differences between the parent country and the colonies."

"And that would be a dreadful event?"

"Undoubtedly."

"It would indeed be terrible to see the fires of civil war, and of a war of invasion, lighting the hills and valleys with the destruction of happy homes, while the red glare of the conflagrations would rest upon the faces of thousands of miserable outcasts, as the reflection of these flames is resting upon ours. Perhaps your depression may be the result of some such apprehension as that."

"It may be—certainly must be—in part. But to think of the blood that must be spilled, the great guns and gleaming swords of the civilized nations, and the whoop and scalping-knife of the impetuous savages!—Julia, what would become of thee? In such a contest neither sex, age, or condition, would be respected."

"Me? Oh, I should not have a particle of fear. I do not think any one could harbour a purpose of harming me. I have never injured any one."

"You know not what would happen."

"No. Nor would I desire to know beforehand. But I think I should meet my fate with a brave heart. Mercy on us!" she exclaimed, starting back and clinging involuntarily to Charles.

The largest tree in the field, which had been for some time completely enveloped in curling flames, fell, with a thundering sound, and with its top toward the young couple.

"Ha! ha! Julia," said Charles, "it is a full quarter of a mile distant."

"It seemed as if it would reach us. Let us return. Why, Solo!" she continued, as her dog sprang up and barked fiercely at some object, apparently but a short distance from them, in the almost impenetrable thicket behind.

"It is a fox, perhaps, or a cat. I could soon ascertain.

Yet it is hardly necessary," said Charles, yielding to Julia's inclination to depart. "But," he continued, somewhat sadly, as they proceeded slowly toward the house, "the horrors of both a civilized and a savage warfare may be in fearful proximity, and we should be prepared for the worst. You are the only friend I possess, Julia—I mean among the white people,—and I shall be very unhappy if any evil befalls you."

"Do you really think there is danger here?" she asked, quickly.

'Not more than there would be elsewhere. My father says the battles will be fought between the cities of New York and Philadelphia. The oldest settlements will be the scenes of the greatest carnage. He deems the conflict inevitable, and I believe in his prescience. No doubt roving bands of Indians will descend from the lakes—"

"And will they join the British?"

"Yes, too many of them. But they have a superstitious reverence for the Moravians, and for their founder, Zinzendorf. With them, if danger assails thee, thou mayest, perhaps, find safety."

"I will remember. But thy father? Why has he not been to see us?"

"He sees no one, for reasons he will not explain. Suffice it that he is experienced in war, and has led thousands to the conflict. His counsel is to be respected. But he will never draw his own sword again. He desires to live and die in the solitude of his chosen seclusion. You will see him some day, I trust; and he will please you and be pleased, I am sure. You will find he has been accustomed to associate with princes; but do not mention this, Julia."

"I will not; but why not?"

"No matter, now. Here is your guardian and Mr. Green coming to meet us. Mr. Schooley beckons me away. Mr. Green will conduct you in. Adieu—if we should not meet again to-night."

They were approaching the huge stile in front of the house, when Mr. Schooley called the young man aside.

"Thou hast been witnessing a grand scene, Charles. The ashes will be good manure, and there will be a larger space for the plough. But it seemed like a pity to destroy so much wood, which would have been very valuable in some places."

"It was a fine sight for Julia," said Charles; "but I have witnessed larger conflagrations."

"When thee dwelt among the Indians, thee, no doubt, saw whole forests in flames."

"Yes, and vast plains, one sheet of roaring fire."

"What destruction of vegetation! and by those, too, incapable of appreciating its uses and value! But I desired to speak with thee, Charles, in relation to thy father."

"My father, sir!"

"Thee need not be surprised. He is my neighbour; and thee knows the Bible says, 'Thou shalt love thy neighbour as thyself.' And how may that be done where neighbours never meet and do not see each other? According to the custom of the country, thy father should have paid me the first visit; but thee knows I am no respecter of etiquette, and I am willing to make the first visit to thy father."

"I will signify your wish, sir," said Charles, somewhat gravely; "but you must be aware that my father never goes into company, and, consequently, that he cannot be desirous of receiving visitors."

"Very true. But thee may say that I wish to see him on business."

"Business? Oh, I will say so, sir. The nature of the business it will not be necessary for me to announce to him."

"Thee may do so. It is in regard to the lines of our land,—a tract held jointly by thy acquaintance Julia and myself, which runs in the immediate neighbourhood of thy father's house. Mr. Green, the surveyor, is of opinion that the house is on our land. And, if it be so, thee knows thy father should be informed of it, as there might be a *gold-mine* involved in it."

"I will repeat your words, sir," was the careless reply of the young man, upon whom the Quaker had supposed the announcement would produce a very different effect.

In short, the frequent conferences between Mr. Green and Mr. Schooley had reference to the whispered rumour that gold existed in vast quantities in the cliff, at the base of which the hut of Mr. Cameron was situated; and it was believed that the white-haired Scotchman had found access to it. Else why did he persist in maintaining so strict a seclusion? And how else could he have obtained the means of bestowing a collegiate education on his son? His man, McSwine, had been sent twice a year to New York, from whom, of course, nothing could be learned; but it was inferred that he carried the precious metal with him to exchange for coin, with which the expenses of Charles, at Princeton, were defrayed.

After a rather embarrassing pause, caused by the surprise of Mr. Schooley, Charles departed for the humble residence of his father.

And in the mean time Mr. Green had improved the opportunity to impart to Julia the fact that a portion of the land occupied by Mr. Cameron belonged, in all probability, to herself; and, furthermore, that it might be the repository of the precious metal so long believed to be hidden in the vicinity.

"If this be so," said Julia, with seriousness, "it would be a pity to deprive him of it."

"Thee must be very generous," said Mrs. Schooley, "not to take what is thine own, for fear of depriving a stranger of it, and one who has no title to it."

"Oh, madam," said Julia, "thou knowest I leave the management of all business matters to Thomas. But, still, I cannot help thinking how great a disappointment it would be for another to relinquish an estate after long supposing it to be fairly his own.'

"But paid for it with thy gold, perhaps: thee must not forget that," said Mary, rising, and going out in obedience to a signal from Thomas, who appeared at the door.

Mr. Green, being left alone with Julia, did not hesitate to touch upon another matter, which he was well assured would not be displeasing to Mr. and Mrs. Schooley, or their thrifty and industrious son.

"In all such matters, Miss Lane," resumed Mr. Green, who really spoke without disingenuousness, "I can have no other object than to promote the interest of my friends. Whatever may be the result of the discovery which we think has been made, I can neither sustain any injury or derive any benefit."

"Of course not, Mr. Green," said Julia; "and you must

not suppose me capable of being offended at any part you may take in the proceeding."

"Oh, I am under obligations to your late respected father and to Mr. Schooley. And, if I might be so bold as to utter a particular wish I have long indulged, regarding the crowning of your happiness—of the happiness of both families——"

"Pray, speak on, Mr. Green," said Julia, smiling. "You have permission to speak plainly."

"Then it is this: that all the lands may descend to the heirs without division. I mean, as the lands are undivided, that the heirs may be united."

"Oh, in marriage!"

"That is it! And Master Richard, I believe, sighs for such a union."

"Mr. Green, I am sure you must be mistaken. He has never said so himself."

"He is diffident. But you may rely upon it."

"But then it would be impracticable, because we belong to different churches."

"You can *thee* and *thou* as well as the rest of them; and I supposed you attended their meetings."

"I have gone to them, but came away no wiser than before, because the Spirit did not move them to speak. No, indeed; I am an Episcopalian."

"I am a Baptist, and would be the last person to advise any one to give up the church of his choice. Still, I think the obstacle could be removed. But pardon me—I will not pursue the subject. Where there is a will there is a way."

Mr. and Mrs. Schooley then entered, and the subject of the impending war became the topic of conversation.

Julia repeated the opinion of the elder Cameron as it had been expressed by Charles.

"Then he seems to take some interest in the world beyond the cliff," said Mr. Schooley.

"Oh, yes," continued Julia, "and he has much experience, no doubt, in wars—and—or—I mean—from his great age I should think so," she added, checking herself.

"Did Charles tell thee so?" asked Mr. Schooley.

"He said he had faith in his father's judgment," replied the startled girl. "And Charles is decidedly of the opinion that the Indians will generally espouse the royal side."

"And Charles's opinion is correct," said Mr. Green. "Although they do not know which side I will take, I have already had a message from King Shingas of the Northern Delawares, and Brandt, of the Mohawks, to be prepared for flight. I have rendered some services to several of the great chiefs, and therefore am I warned by them. Yet I do not think there is any immediate danger."

"But I shall take neither side," said Thomas. "That is, I will commit no violence on either side, although I shall be rejoiced when the rebellion is put down, as I have no doubt it will be. And if the Indians fight for the king, they will hardly molest me—a loyal subject."

After relating to Julia the manner in which he had obtained the friendship of the Indians, Mr. Green withdrew, promising to attend Mr. Schooley during his interview with the elder Cameron.

CHAPTER V.

THE HERMIT—HIS SECRET—SCENE AT THE TREE—SOLEMN VOWS—MOODY'S APPEARANCE.

CHARLES determined to seize the first opportunity, both to propose to his father the reception of friendly visitors and to expostulate upon the impolicy of occupying so mean a house.

It was with this bold resolution that he arose the second morning after his interview with Mr. Schooley, and occupied the rude seat opposite his father at the morning repast. Mr. Cameron was not exceeding sixty years of age, although his bleached locks and profuse grizzly beard had created the impression that he was much older. His form was tall and erect, and his frame, though not robust was not fragile. His face was very pale, and his eyes dark, clear, and piercing.

Hugh McSwine moved backward and forward between the table and the broad fireplace, serving his patron and his son.

After partaking of the viands in silence, Charles broached the subject of erecting a better habitation. His motive, he delicately hinted, was the comfort of his parent, and not a matter of convenience to himself, for he had been accustomed to the rude wigwam of the children of the forest. And he regretted that his indulgent parent had not used a portion, if not the whole, of the money expended on him at college, in the erection of a better tenement.

"Do you suppose, my son," said Mr. Cameron, "that this is to be your permanent abiding-place?"

"No, father. Yet the woods, the rocks, the streams, and the skies, here, are no doubt quite as pleasant as elsewhere, and I could soon become attached to them and feel that this was my home. But it has ever seemed to me that I was destined to mingle in more stirring scenes than those likely to occur in this quiet valley. I have dreamed of going forth to battle——"

"Nature—NATURE, sir!" said McSwine.

"Peace, Hugh!" said Mr. Cameron.

"But when I returned, it was to some such place as this, surrounded by crags and deep impenetrable forests."

"And such may be thy destiny. But, until you shall have returned in safety, where is the necessity of a better house? If you did not return to inhabit it, it would be tenanted by strangers."

"It would be occupied by you, sir. Oh, I assure you, I feel many a bitter pang after lying long on my sleepless couch, imagining I have achieved honours in battles or science, to revert in thought to the mean hut which shelters the head of my parent. If we are poor in purse, still McSwine and myself have strong arms, and there is abundance of material, both wood and stone."

"I might have a better house, Charles. There is gold sufficient in my chest to build one. But wherefore? I am comfortable, and have my health. I could convince you that my abode would be less agreeable in a better house, and will do so very soon."

"But, sir, this hut is made the subject of contemptuous remark by the people."

"I know it. I desired it."

"Will you not tell me why such was your desire?"

"Not now; but soon."

Charles then delivered the message from Mr. Schooley, and repeated the request that a meeting might be had at an early day.

A startling frown darkened the pale brow of his father; but it vanished when he learned the object of the Quaker's pursuit was merely gold, and a smile of derision parted his lips.

"Ah!" said he, "the Quakers retain but a limited portion of the Old Testament. The command that 'thou shalt have none other Gods but me' is received with certain reservations, according to the monitions of the spirit. But, less wise than the Indians, it may be doubted sometimes whether they know the difference between the promptings of the Kacha and the Malcha Manito."

"Ha! ha! ha!" was heard in guttural sounds.

"Peace, Hugh!" said Mr. Cameron. "It is the same thing throughout the earth. Many men make choice of a religion for their worldly convenience rather than their eternal welfare. But this prying Quaker, and the cupidity of the idle gossips of the country, would fill my poor house and overrun the premises. I will see him, however, under the elm at the margin of the brook, and treat with him as the savages did with Penn; only, he must offer me no gaudy presents."

"I will inform him, sir. But, father, may I ask why it was, when I mentioned the request of Mr. Schooley, your brow contracted and your frame seemed agitated?"

"You may," said his father, after a long pause. "There could be no better time than the present, perhaps, to make known to you——"

"Right!" exclaimed McSwine, clapping his hands.

"Peace, Hugh! Close the door and barricade it," said the old man; and then, turning to his son, while Hugh lighted a torch, (for no particle of the glittering sunlight now penetrated the hut,) he proceeded:—"Charles, you have no doubt met with many of your name and country. There are hundreds of them driven forth by tyranny from their native soil and dispersed over the world. Did you not learn from the books in the college library, or from Dr. Witherspoon, that there was once a race of lords of this clan, each of whom led to battle a thousand followers?"

"I did, sir. And the doctor referred to them in the last conversation I had with him. He told me to be worthy of my name."

"A noble, a glorious name and lineage!" exclaimed McSwine.

"Be silent, faithful Hugh!" said his master. "He advised thee well, my son."

"But, father, can it be possible that I am a lineal descendant of the lords of the clan Cameron?"

"It is. You are the last of the line in more respects than one."

"How, sir?" cried Charles. "Was not the 'Gentle Lochiel,' as his prince called him, stricken down on the fatal field of Culloden, as had been predicted by the Highland seer?"

"He was stricken down, but rose again; and the seer spoke falsely."

"The seer said he would die at the stake," said McSwine, despondingly; "and it may yet come to pass."

"Peace, Hugh!" said his master.

"Then he must be living still," said Charles.

"He does," said his father. "After the escape from that fatal field, he entered the service of the King of France. He fought against the armies of the British tyrant both in Europe and America."

"America!" said Charles. "Am I—can I——"

"Thou art his son. I am Lochiel!"

Charles threw his arms round his father's neck, and long remained silent.

"Yes," continued his father, gently disengaging himself, "I am the Gentle Lochiel, and thou art my son. But know you not there is a price upon my head? A reward of a thousand guineas was offered for my arrest, and it has not been revoked."

"But, father, George II. has descended to the tomb, and surely the decree would not now be enforced if you were apprehended."

"You know not that. My brother returned to Scotland, many years after the battle of Culloden, for the treasure of the family he had secreted. He obtained it, and it was transmitted to me in Paris. But he lingered in Scotland, supposing the enmity of the usurpers might be extinguished. He was arrested—executed! He and I were among the proscribed, and were already condemned to death. No trial was accorded him. The king had only to sign the death-warrant, which was done, while he uttered hollow regrets—merely enticements, hoping I, too, would return to the land of my fathers. His crown sat uneasily on his head while an honest chieftain asserted that he had no title to it! But enough of that. When peace was made, I did not return with my regiment to Europe, because the Indians had stolen my son. I sought you and found you. But then the last of the royal Stuarts had been arrested and conveyed from Paris by the orders of Louis, and I resigned my commission, (which was not accepted,) resolved to bestow an education on my son and die in some peaceful seclusion. Now you know the reason of my standing aloof from society. The thousand guineas would induce many a wretch to cut short my existence. You need not frown. You could not prevent it, but you might avenge me."

"I will be avenged upon King George!" said Charles.

"I know thou wouldst, my son," said the old man. "I know you would contribute to sever this vast country from his empire. It will be lost to him and his line forever without our instrumentality. Such is the decree of Providence, who rewards or punishes every good or evil action. But more of that hereafter. Let it suffice that I have ample intelligence of the great political events, and can, from my obscure hut, notwithstanding the umbrage I conceived, wield no mean influence at the court of Versailles. As for thee, thou art already, I fear, entangled in the silken fetters of love——"

"I, father?"

"I think so. What think you, Hugh?"

"Gone! noosed!" said McSwine, grimly smiling.

"And, pray, how was such information obtained?" demanded Charles, with a burning blush suffusing his face.

"Ha! ha! Ask Solo!" said McSwine.

"Solo? Ha! were you in the thicket that night?"

"I was," replied the shaggy, broad-shouldered Scot.

"Beware how you dog my trail, McSwine!" said the indignant youth. "If my tomahawk had been in my belt, your brains might have manured the roots of the brambles!"

"It was not without my permission, Charles. But the lady, as I have learned——"

"As you have learned, father?"

"Oh, yes. The mode of obtaining my intelligence is no doubt sufficiently mysterious; but it is ample and reliable. I say I am gratified to learn the lady is altogether worthy of the son of Lochiel. I shall not oppose the union, when the time arrives for its consummation, should I survive to see it,—for the event cannot transpire immediately. It will be obstructed by others, and in the mean time I may be seized and led to the block."

"Never!" said Charles. McSwine pointed significantly toward the dying embers on the hearth.

"I understand you, Hugh," said the old man, smiling. "Charles shall know all. Follow me, my son," he continued, lifting the torch, and striding toward the broad fireplace, that had been apparently cut from the solid rock, being a portion of the perpendicular cliff against which the hut was constructed. After removing the soot on one side of the rock, and introducing a strong iron bar into an orifice hitherto concealed, the entire rear wall, in one piece, began to swing forward on hidden hinges, like the ponderous door of a vault. The torch was then extinguished, and Charles was amazed to behold the subdued rays of the sun falling across the passage revealed within.

In silence he followed his father, and the next moment was standing in an elegant room, with an arched ceiling, through which the rays of the sun were streaming in a hundred places. The floor was strewn with rushes, and in the corners were several couches covered with velvet. The walls were hung with Gobelin tapestry, commemorating events in the history of Scotland and France. A small ebony table on one side was covered with books richly bound; and on the other, supported by a small stand, was an open Bible and an Episcopal prayer-book. In the centre of the room gurgled a stream of transparent water, which filled a pool hollowed in the rock, and then flowed out at the side by a channel cut in the floor. In the pool disported a number of speckled trout, seemingly familiar with the presence of man.

"This is not the work of enchantment," said the exiled chief, gazing at the surprised countenance of his son, "but partly of these hands. It is never good to be idle. While Hugh tilled the soil and you were at college, it was my daily task to excavate the rock and provide a refuge. You may learn from this the magnitude of results obtained by incessant application, however slow the progress. If the idea be conceived, unceasing application will sooner or later accomplish the end. But you have not seen all." He then led the way into two smaller rooms, some ten feet square, and both likewise illuminated by rays of the sun struggling through small fissures. In one of these rooms—the centre one, for they were in a suite, after the plan of the palaces in France—were arranged a great number of warlike implements. In the farthest was the wardrobe and the treasure, the latter secured in a strong iron-bound oaken chest. The lid was lifted, and Charles beheld several bags of coin. There were also costly jewels, and pieces of massy plate, the presents of princes and the heirlooms of the family.

"This is thy heritage," said the exile. "If it please thee to build a finer house, have thy will; but thy father will still abide in his stronghold."

"No, sir!" said Charles, with firmness. "Every thing shall be subject to thy will—not mine. Thou wert right in constructing such an abode. And, if I were thee, I would not see Mr. Schooley, nor satisfy the curiosity of prying neighbours. Permit me, sir, to turn back all intruders. Against me no accusation can be brought; but some one whom thou hast met in foreign lands might recognise thy features."

"No, no. Hugh will watch and guard the premises. He is faithful. And they may not know me. I had no exuberance of beard, and my hair was dark, until thou wast stolen. No, no! there is no danger now; and I will see this Quaker under the elm. No doubt they believe I find gold in the cliff, since they must have observed the dust from my excavations swept away by the freshets. Let us return to the humble hut. Hasten to thy friend, and say I will see him."

Charles was impatient to deliver the answer of his father, but paused near the door of the hut, and carefully surveyed the premises. The hut, as we have said, was built against a perpendicular portion of the cliff. It was where the range had been divided at right angles by one of the narrow ravines that opened into the larger valley, which ran parallel with the principal ridge. Thus the tenement was above the reach of high-water, and the rooms excavated in the rock received their light from the many perforations in the cliff fronting on the largest stream, and were quite inaccessible to any one without. There were a few well-cultivated acres on one side of the small brook, on which were a rude stable and cow-house. And in this manner the recluse lived in security and independence.

Charles directed his steps toward the abode of Julia with feelings very different from any he had hitherto experienced. His hatred of the king became inextinguishably violent, and he was glad he had resisted the artful suggestions of Governor Franklin.

When he drew near the house, Paddy addressed him.

"What is it, Paddy?" he asked, pausing near the garden.

"Nothing matarial, Misther Charles, only we've no wathermelons in Ireland, and, as I niver seed 'em grow, I can't ricognise thim whin I mate them face to face. They tould me they growed among the savages, and I thought you might be famaliar with 'em, and would be oblaging enough to say which is which."

"That is a watermelon-vine at your elbow, Paddy," said Charles, laughing very heartily.

"Be my life, I thought so, though I niver saw one before."

"But you are cultivating it in a most singular way," continued Charles, much diverted on finding the imported gardener had driven a long stake in the ground and wrapped the vine around it.

"I shouldn't wonder, Mr. Charles; for what is right in a savilized country is wrong in sich a wild place as this. And it reminds me of the corn Lord Bute, whose gardener my father was, tried to raise in Scotland. His lordship tasted the laves of the bush, and they cut his tongue. He had thim biled, like granes, and tasted thim sasoned, but threw thim to the pigs. Well, Mr. Charles, the great philosopher, Franklin, the nathural father of the prisent governor of this colony, was there, looking on, laughing and whaspering something to her ledyship. At last he hinted that the car ought to be biled and aten, as it was done in America. 'Och,' said his lordship, 'is that the way? I thought the grane was the sade, and not to be aten, but planted.'"

"Paddy," said Charles, "when the Indians get you, if you tell them that tale it may save your scalp."

"I wouldn't spind my breath on such blackguards," was Paddy's reply, as he proceeded to detach the vines from the poles, and muttering something about the "falthiness" of permitting fruit to grow on the ground.

Mr. Schooley and Mr. Green did not delay when informed that Mr. Cameron would receive them. They mounted their horses and trotted briskly away. And, while Mrs. Schooley's foot was in rapid motion at the little wheel, furnishing the threads for the loom, Julia and Charles wandered away toward the grove near the end of the lane.

On one side of the lane, Richard and the negroes were at work planting the late corn.

"I suppose, Julia," said Richard, his hoe suspended in the air, as the couple passed slowly along, "thou hast been telling thy friend about our claim to the land. Thou mayest promise, if there be much gold in the cliff, that a share of it shall remain for his father."

"Oh, pray don't be too liberal, friend Richard," said Charles. "My father don't value gold as much as you do the common dust; and as for me, no doubt Julia will speak kindly in my behalf."

"Do so, Julia," said Richard; "and whatever thou dost promise will be approved by me."

The amused couple pursued their way, and never paused until they reached the great sycamore on the margin of a trout-brook at the eastern extremity of the farm. Here they sat upon a moss-covered stone partly buried in the soil, placed there, perhaps, by human hands, to mark the spot of a battle between hostile tribes of the forest. Animals, arrows, and birds, were cut on one side of its surface. On the other, and almost illegible, were rude figures of men wielding the tomahawk and scalping-knife, besides many nondescript marks and characters. Charles read the meaning, and not only understood the number of warriors that had been engaged, but the name of the tribe which had conquered. He could not tell when the conflict had taken place, but it was evidently at a remote period.

"Ha!" he exclaimed, upon lifting his eyes and beholding recently-made figures on the smooth bark of the sycamore, "a Seneca chief has been here within the last twenty-four hours!"

"And with an evil intent, think you?" asked Julia, with emotion, observing the excited gaze of the young man.

"I fear so, Julia," said he. "He threatens us. Do you not see the serpent winding round the eagle, and the arrow piercing the antelope?"

"And they call you the White Eagle and I the Antelope! Why should they threaten us?"

"They would have me with them again. And they suppose the Antelope withholds me from returning to the Brown Thrush, the sister of Thayendanegea.'

"And perhaps she loves you!"

"She called me brother."

"But I have learned that the white captives often marry their brown sisters."

"True. But I will never do so."

"But does she not love thee?"

"She does. But what then?"

"Fly to her!"

"No."

"Why not?"

"Because, Julia, I love only thee, and will remain."

"You never said so before," replied the girl, after a long pause.

"But I have long felt it, and you could not have been wholly ignorant of it. Even Shawuskukhkung, who came hither with me, and is now on the lakes, pleading with his kindred to remain at peace, observed it. Mr. Livingston suspected it; and now I avow it. Oh, do not drive me back to the wild forest! I never regarded the Brown Thrush otherwise than as a dear sister. Do not drive me away. I am not the outcast they suppose. My father is of gentle blood. Only permit me to love thee, and let thy friendship continue, and that is all I will require, until a proper time arrives for me to claim your hand in the face of the world."

"Charles, you know I have ever esteemed you; but I cannot promise."

"Not promise to continue your friendship? to ramble with me as usual over the hills and through the valleys? —to——"

"Oh, I think I may promise that—but——"

"That is all I ask at this time. I know that, until you arrive at a certain age, your guardian has power over you. This both himself and Mrs. Schooley have repeatedly assured me."

"He possesses the power of withholding my fortune until I arrive at a certain age, if I marry without his consent. That is all. But I promised my father to be guided by his advice until I had attained my majority, and, you know, long years must elapse before the fulfilment of that period."

"True. But the time will come. I asked nothing but a continuance of your friendly regard until a proper moment arrived for me to apply to your guardian. There was one other thing, however:—that you would make no pledge, under any circumstances, to Richard."

"To Richard! Do you know the Quakers must marry within the society?"

"I know it; and I know also there are many ways of whipping the devil round the stump."

"They would not attempt to whip me; but surely you could not mean such a thing."

"No, certainly not; the allusion was to the Malcha Manito, which may sometimes be mistaken for the Good Spirit in one's breast; and, according to the Quaker doctrine, its monitions might be the highest decrees—higher than any human laws. But you do not promise!"

"I do, Charles! And let it be a solemn compact!"

"Solemnly between us!" said Charles, pressing her hand against his heart. "For, Julia, the time may come when we must be separated,—when I may be a captive, or an outlaw with a price upon my head; for I will never draw sword or wield tomahawk in behalf of King George.

CHARLES AND JULIA SURPRISED BY MOODY — P. 56.

Mr. Livingston, Mr. Stockton, Doctor Witherspoon, and most of the leading characters, will resist the tyranny of the king. And my father says that when a rebellion is headed by the great personages of a coun'ry, after due deliberation and formal confederation, the people must win their freedom."

"The devil he does!" said a broad-chested, red-haired man, of vigorous step and scowling features, who came from the opposite side of the huge sycamore and confronted the unsuspecting pair.

"Who are you?" demanded Charles, leaping up and grasping his tomahawk, which he had carried in his belt after hearing the history of his father.

"I am a loyal subject of King George III., and you are a rebel!"

"And you have been eavesdropping? But you shall not repeat what you have heard!" And the youth hurled his tomahawk at the head of the intruder. Julia uttered a scream at the moment, and strove to defeat his aim. She was successful. The instrument penetrated the tree several inches above the mark, and remained firmly fixed in the wood.

"Now is *my* time!" said the stranger, pale and quivering; for the assault had evidently not been anticipated, and he had made but a hairbreadth escape."

"Nay! do not fire!" exclaimed Julia, throwing her slight form between his rifle and her lover. "I saved thy life," she continued, "and you shall not take his without first killing me!"

"I believe you would die to save him," said the stranger, lowering his gun. "But you must teach him better manners than to throw his tomahawk at every one he meets, and before he learns whether they are his friends or his foes."

"Sir, you could not be the first," said Charles; "and I defy thee still, although unarmed."

"Merely because I happened to hear the words you were speaking to this maiden? Know, sir, that the tree is hollow, the entrance being on the opposite side. I was in it before you came hither."

"And what were you doing there?"

"I will tell you, seeing you have no secrets from me.

Know, then, that I, too, can read the picture-writing as well as yourself—nay, better, for I understood by the figures that the Seneca chief would return in a few hours. I fell asleep awaiting him, and was awakened by you. I know you both, and will not retain the advantage. I am Bonnel Moody, at your service, and bear a commission in the service of the king. And I am now on duty, being sent hither by one of the royal governors to ascertain the sentiments of the people."

"And you have learned the sentiments of one of them," said Charles, smiling.

"But sentiments change, like the seasons; and, when you hear what I have been charged to speak to Mr. Schooley, perhaps your opinions may be modified. My mission is to spread information as well as to obtain it; to conciliate, rather than to incense. Hence, I trust there will be no further strife between us."

"I thank you for those words, Mr. Moody," said Julia.

"And fear not that I will repeat the speeches I have heard, unless forced to do so in the discharge of my duty," continued the intruder, with a slight smile.

"I warn you, sir!" said Charles. "Utter but one word you have heard, and we are deadly enemies forever. Let us return, Julia. You still tremble."

Charles had not gone many paces before he was overtaken by Moody.

"Take your tomahawk, sir," said Moody, placing the glittering hatchet in the hand of the youth. "You have a strong arm, sir. I could hardly loosen it. And, as the maiden may not always be present when we meet, I hope it will never be aimed at the same target again. Let us be friends."

"It cannot be. Avoid my path, and I will not seek yours."

"It must be as you decide," said Moody, gravely. "But I may keep your company until we arrive at the house, since I have important messages for Mr. Schooley."

"He is not at home, sir," said Julia. "He and Mr. Green have visited Mr. Cameron, Charles's father."

"The old man of the gold-mine? Then I will join them there; and I know a nearer way than through the lane. A fair morning to you both," he continued, bowing very low, and striding through the wood in a divergent direction.

"And be careful that you do not again play the eavesdropper," said Charles; "for Hugh McSwine has a sharp tusk."

"Do not irritate him, Charles!" said Julia, clinging with increased tenacity to his arm.

"Julia," said Charles, in a sad tone, "that man is the only witness to our vows."

"No, Charles. One in heaven heard them! They say such vows are registered in heaven, and there is no reason to doubt it. And if it be so, it must be a grievous thing to break them! I hope you made no similar pledges to the sister of the Mohawk chief."

"Indeed, no, Julia. And she will acquit me of it; but she knows not of my regard for you. She is meek and forgiving, and seldom swayed by passion; but her brother is sometimes fierce and furious. He loves me, but would kill me rather than lose me; but we must be separated."

"And will he not kill you?"

"Not if I can help it. But he is patient, too, at times, and prudent and wise, as well as affectionate. He is only terrible when in one of his ungovernable spasms. He still hopes I will return and marry his sister; and I do not think he would listen to the words of this Moody, if he were to repeat what he heard at the sycamore." In this manner they conversed until they were joined by Richard, who, having faithfully done a half-day's work, was repairing to the house for his dinner.

CHAPTER VI.

THE SENECA INDIAN—ATTEMPT TO ARREST THE REFUGEE—
RIVAL LOVERS—BLUE PIGEON'S MESSAGE.

CHARLES accepted Richard's invitation to dine with him. Rose brought in the smoking fowls and other viands, and they fared sumptuously.

Before the dinner was over, and when even Mrs. Schooley herself was smiling at the idea of the Irish gardener planting poles for the watermelon-vines to run on, (an account of which Charles was entertaining the family with,) Paddy himself made his appearance in a most unlooked-for manner. He sprang into the room and overturned the table, over which he fell, sprawling to the floor. Before any one had time to demand an explanation, he bawled out, "Indians! the savage Indians!"

'Where?" asked Richard, jumping up, and manifesting some alarm.

"Be calm, Richard. Thee need not fear," said Mrs. Schooley. "Thou knowest the chiefs have often been the guests of thy father in Burlington, and thee need not fear them here."

"How many did you see?" asked Charles.

"I don't know how many, Misther Charles," said Paddy. "But one of the blackguards was laning over the palings close be my head when I was sticking the marrow-fat pays. He was as close to me as I am to you at this moment."

"Then it could not have been his purpose to kill you," said Julia, "or he might have done it easily."

"Och, and I should niver have been the wiser! What a country to live in! Nothing but rattlesnakes and blackguard Indians!"

"Thee must not term them so, Patrick," said Mrs. Schooley; "for, if they should hear thee, they might do thee some mischief."

"I will call them gintlemen if they'll only let me sculp

alone. I hope they did not hear me. I'm sure I beg their pardon if they did."

Charles stepped to the door and uttered a friendly call in the Seneca language; and the solitary Indian, who had so much alarmed the gardener, approached from the position he had occupied when Paddy beheld him, and from which he had not moved. He entered the house, shaking hands with all the inmates, and uttering the usual "How do?" Paddy hesitated and squirmed a great deal, but yielded when told by Charles that if he refused to extend his hand it might be considered as a token of hostility.

The Indian wore upon his garments a great many bears'-claws and porcupine-quills; and behind, hanging from his feathered head-dress, was the skin of a large rattlesnake, reaching nearly to his heels. The rattles were still on the lower end of it, and at every motion of his body they gave forth the startling sound so terrifically familiar to the ears of the first settlers of every portion of our country.

The Indian was invited to eat as soon as Rose could re-adjust the table. When he had finished eating, Mrs. Schooley lighted his pipe, and Charles smoked with him.

"My Seneca brother," said Charles, in the Indian language, "has threatened the White Eagle. It was done in sport, was it not?"

"The Rattlesnake listened to the voice of the great chief, Captain Pipe, and did his bidding. The Rattlesnake does not aim his fangs at the White Eagle."

"The White Eagle is glad to hear it, and he smokes the pipe of peace with his brother. But he would have the Seneca chief listen to his voice also. He would have him say to the great Captain Pipe that he fears him not, nor any other captain who threatens at a distance; but, that if the Antelope should be molested, the White Eagle would soar to the top of the highest mountain, whence he could see his farthest enemy; and the bird of the fleetest wing would soon alight upon him."

The Seneca promised to deliver the message, and at the same time declared that Thayendanegea was entirely ignorant of what had been done to offend his brother.

Charles learned from this Indian, who was but a minor chief, that the colonists had taken the fort at Ticonderoga, and that preparations for war were being made everywhere in the North.

The Seneca soon after set out in quest of Moody, for whom he had certain messages.

Meantime the interview with the mysterious occupant of the humble hut took place under the elm on the margin of the stream that swept along the base of the cliff. Mr. Cameron did not apologize for not offering to entertain his visitors within the house, but proceeded to business without delay. And when he exhibited his title, (it was for five thousand acres, to the utter astonishment of Mr. Schooley,) derived from the heirs of Edward Byllinge, one of the original purchasers from Lord Berkeley, who had his title from the Duke of York, and produced a plot made by John Rockhill, a noted surveyor still living, neither Mr. Green nor the Quaker had a word to say against the correctness of his lines or the validity of his title.

"And now, gentlemen," said the exile, "I believe our business is at an end, and we must part as strangers. If this examination into my title had not been made a pretext for inspecting my premises, I might have desired a more social intercourse with my neighbours. I know it is believed that gold exists in these rocks; but such can only be the supposition of the ignorant; for any one at all acquainted with chemistry would know that the substances found in this region resembling the precious metals can be nothing more than worthless iron pyrites."

When he ceased speaking, Moody, who, as usual, had been a concealed auditor, came forward and placed sealed packets in the hands of Mr. Schooley, whom he knew by his Quaker hat and coat. He then wandered carelessly aside, while Mr. Schooley broke open the seals. They contained letters both from New York and Burlington. Moody had just arrived from the former place, and the Indian (who now made his appearance, "how-doing" and shaking hands) from the latter. From Governor Franklin he brought a commission, creating Thomas Schooley a justice of the peace.

The Indian, true to his instinct, followed Moody's trail, and entered the small ravine which opened into the valley where the interview had been held.

"No, mon! I tell ye no! Gae bock, or I'll dirk you!"

Such were the words spoken a moment after, in a loud voice, by Hugh McSwine. And when all eyes were turned in the direction of the hut, Moody and the Indian were seen retreating, driven back by Hugh.

"If you scratch us with your Scotch dirk, I'll send a ball through you!" said Moody, half presenting his rifle.

The Indian uttered one of his warwhoops and brandished his tomahawk. Mr. Schooley and Mr. Green became much excited. The first, by virtue of the commission he had received, besought and even commanded the white man to keep the peace; while the latter, who knew something of the Seneca language, warned the Indian against shedding blood. The white-haired exile lifted a small horn to his lips and sounded a shrill blast, which was answered by another from the hut of a Mr. McArthur, living near the summit of the range of hills. The faint echoes of several other blasts were then discernable in the distance, but did not seem to be comprehended by Moody, who was still intent upon the execution of his purpose.

"I call upon you, Mr. Schooley," said he, "by virtue of your commission, to arrest these men in the name of the king. Here is a paper given me several months ago by Sir John Johnson, in which is described a certain fugitive from justice, and for whose arrest and delivery into the custody of any of his Majesty's officers a reward of one thousand guineas has been offered."

"Dost thou suppose this Hugh the one?" asked Mr. Schooley.

"No; but the pale Scotchman, if his hair were not so white, would answer the description," said Moody, lifting the paper before Mr. S.'s face.

"Art thou the man?" asked Mr. Schooley, turning to Mr. Cameron.

"What man?" was the reply.

"The Highland laird who fled with the Pretender," said Moody.

But the exile made no reply, while Hugh gazed steadily up the ravine.

"I see," continued Mr. Schooley, having adjusted his spectacles, and holding the document before his eyes with both hands, "I see that John Johnson, known as Sir John, hath been charged by his Majesty's ministers to seek a certain fugitive, supposed to have taken refuge in the hills of New Jersey, whose description followeth, &c. Truly, my friend," he continued, turning to the exile, "thou dost answer the description in every thing but the colour of thy hair. The name, too, is the same; for every one knows that the rebel Lochiel was the chieftain of the Camerons. And this paper further sayeth that there is quite a number of Scotchmen hidden in these parts, and they are supposed to possess several very valuable jewels rightfully belonging to the crown of Great Britain, but which were seized and carried away by the second James Stuart in his flight from the kingdom. One of said diamonds is valued at five thousand pounds. Bless my life! What canst thou say to all this?"

"Not one word will I say to you," replied the chief. "If it must be answered, let it be before a proper tribunal."

"Proper tribunal! Thee forgets I am one of the king's justices of the peace."

"I do not recognise the king's authority. What say you, my friends?"

"Down with the Usurper!" was the cry of some half-dozen voices; and the next instant a number of the brawny sons of Scotland, armed with dirks and rifles, emerged from the bushes and stood in a line before the amazed magistrate.

"What men are these?" demanded Thomas.

"They are the Scotchmen alluded to in this paper," said Moody; "and they are too strong for us," he added, in a whisper.

"They are the SONS OF LIBERTY," said Mr. Cameron.

"Sons of Liberty!" said Mr. Schooley, in astonishment. "William Franklin urges me, as a loyal subject, to prevent the organization of such a body in this section, and says it is believed a secret association, calling themselves by that name, are pushing their ramifications into every township."

"My friend," said Cameron, with a smile, "your labour will be fruitless if it is the design to suppress the Sons of Liberty. As for you, sir," he continued, addressing Moody, "go back to the miserable cave which is the repository of the plunder taken by thee in the name of the usurper styled King. If thou wouldst lose thy life in his service, die like a man in the heat of battle, or else bury thyself in the murky shades of the swamp, so that thy name may never more be mentioned. And thou, son of the forest," he continued, turning to the Indian, "fly far beyond the trail of the white man. Hunt the deer, the moose, and the buffalo, in the primeval forests, or on the interminable plains, beyond the reach of civilization. Avoid alike the faces of the English and the Americans. No matter which side you may choose,—no matter which party may be victorious,—a union with either will be thy destruction. Render that into his own language," added he, speaking to his son Charles, who had silently joined the party, and was now standing beside his father.

The chief listened attentively—as Indians ever do—to the speech intended for the ears of his race. When it was finished, he merely replied that all the lands and rivers had been given to the red man by the Great Spirit, and he would be unworthy the gift if he fled before the invaders from beyond the broad water.

During this scene Mr. Green remained silent, but did not seem surprised. He had much land, and was not disposed to place it in jeopardy by hastily taking sides with either party. Charles was indignant, and so greatly excited, it was with difficulty his parent could restrain him from making a desperate assault on Moody.

Of course the statue-like Sons of Liberty, who had descended from the hills, and now stood in imperturbable composure, each grasping his gun, put to flight for the time the purpose of making the arrest in the king's name. Moody slowly withdrew, in company with Mr. Schooley; Mr. Green and the Indian followed, while the exiled chief motioned his small band of Highlanders to return to their homes. He then entered his hut, and laid before Charles some papers he had just received from New Brunswick by the hands of one of Hugh's runners,—a red-haired boy, of an idiotic appearance, but of reliable shrewdness, called Skippie.

By these documents Charles learned that he had been appointed captain of a company of minute-men, to be raised in his county. The Convention had likewise imposed a tax of £10,000, to be paid to agents named by the committees; and until such appointments were made the captains were authorized to act, and were to correspond with the standing committee of patriots:—James Kinsey, John Wetherill, John Stevens, Richard Stockton, &c.

Governor Franklin was declared a public enemy by Congress, and his seizure ordered—by the advice, it was said, of his own father. And malignant persons asserted that the wise philosopher and his son made a politic choice of different sides, so that the one who chanced to be of the victorious party might save the other.

The Continental Congress decreed that if the Quakers could not conscientiously take the oath prescribed by them, they might subscribe a declaration as follows:—"*I agree to the above association as far as the same is consistent with my religious principles.*" As many believed it a Christian duty to be true to the king, they found no difficulty in signing when hard pressed. Such was the case in many localities where the whigs were the most numerous. But those who refused were to be disarmed, to give security for their peaceable conduct, and to "pay the expenses attending thereon." And the captains in the township, or the county committees, were to attend to the matter without delay, and were empowered to arrest and imprison dangerous persons at discretion; and all who would not muster when required, armed as the law directed, were to pay ten shillings for each offence, recoverable by a distress warrant.

"Now you are invested with quite as much authority," said the elder Cameron, smiling, "as the Quaker guardian of Julia Lane."

"It seems so, sir," said Charles; "but I shall be embarrassed in the exercise of it."

"You will accept the appointment, then?"

"Certainly, if you advise it, since Mr. Livingston accepts the appointment bestowed on him."

"You have my permission. And I would advise you to enroll your company with as little delay as possible, and lodge this Moody in the new jail at Newton,—else he will attempt to capture your father, not from motives of duty, but for the sake of the reward."

"True, sir!" cried Charles, starting up. "It must not be delayed. As I came from Mr. Schooley's, I crossed a trail in the woods, which arrested my attention. A dozen men had passed since morning, and they were evidently seeking to conceal their presence. It was not a mile distant, and they must be lurking in this vicinity."

"Were they Indians?" asked his father, in some concern.

"No, sir. I marked their footprints. They may have been guided by one, however. It is the tory gang of this Moody. I must be up and doing, sir, for we cannot tell what moment they will fall upon us."

"Stay," said his father. "You must remain till morning. It is now growing dark. You know we are impregnable in our defences. To-morrow, when the sun again illuminates the paths, you may seek these robbers. Hugh, barricade the door; but first admit the bloodhound. He seems to snuff the foe," he continued, when the whining animal was called in and the lighted torch revealed his gleaming eyes as he crouched beside the door.

"They will attack us to-night!" said Charles.

"They would depart in peace, if I would only accompany them," said his father.

"Rather let every one of them perish! What say you, Hugh?" exclaimed Charles.

"Kill!" was Hugh's reply.

Charles was permitted by his father to prize the ponderous stone door slightly open, so that they might readily escape in the event of a sudden emergency.

Hugh prepared the supper, which was heartily eaten, as if the presence of danger could produce no diminution of appetite.

Time wore on until the usual hour for rest, and still the apprehended assault had not been made.

"They must have abandoned the project," said Charles, breaking the silence which had prevailed for some moments.

"Perhaps not," said his father, rousing from one of the prolonged reveries to which he was addicted, and taking up one of the jewelled pistols that lay on the table, which had been presented him by the unfortunate Charles Edward. "But no matter," he continued; "there will be strife sufficient before this contest is ended. And the usurper will lose. Unlike the civil wars suppressed by tyrants, we here see the instigators of the revolution assuming the posts of danger. When cowards urge their instruments to rise, keeping themselves beyond the reach of injury, their enterprises fail. It was thus with many of the Jacobites. They not only kept aloof themselves, but would not consent for the king to take the field in person. His son could not sustain his standard. But it is different here. Every man of note who sanctions the movement throws his head into the scale. The usurper's empire will be ruptured. America will be lost. And the last of the royal line of Stuarts, degenerate as he is, will have the melancholy satisfaction of witnessing it."

The bloodhound bayed twice, and sprang against the door, which he gnawed with his teeth.

"I thought so!" said the exile; "and it is quite likely the leader of the party has been listening to my words."

"It is certain!" said Moody, without. "We have heard enough. I have with me some fourteen men, and resistance will be in vain. In the king's name, I bid you open the door."

"The devil's name would be quite as potential here as the king's," said Charles; "but neither will avail."

"We will see," replied Moody; and the next moment a dull, heavy blow sounded on the door, and nearly prostrated it. They had lifted up a heavy log and projected it forward like a battering-ram.

"Awa' with you! awa' with you, mon!" said Hugh, "or——"

"Or what?" demanded Moody. "We are armed, and quite ready to meet you in that way. But we do not wish to take the life of the prisoner, if we can avoid it."

"No," said the aged exile; "there might be some difficulty in proving my identity and in obtaining the reward."

"If you have money," said Moody, restraining his men during the parley, "we will listen to terms. Have you no disposition to offer a ransom?"

"None whatever!" said Charles, and then fired his rifle through the door. The log, held in readiness for the renewal of the assault, was heard to fall, and doubtless one of the assailants had been wounded.

A moment after, ten or twelve shots were fired by the party without, and the door was riddled with their bullets; but no injury was sustained by those within, who had anticipated such an occurrence.

"Father," said Charles, "as they have a great superiority of numbers, would it not be well to summon our friends from the hills?"

"It would be well, but it is not practicable. However,' continued the old man, "these assailants will not be able to injure us."

"You are mistaken!" cried Moody, ever listening.

"Then do your worst! we defy you!" said the elder Cameron.

"What will they do?" asked Charles, to whom it was apparent they were not resorting again to the heavy timber with which to force the door.

"They will try to burn us out," said his father, in a whisper.

"They may destroy the hut," said Charles, "but not injure us."

"They can do no more than burn the outside shell," said his father, smiling. "Do you not observe how heavily and completely the interior is plastered? The cement is thirteen inches in thickness. The logs outside will burn and fall to the ground; but the house itself will remain, to astonish them, and to furnish stories for the superstitious. Come; let us retreat into the rock. I hear the crackling flames already, and the light will bring down my little clan on their rear. Come, Hugh, unless you would be roasted like a wild boar."

"Let me stay, sir, until I feel too warm," was McSwine's reply; and the father and son retired into the excavated rock.

Very soon the cliffs of the valley, the crests of the hills, and the tops of the distant woods, were tinged with the crimson glare of the burning house. The wolves ceased their howling, and the owl, stricken blind, flapped down to the earth in mid career.

"Open the door, before it's too late!" cried Moody.

"Hoot, mon, what're you impatient about?" was the response of McSwine.

"Where are the others? Why don't they speak?"

"Gone, mon, where you canna' hear 'em."

"Are they smothered? suffocated?"

"It's nane o' your business."

"You seem to take it very coolly."

"Yes, I am smoking in the chimney-corner."

"Smoking, are you? I guess you'll soon be burning."

"I'm smoking my pipe, mon, and you're ower impudent to be disturbing ane."

This was true. McSwine enjoyed his pipe when the roof was in a blaze and the consuming logs were falling from the sides of the hut. Yet it was rather warm within to be comfortable; but the surly Scot determined to bear it. He posted himself in the fireplace for the benefit of the draught; but the current of heated air forced him at last to step through the aperture and join his master. He did not remain long, however, before the heat diminished in intensity as the burning logs fell away, and he was able to breathe again in the hut, which he re-entered, closing the stone door behind him.

"The old boy must be roasted too, by this time," said Moody.

"The de'il you say!" responded McSwine.

"He *is* the devil, I believe!" cried one of the gang.

"Knock a hole through the infernal lime," said Moody, "and let us see him."

This was not an easy matter. Failing to accomplish it, they once more resolved to assail the door, which had escaped the flames by being deeply sunk in the wall. But, before the first blow was aimed, McSwine sent another bullet through, and the timber was again heard to fall.

"He's broken my arm!" cried one of the men, "and I'll have nothing more to do with 'em."

Shortly after, several shots were fired on the right, and then could be heard the tramp of running men. Another minute, and all was quiet. The Highlanders, aroused by the light, had come to the rescue of their loved chieftain, and at the first discharge Moody and his robbers made a precipitate retreat.

In the morning Charles was eager for an immediate pursuit. But the aged chief forbade it. Before attempting to punish Moody, it would be prudent first to ascertain precisely the sentiments of the people:—whether, indeed, the Federal Congress or King George on such a question would have the greatest number of adherents.

Yielding to the counsels of his parent, Charles strove to suppress the deadly rage he felt, but harboured a settled determination to punish the knavish miscreant on some future occasion. He then aided in rebuilding the hut. Like a block of granite, the lime and cement, though blackened, and in many places cracked and scaled, still remained standing, and the redoubtable Hugh said it would bear another siege of fire. It was thoroughly repaired, however, with all possible expedition.

During the day, and as the news of the assault spread over the country, it was gratifying to Charles to receive tenders of assistance from many persons hitherto total strangers to him; and it soon became apparent that Moody had but few sympathizers and abettors in the neighbourhood. On the contrary, although Lochiel's identity was no longer doubted or denied, no one stepped forward to arrest him, tempted by the munificent reward. This was a cheering sign, and Charles lost no time in communicating to the people the substance of the documents he had received from the Colonial Convention. Although at first many remained unmoved, preferring not to commit themselves at that early stage of the rupture, yet it was apparent that in any test of authority between the king and the Congress the latter would have the preponderance.

Emboldened by such indications, Charles commenced canvassing for volunteers, and before the eve of the third day he had the names of forty "minute-men" enrolled on his list. His sergeant was a herculean Irishman, by the name of Timothy Murphy,—a well-digger up the county, whose life had been saved by Charles when in the hands of the Indians.

One day, leaving Tim in charge of the recruiting service, the head-quarters and rallying-point being in the vicinity of his father's hut, where a temporary encampment had been built both for the shelter of men and horses, Charles set out in the direction of Mr. Schooley's plantation.

Charles was surprised, when approaching the smithy of Van Wiggens, now in full blast, to find a sign hung out in front of the dwelling with a huge bear roughly painted on it.

"What does that mean, Will?" asked Charles.

"My Joan's doings," said Van Wiggens, wiping the perspiration from his fat cheeks with his leather apron, blackened with the dust of the shop. "You see, dese cross roads are dravelled more and more, and te people keep stopping at our house and living on us. So Joan has set up a davern, and *I* painted te Black Bear sign."

"I hope the entertainment won't be as rough as the sign, Will."

"Dat's uncertain, and tepends on te sort of guests dat come. She's a fine laty, captain." he continued, in a whisper, "but she's a Tartar! As soon as she was mistress of her own house, she began to scold me about every ding. And ten she flung her shoe at me te oder day for telling some dravellers our ages."

"She did? That's strange. Your ages?"

"Yaw. I'm dirty, and she's dirty-two."

"Women don't like to have their ages told, Will, if they are older than their husbands. But thirty-two is nothing to be frightened at. I suppose you gave her a taste of your authority, as the Indians do their scolding squaws."

"No, captain; dey always said Vill Wan Viggens and his dog" (a small brown animal of mongrel breed, crossed principally with the cur) "didn't fear man or teiffle—but didn't say voman."

"I understand. Well, Will, suppose you join my company?"

"Keep tark!" replied Will, in a very low whisper; "I see Joan's cap bobbing up in te pea-patch. I can't stand it much longer—tam if I do! She owns a pig nigger, you know, who larnt his drade in Burlington, and she says he can shoe a horse better as me. Tam if I don't go mit you! Captain, when you're ready to go after te red-coats or te savages, send a note here for Vill and his dog."

Charles shook hands with the poor hen-pecked blacksmith, and promised not to forget him and his dog.

He soon after fell in with Richard Schooley, resting on his plough in a corner of the fence. Richard stared at him in silence, and with something like an expression of anger on his stoical brow.

"Richard," said Charles, seeing his nod of salutation had not been returned, "what makes thee so grum today?"

"Thee knows well enough," said Richard, with a sigh.

"I do not, upon my word."

"Thy word don't signify."

"What? Do you mean to doubt my veracity? Do you give me the lie?"

"I did not give thee the lie."

"But to doubt my word is pretty much the same thing. Never do it again, unless you wish to quarrel with me."

"Thee knows we never quarrel."

"Then what the devil is the matter?"

"Don't use profane words, I beseech thee. But, to be plain with thee, hast thou not striven to win Julia's heart away from me?"

"I have sought to win her esteem, because I respected her. Have you really loved her, Richard?"

"Oh, deeply! almost desperately! and if thee would not see me miserable, thee will forsake her and seek some other maiden."

"I am sorry to hear you say so, Richard. But still, if it should so happen that Julia be loved by me also, why not seek some other maiden yourself?"

"Thee knows we were children together; and thee must know that both my father and mother told me that Julia was to be my wife."

"Indeed! But then thee knows that Julia and I were companions at Mr. Livingston's when she was a young lady and I a young man."

"I know it! And my mother always said that evil might come from such indulgence."

"Thy father, her guardian, had no right to restrict her in the choice of a residence or in the selection of companions. There is but one way, I fear, Richard, to settle the difficulty."

"If thee knows any way, so I can espouse the maiden, I will be obliged to thee."

"Would the maiden espouse thee, Richard, if I were removed out of the way?"

"I think she would, in time, if father could persuade her to attend our meetings."

"Oh, is that all? Well, the way to adjust the difficulty between us is, I suppose, to fight a duel. The survivor will then have no rival."

"Thee knows I durst do no such thing!" said Richard, with an encrimsoned visage; "and thee does very ill in naming it."

"I beg your pardon, Richard. But declare thy passion to Julia, if thou wilt, and receive her answer. Know that I love her as well as thyself. She must be the arbiter of her own fate."

"Stay!" said Richard, seeing Charles about to move on. "If thee marries her, thee being a rebel as Mr. Moody says, thou wilt bring her to beggary, for all her lands will be confiscated."

"Fool!" ejaculated Charles. "The Malcha Manito is now moving thee. Gold is thy god, and the god of too many of thy persuasion. I thought thee capable of worshipping the lovely Julia——"

"Thee knows we never worship any mortal being," said Richard, interrupting him.

"Oh, yes, I know it. You merely sought her estates. But learn, sir, that her union with me might be the only means of saving them. Congress can confiscate as well as the king. Follow me to the house; I have more to say on this subject."

Charles put spurs to his steed, and never paused until he reached the stile in front of the dwelling.

He was met in the entry by Julia, who chanced to be passing out, accompanied by her faithful dog. She wore a troubled countenance, which soon vanished, however, in the hearty greetings that followed.

"Meet me at the sycamore," Charles whispered, as he passed on to accost Mr. Schooley, whose approaching step his keen ear had detected. Julia vanished in silence, which was a sufficient response for the lover.

"Good-morning, Charles," said Mr. Schooley; "I have wished to see thee on serious matters," he continued, as he led the young man into the sitting-room, where Mrs. Schooley's foot was propelling the incessant spinning-wheel. She nodded her staid chin at him, and stared a brief moment through her spectacles.

"I am sorry, Charles," said Mr. Schooley, when they were seated, "that thy father is truly the rebel laird who waged war against the King of Great Britain."

"And I am proud of it, sir!" said Charles.

"I hope thee will be calm. Thee knows it is a grievous offence for one to take up arms against the sovereign."

"King George was not the rightful king. Thou knowest,

Thomas, it was the Stuarts who granted religious liberty to the outcast members of thy society when they landed in this country.'

"That is true; but we are bound to honour the rulers set over us, without discussing their right to govern."

"Very good, Thomas," said Charles, quickly; "and if you remain of that opinion long, you and I will concur in honouring the Congress, which will soon be omnipotent. King George III. has ceased to reign in America. I renounce all allegiance to him!"

"What! what dost thou say?" exclaimed Mrs. Schooley, the thread snapping asunder in her fingers and the wheel abruptly pausing in its revolutions.

"I say," continued Charles, "so surely as thy wheel has ceased to revolve, Mary, a great revolution has begun in this country."

"Thee is mistaken! thee is mad!" said she, her foot again violently in motion.

"Yes, thou art greatly in error, Charles," said Mr. Schooley; "and I desire thee to pay particular attention to what I am going to say. Thou knowest I am a magistrate, and it is my duty to arrest any offender that may be pointed out within the limits of my jurisdiction. Thy father confesses he is the individual described in the document that Bonnel received from John Johnston, called Sir John. Thy father hath resisted the king's authority——".

"Certainly," said Charles; "he resisted the king's claim to the throne."

"Thee knows how deadly an offence that was. Well, it is incumbent on me to discharge my duty, else my commission becomes derelict. Thee knows, if thy father be taken, he will not be entitled to a trial, as he hath been condemned already. The king's signature will merely be required to his death-warrant, and 'then he must be executed. Such, thee must know, was the case with his brother, Dr. Cameron. Now, inasmuch as I dislike being made the instrument of the vengeance of the law, and as I have still a regard for thee, notwithstanding thou hast done very wrong in attempting to woo away my ward, I confess to thee that I feel an inclination—which the monitor within seems hourly to strengthen—to decline the commission sent me, and remain an inoffensive spectator of the scenes of violence and bloodshed which I very much fear will be the result of the rebellious conduct of the politicians."

"I think, Thomas," said Charles, "that thou art moved now by the right spirit, and that thou wilt do well in yielding to its monitions."

"But then, Charles, thee knows, if I would keep myself entirely aloof from implication, there must be an utter severance between every member of my family and those who foolishly embark in the rebellion."

"I understand thee, Thomas. Thou canst not see that this outburst is a revolution, instead of a rebellion. And thou wouldst stipulate that I should cease to visit Julia, the only Christian friend I ever knew besides my father, so that her fortune—which I do protest forms no portion of my motive in seeking her hand—may remain with thine, and become thy son's when thou art dead (and all must die) and canst not even be a witness of the happiness his wealth is to secure him? Oh, Thomas, Thomas, I very much fear, after all, the invisible spirit within, which furnishes thee the law for thy conduct, is sometimes a very dangerous and irresponsible monitor—the devil himself!"

"Thou art uttering a vile profanation!" cried Mary, dropping her thread and silencing the wheel.

"I am sorry for thee!" said Thomas.

"Be not uneasy on my account," continued Charles; "but tremble for thyself. Mammon and the true God cannot be honestly worshipped at the same time or by the same individual. In regard to Julia, in heaven's name, let her be the arbitress of her own fate! Let her decide for herself in matters pertaining to her affections. Her father never supposed he was delegating to you the privilege of choosing a husband for his daughter; and, if it had been his purpose to bestow her lands upon your family, he might have done it in a more direct manner. No, Thomas; I will make no such compact with thee."

"Then thee knows the consequence. I must not be implicated with my ward if she casts her lot among the rebels. I must convince John—called Sir John—that I am a loyal subject. I must deliver thy father into the custody of his Majesty's governor of this colony."

"Very well. But, Thomas, thy messengers travel very

slowly, else thou wouldst have known, as I do, that William Franklin, late his Majesty's governor, is now a prisoner, having been declared a public enemy by Congress; and his successor will be my friend, and Julia's friend, and my father's friend, William Livingston."

"Thee seems to be in earnest," said Thomas, in perplexity. "Thou hast never attempted to misrepresent any thing, and I must do thee the justice to say so."

"What I say is the truth. And now *I* have a duty to perform. By these orders it is my duty to require thy signature to this," continued Charles, placing a form of the Declaration on the table; "and power is given me to arrest those who decline it, if they do not give security for their good conduct. Be not so pale, Mary, for thou art not in danger. I will be his surety. I do not believe that Thomas advised the attack on my father's house——

"Thee speaks truly, Charles," said Mr. Schooley.

"No. I have never known one of thy society to counsel violence."

"That is just, Charles," said Mary.

"But it cannot be denied that the measures they advise are sometimes calculated to produce bloodshed."

"What does thee mean, Charles?" asked Thomas.

"I mean, that although the slaves at Amboy were incited to insurrection by the abolition declarations and teachings of John Woolman, the pious tailor remained in his shop at Mount Holly instead of heading the negroes. Several were executed; and it strikes me that the blood which was shed—both that of the negroes and their victims—flowed in consequence of Woolman's intermeddling."

"John was a conscientious man," said Mary, who knew him well; "but it was an unintended wrong to speak such dangerous things to our slaves."

"Whatever might have been the intention, the result was most lamentable," said Charles. "Yet, I repeat, I have never known a Quaker to participate directly in acts of violence. But they are not slow to grasp at the wealth squandered by others; and, consequently, I think they should not be exempted from contributing something to defray the expenses of a just war, in which the government that protects them may be involved, even if they are opposed to the shedding of blood. Therefore, if thy son

Richard will not join the ranks, armed as the law directs, he must be prepared to bear the expenses of a substitute.'

Charles then mounted his horse and galloped to the sycamore overshadowing the Council Rock; and when Richard joined his parents a few minutes after, and learned what had been said in relation to him, he could only stare in blank amazement.

Julia had been some time awaiting Charles.

"Your guardian will be quiet now, Julia," said Charles, exhibiting his papers and assuming an air of authority. "Instead of arresting my father, he is indebted to my forbearance for escaping an arrest himself. I acquit him, however, of any participation in the incendiary assault. As much as I dislike the Quakers, I do not think any of them would be capable of sanctioning such acts as that."

"No, indeed," said Julia; "at least, I am sure Mr. Schooley would never participate in them. But what did they say respecting *me?*"

"Oh, a great deal. They desired me never to see you more."

"*Indeed*, Mr. Basilisk! They fear you will fascinate me, I suppose."

"Or rather that I will envenom your heart against Richard! But the fellow is large enough to muster; and, since he will remain at home and fill a labourer's place in the field, I intend to make him pay for a substitute in the little army under my command. Yes! before they knew their idol William had ceased to govern or to enjoy his liberty, they proposed—I mean Mr. Schooley proposed—to resign his commission, and thereby suffer my father to escape arrest, and the executioner's block, as a sort of equivalent for my relinquishment of your society."

"Surely they put a very high estimate upon it! But then they have almost intimated a purpose to relinquish it themselves; for my good guardian has hinted at the necessity of returning to Burlington, since we too may be liable to such outrages as happened on your father's premises."

"And what could you say in reply to that?"

"I read to him Kate Livingston's letter brought by the last express. She writes that her father thinks it will soon be unsafe for her to remain in the old settlements, and she has a strong desire to be here with me. She is enchanted she says, with my descriptions of life and scenery in the forest."

"But did not Thomas say something in behalf of poor Richard?"

"Not directly. But both he and Mary expatiated on the beauties of Quakerism, and seemed anxious I should join the meeting. That obstacle removed, Richard's superior merits would doubtless secure the inestimable prize. But why do you stare so? Oh, there are new pictures on the tree! Read them for me," she added, when they had risen.

"Blue Pigeon has arrived with a message from my mother!"

"From your mother? Oh, yes, I remember; you told me she was ever indulgent and affectionate, and they called her——"

"Gentle Moonlight. And she was truly gentle. And Blue Pigeon was one of my most loved companions."

"But here is the song-bird again—the same painted by the other Indian. Its mouth is open, and it sings for thy return."

"My sister joins my mother in the message. I will know more when I see Blue Pigeon."

"Is it right to call the Thrush thy sister? Have you not said the mother who adopted thee was only the aunt of Brandt and his sister? How, then, can they be your sister and brother?"

"Gentle Moonlight," said Charles, with emotion, "lost her husband in battle, and her only child, a little son, sickened and died. This was before my capture. After her bereavement, Brandt and his sister called her mother; her affection was bestowed on them, and they seemed to love their aunt almost as well as their true mother. Their mother, seeing this, prevailed on Sir John Johnston to procure a white captive for her sister, on whom her love might be lavished. Sir John complied, and I was the captive. Gentle Moonlight loved me as fondly as she had done her own lost son, while I was taught to call Brandt my brother and Brown Thrush my sister."

"And they now wish you to return—to marry Brown Thrush, and remain with them—to——"

"Ah, Julia! how can you utter such bitter words? Am I not free?—a man—and a white man? Have I not found my father?"

"Oh, very true! But do not the rules among the Indians require an unconditional compliance with the requests of mothers? Do not all inheritances, titles, and wealth, come from the mother? Do not the mothers contract the marriages and the maidens sometimes make the proposals?"

"Very true; but Gentle Moonlight is not really my mother, and I am no Indian."

"And I have learned that the Brown Thrush and her brother are the children of the British knight."

"It is so said, but I doubt it. They have very fair complexions, it is true; but I have seen hundreds of the children of the forest as fair as themselves."

"Then, as Moonlight is not thy mother, as thou hast found thy father," continued Julia, archly, "and as thou hast no Indian blood in thy veins, thou wilt remain?"

"I do not know what may be required of me. I must see this runner, this old playmate of mine, and hear what he has to say. But, Julia, whatever I may do, whatever may be my fate, you alone have my heart. It is thine. But still I must feel a brother's affection for my forest sister. A more gentle and loving creature does not exist. She would have died for me, and———"

"She loves you! She loves you! But it is no fault of thine. Poor, unhappy girl! I wish she were my companion here, or I were with the Gentle Moonlight———"

"Nay, Julia, you know not what you say! You know not how soon the Iroquois may be hurling the tomahawk at the heads of our race and kindred. Then the brave and terrible brother of the Thrush, and the nephew of the Gentle Moonlight, will be upon the war-path. He will descend the valleys with yells of vengeance for the ills the Indians have suffered at the hands of the white man. And the Gentle Moonlight and the singing Thrush must be witnesses of the tortures inflicted upon prisoners. They will be chilled by the howls of the Malcha Manito which dwells in the shrivelled bosom of Queen Esther—the remorseless Catharine Montour———"

"Oh! name her not! I have heard of her cruelties—and she not an Indian!"

"No, Julia. The whites are as capable of committing monstrous cruelties as the poor Indians. But I know *you* could never become a second Catharine Montour, or desire to witness her savage fierceness. She is the daughter of the French governor, Frontenac, it is believed, and was made queen by the Senecas. She carries a war-club and scalping-knife, and slays the miserable prisoners with her own hands!"

"Horrible! No; I would not behold her. Nor would I have thee see her. But I fear this messenger will summon thee away."

"I would not obey any summons of hers. She is a Seneca. Among the Indians I am of the bird tribe, having taken the name of White Eagle, which was conferred by Gentle Moonlight when they made me a chief. I was under the usual age, but had saved the life of Brandt. I will tell thee the manner of it some other time. Queen Esther's totem is the wolf."

"Then you might intermarry with the feathered tribe," said Julia, smiling; "and of course the thrush is one of them."

"No," said Charles; "it is not permitted for those of the same totems to marry."

"Indeed!"

"But then," he continued, "my forest sister's totem is the turtle, or tortoise."

"And, then, you might marry her?"

"Perhaps, if I desired it. But see! Solo is bristling up, and growls. Behold, yonder comes Blue Pigeon! He has sought me at my father's house, and returns to the tree. Be quiet, Solo! And my poor horse, Yameder, pricks up his ears. Will you remain? You may, if you desire it; but you will not understand our language."

"Yes, I will remain."

When the Blue Pigeon recognised Charles, after a long pause, he sprang forward and clasped him in his arms; and, upon being informed that Julia was the Antelope of whom he had doubtless heard Brandt speak, he offered his hand, and uttered the word "sister" in good English. And Julia, struck by his noble features and perfect form, called him "brother."

"Now, my brother," said Charles, "my ear is open. I am ready to hear the words of my mother."

"The Gentle Moonlight," said the young warrior, "has been weeping. Like the dew-drops on the leaves at early morning, the tears have stood upon her face. Her sister's children have striven to comfort her, but they have another mother. 'White Eagle,' said she, 'has no mother but the Gentle Moonlight, and she beholds not her son.' She waited very patiently until the moons were ended during his stay at college. Then she sang with joy, and the Brown Thrush also sang with her. But the wings of her noble Eagle did not cleave the air of the mountain. The dew was not wiped from her face by the feathers of her darling boy. Thayendanegea said the White Eagle had come within a short flight of his mother, but was perched near an Antelope that had charmed him. Then Queen Esther summoned a council of the warriors, chiefs, and sachems, and proposed that the Five Nations should invade this country and burn and slay. But their ears were closed to her words. It was the land of the *Sagorighwiyogstha*, (Doer of Justice,) and if the Indians loved the young White Eagle, why should not the pale-faces love him too? Then Gentle Moonlight was permitted to speak. She said her son had never disobeyed her. He had said, when his white-haired father led him away, that he would never cease to love his forest mother. And he never lied. She would therefore summon him to her presence, and if he still loved her he would obey. If he loved the Antelope too, still he would come to the Gentle Moonlight, and return again to his new charmer. He might do so, if he desired it. But he must come to his mother, or she would die. Such were her words, my brother, and I have given them truly to you."

"Blue Pigeon, my brother," said Charles, "you have seen the dew-drops fall from my eyes when you repeated the words of my mother. She is the only mother I have in the world. She loved me ever as the dearest of mothers only can love. She loves me still. Moons may wane, but a mother's love does not decline. The White Eagle still loves the Gentle Moonlight. My brother, look at my face and repeat my words to my mother. Say I will love her always. But her Eagle cannot say at the present time when he will fly to her wigwam;—whether it will be this moon or the next. But he will come. He never lies. He must first see his white-haired father, and hear his counsel; and he must take leave of the Antelope, who will be sad at his flight. Go, my brother. Return to the forest by the clear waters where you and I have hunted the deer and the bear. We were very happy then. I shall again behold the wild scenes through which we loved to roam. Tell my mother I often see her in my dreams. I awake and find myself near the torn fields of the white man. I hide my face and try to dream again. I would dream forever. Farewell, my brother. I have finished until we meet again."

Charles remained in a profound reverie after Blue Pigeon had departed, which even Julia did not seek to break until the silence became painful.

"Is it not as I conjecture?" asked Julia.

"Precisely," said Charles. "My mother has sent for me."

"And you have declined going?"

"No, Julia. She consents to my return hither after seeing her. I have sent her word that I will come; but I could not say when. I must consult my father, and also General Livingston."

"They will keep you with them or kill you if you again put yourself in their power," said she.

"No—I fear nothing. They durst not injure me. War is not declared by them. I may prevent it. If not, I can return hither."

"But will they really consent to it?"

"I suppose so. If not, I could easily escape. Adieu. I must see my father and send his runner, the boy Skippie, to General Livingston, or Governor Livingston, or whatever his title may be by this time. Have your letter for Kate in readiness; but do not prevail on her to urge her father to decide against my visit to the lakes. It is only a few days' travel. At this season the Indians are at home, petitioning De-o-ha-ho, the spirit who presides over the growth of corn, beans, and squashes. In the fall they might be in the great western hunting-grounds beyond the Ohio, whither Gentle Moonlight sometimes accompanies them, for she used to take me thither."

"And you have seen the 'Dark and Bloody Ground' in Kentucky?"

"Yes, and a fairer land the sun never shone upon. Many a happy day have I passed under its maples, and many a blissful dream of Kentucky still illumines my slumbers. Adieu!"

He galloped away, while the maiden, with a throbbing bosom, gazed after him until he vanished from her sight. She then turned her footsteps toward home, warbling a plaintive ditty, and thinking of the Indian maiden who bore the name of one of the sweetest of wild-wood songsters.

CHAPTER VII.

PADDY TOMAHAWKED AND SCALPED—CHARLES STARTS ON HIS JOURNEY WESTWARD.

As had been predicted, William Livingston had been appointed governor by the people's Colonial Legislature; and at the moment when Skippie was admitted into his cabinet the governor was inditing a letter to Charles, urging him to make an excursion into the Indian country for the purpose of ascertaining the intentions of the tribes regarding the war with the mother country, which was now waged in earnest; so that the visit of the young man to the fondly-remembered scenes and friends of his youth was to meet no impediment in that quarter.

And soon after Skippie's return the father of Charles yielded a reluctant consent to the journey. Mr. Schooley, whose discretion led him to adopt an obscure and inoffensive position between the contending parties, but who could not be induced to relinquish the idea of marrying his son Richard to Julia, heartily approved the project. But Julia's objections remained to be overcome. Charles met her almost daily at the sycamore-tree, and was still beguiled of many weeks which might have sufficed for performing the journey.

Meantime, there were rumours of preparations on the part of the Indians to attack the settlements. These accounts, so far as it regarded the readiness of the Iroquois to commence active hostilities immediately, were discredited by

Charles. He rightly attributed them to the instructions of Moody and other tories, issued by the agents of the crown as a means of keeping the people in continual alarm and preventing them from sending succours to the American army.

Nevertheless, it was a well-ascertained fact that several small parties of roving savages had committed depredations near the Gap and in the valleys on both sides of the Blue Mountain. A number of horses had been stolen and one or two men had been killed.

Poor Paddy was rendered very uncomfortable; and Mr. Green related some new story of Indian warfare every evening; and, at the conclusion of his horrible tales of tomahawking and scalping, he never failed to predict that such scenes would soon be re-enacted in that vicinity.

To such a degree had Paddy's imagination been wrought upon, that he was often seen running across the garden upon hearing any unusual noise. His mind seemed to be filled with fears of snakes and Indians. One day, when Mr. Schooley, Julia, and Charles were sitting in the hall, where the hum of the small spinning-wheel and the bang of the loom assailed their ears, they were startled by the entrance of Rose, who, with dilated eyes, said Paddy was mad—stark, staring mad—in the garden, and was then dancing.

"Does thee say dancing?" asked Mr. Schooley, rising indignantly; for any thing like dancing was an abomination in his sight. He was followed by Julia and Charles and the Newfoundland dog.

Sure enough, Paddy was seen springing about in every direction, and sometimes leaping up perpendicularly; and he seemed to be continually striking at something with a hoe.

"What hast thou there, Patrick?" asked Mr. Schooley.

"Och, yer honour, a hundred divils! It was the great sarpint they tell of in the Apocalypse. It came out and lifted its head and looked at me face, and so I struck him across the back and cut him in two."

"And then thee killed it, I suppose?"

"And would ye suppose it? Take that, ye blackguard!" he continued, cutting at it again, and then jumping aside. "Kilt him? Divil a bit, saving yer honour's prisence. But what d'ye think he did when I cut him in two?"

"Thee must tell," said Mr. Schooley, "for I never guess."

"Then see here, Miss Julia," he said, as she approached; "as I hope to save my sowl, when I cut the baste in two, both ends began to run afther me! and when I cut them in two, all four of 'em crawled toward me. And I kept cutting till there was more than a dozen, and all from one!"

"It was a joint-snake," said Charles, looking down at the writhing particles of its body.

"Take care of his head!" cried Paddy, "for it won't die, and can run when it's not longer than Miss Julia's swate little toe. And it's a jint-snake ye call it? Well, I niver seed the likes before."

"Patrick," said Mr. Schooley, "it was an unoffending creature, and thee did wrong to molest it."

"Then I'm sorra, yer honour; but I was jist thinking of the bloody Indians, who they say will snake up behint and strike ye on the back of yer head wid a hard iron tomahawk. And——"

"Patrick," said his master, "I see the cows in the orchard, trampling the new-mown hay. Go and drive them out."

"And, Paddy," said Charles, "keep a good lookout for Indians."

"Och, but you're joking now, Misther Charles, for I'm sure you'd niver be guilty of saying sich things if you thought any savages were about."

Paddy set off in a brisk trot, while the rest, amused, gazed after him. He had not gone more than fifty paces before he stumbled against the teeth of a rake that had been left lying on the ground. The handle flew up and struck him a smart blow on the back of his head, and, uttering a piercing cry, he fell forward on his face and lay quite still. Supposing the man might be injured by the blow, Charles and Mr. Schooley hastened to him, while Julia followed at her leisure.

"What's the matter, Paddy?" asked Charles.

"Patrick," said Mr. Schooley, deliberately, "art thou suffering any pain?"

"Why don't you speak?" demanded Charles, endeavouring to turn him over so that his face would be visible; and, after several efforts, he succeeded.

"Murther! murther! murther!" cried Paddy, in such stunning tones that even Richard, in the most distant field, heard him distinctly, and paused in mid-furrow.

"Where art thou injured, Patrick?" asked Thomas; and then added, since Paddy did not reply, "I saw thee receive the blow, but did not think it could injure thy head."

"St. Pater and the Howly Vargin!" cried Paddy, with his eyes convulsively closed; "I'm dying, dying, dying!" and the last utterance was the loudest.

"If you are dying, Paddy," said Charles, "be kind enough to tell us what killed you."

"The Indians!" he yelled. "I've been tomahawked and sculped! One of 'em was standing behint an apple-tree and hit me on the back of me head! Then another sculped me! Oh, the blackguards!"

"Nonsense!" said Charles, after a burst of hearty laughter, in which Julia joined, and which could not be wholly resisted by the sedate Thomas. "Do you not see we are laughing at you? Open your eyes, man! We are not Indians. It was a mistake—a dream."

"A drame was it?" cried Paddy, sitting upright, and opening his eyes. "But drames don't hurt," he continued, placing his hand against the wounded part. "Och, murther! I'm sculped!" he cried again, upon beholding blood on his hand. He fell back and closed his eyes once more.

Charles, upon examination, found he had received a slight contusion, from which flowed a few drops of blood.

"Here, Paddy," said he, "is the Indian. Open your eyes and see him. He is our prisoner."

"He is? And you've taken the blackguard? Why, Mr. Charles, that is a rake!"

"It is the Indian that tomahawked and scalped you, Paddy, for I saw him do it."

"Saw the rake do it! And you mane to say, Mr. Charles, that I hit the tathe with my fut, and the helve came up and struck me behint? And I'm not kilt, then?" he continued, rising to his feet.

"No, Patrick," said Mr. Schooley, looking quite angry, "and yet thee has alarmed the whole plantation. To-morrow, and the next day, it will be the same thing. There is no peace where thou art. Thee must leave——"

"Lave! Did your honour say lave?"

"Thee must leave such idle alarms to the women."

"Yes, leave them to us, Paddy," said Julia.

"And it's cowardice you'd be afther charging Patrick Pence wid? Och, Mr. Thomas, if you could only saa me blood up onct! Och, murther! look at that!" And Paddy having pressed the back of his head again, a few more drops of blood stained his hand. He did not lie down, however, but resumed his work in the garden.

Months had now passed since Charles had promised to visit his Indian foster-mother, and he still lingered in the valley where dwelt his father and Julia. His father, having at first given permission for the journey with great reluctance, at length urged him to set out, since Governor Livingston desired it and he had pledged his word to make the visit.

Finally, the day of setting out was appointed a fortnight in advance, and every preparation was made for the event. Charles decided to resume his Indian dress; and, as Julia superintended its completion, it may be presumed it was not deficient in tasteful decoration.

Sergeant Murphy was to be left in charge of the company which had been formed. The men had been assembled several times for parade, armed with their own rifles, and then dismissed to their houses. No orders came for them to march away, and Governor Livingston had intimated that it might be necessary for them to remain in their own county. Richard Schooley had failed to muster; and his father did not neglect to pay the fine which Murphy was charged to collect.

Mrs. Van Wiggens's tavern and shop prospered very well. Her husband, as he had feared, became a mere cipher under the thumb of his tyrannical spouse. But, about the time of the departure of Charles, he was recalled to the plantation of his patron to act again in the capacity of overseer, in the place of Peter Shaver, who had been his successor in office, but who, becoming dissatisfied with his Quaker employer, as it was supposed, or his wages, had absconded. No one knew whither he had gone. The last time he had been seen was when setting out one morning on his crop-eared Indian pony with a bag of grain, which he said he intended to have ground at a mill some miles distant. His object was professedly to ascertain if the

Quaker miller they usually patronized had not been in the habit of taking excessive toll. Peter was a short, fat man, something like Van Wiggens, and hence was distinctly remembered by all who had seen him. If he had not absconded, the supposition was that he had been killed.

And so Van Wiggens was now relieved of the tongue-lashings of Mrs. Van Wiggens during the day, and was a curious witness of the preparations made by Julia for the decoration of the young chief, as Charles was often termed. And more than once he took occasion to intimate that, if Peter Shaver should return before the day appointed for commencing the journey, he would rather go into the Indian country with the White Eagle than return to his wife. But Peter did not return.

At length the day of departure arrived. Charles had taken leave of Julia under the sycamore-tree, decked in his elegant Indian costume. His head-dress was surmounted with white feathers; his buckskin coat, leggins, and moccasins, were studded with beads and spangles, or stained porcupine-quills. His embroidered blanket was folded carefully and strapped behind the saddle, on which he sat with the erectness and grace peculiar to the Indians and those who have dwelt among them. He had his rifle, his tomahawk, a dirk that McSwine had thrust into his belt, and—what was shocking to some of the inhabitants—a scalping-knife. These, with a few indispensable utensils for cooking, comprised his equipment.

His aged father bestowed his blessing upon him, and, turning sadly away, shut himself up with his books. Charles, directing his steed toward the west, disappeared in the forest, followed by the cheers of his friends and by the light pursuing step of Skippie, the sandy-haired boy, of whom it was said he never spoke with his tongue so much as by his looks and features.

CHAPTER VIII.

ONE CRYING IN THE WILDERNESS—THE PANTHER AND TURKEY—PETER SHAVER—GENTLE MOONLIGHT AND BROWN THRUSH.

ONCE more in the solitude of the forest, Charles loosened the reins and permitted his noble steed to walk leisurely along the narrow path. It was one of the old war-paths of the Indians, leading to the great lakes of the Northwest; and, although it had become overgrown and indistinct to those unused to the wilderness, the young man had no difficulty in discerning it.

The birds sang on every bough or flitted gayly from tree to tree. The hare sat upright in the wild grass, gazing without alarm at the solitary wanderer. The doe and her spotted fawns emerged from the tangled thicket, and drank of the cool limpid water at the gurgling brook; and the sun rode gloriously over all in a cloudless sky, gladdening the myriads of joyous insects that basked in its genial rays.

A balmy breeze cooled the fevered temples of the wanderer; and, as he looked upon the inspiring scene of mountains, woods, and streams, sweet memories of the happy days of his sunlit childhood flitted athwart his mind. They came like phantoms of pleasant dreams which too quickly vanish. But he strove to prolong their presence; and, while he luxuriated in the vision, consciousness of his present condition gradually faded away. Thus he was again completely a child of the wilderness, and oblivious of the flight of the passing hours, until the hooting of the owl and the darkening of the glades admonished him of the approach of night. His noble steed, too, had been reared among the Indians, and seemed to have an instinctive knowledge of the direction his rider wished to pursue; for Charles had long ceased to notice the ancient encampments, the intersecting paths, and the moss upon the northern side of the trees.

Nevertheless, after drawing rein and dismounting to prepare his diminutive encampment, Charles became aware of his location. He had descended the western side of the Blue Mountain, and was now upon the narrow bottom of one of the small trout-streams emptying into the Delaware, some few miles distant. It was in the midst of a clump of gigantic trees, whose huge trunks seemed like vast columns supporting the blue vault above. There was but little undergrowth, except the wild grass, upon which the steed was turned loose to graze. No fears were entertained of the faithful animal deserting him. The horse of a solitary traveller becomes attached to his master, and will not relinquish his society.

Charles was at no loss in the forest to provide for his comfort. With his tomahawk and knife the framework of his camp was soon completed. The small forks and poles were furnished by the thicket fringing the base of the mountain; while the dry bark torn from the trunk of a gigantic hickory-tree sufficed for the roof to shelter him from the dew, and also for fuel with which to cook his simple repast. The rear of the camp was protected by the trunk of a large fallen tree, and at the opposite end the fire was kindled; and, while his meat hung before the crackling fagots, he gathered rushes from the margin of the brook and elastic twigs from the pendant boughs, with which he prepared his couch.

While partaking of his frugal meal, the young man several times observed his horse lift up his head and look in the direction of the thicket already referred to. The animal exhibited no signs of alarm, and always, after gazing a moment, resumed his browsing. Charles did not suppose it an object worthy of attention. It might be a wolf, a fox, a raccoon, or some other animal attracted by the light of the fire or the odour of the meat, and from which there was nothing to fear. If it had been a bear or a panther, (and neither of which would be likely to assail him,) his horse would not have retained his composure. And thus this noble animal not unfrequently discharges the duty of a faithful sentinel.

Later in the night the moon arose in brilliance, and her silvery rays glimmered tremblingly through the thick foliage slightly agitated by the gentle breeze. The beetles chirped pleasantly in cadence with the mournful wail of the whippoorwill, and the soft approaches of soothing slumber began to lull the senses of the youth. Spreading his blanket on the couch, and happening to cast his eyes over the fallen trunk near which he was about to place his head, he beheld the face of Skippie.

For a brief interval Charles remained perfectly still and silent, for he had acquired the Indian habit of suppressing the symptoms of any sudden emotion.

"Why are you here, Skippie?" he demanded.

"He did not say no," was the answer.

"My father?"

To this Skippie nodded affirmatively.

"And you asked his permission?"

Again there was an affirmative nod.

"Then come in and eat; and afterward lie down and sleep."

Skippie did his bidding in silence. This youth—or rather dwarf, for the wrinkles on his forehead indicated that he had long since passed the age of adolescence—was one of the clan Cameron, and had joined his exiled laird in Canada, and acted in the capacity of page to his mistress until her death. Afterward he became a constant attendant on the exile, and Charles was aware that he had been of great service to his father in procuring news from distant points, (for, although exceedingly small, he was very active, and seemed insensible to fatigue,) and in warning him of approaching danger on several momentous occasions. And not the least valuable of his qualifications as a runner—a term familiar in the Indian country—was his uniform taciturnity. He heard every thing; but nothing was ever learned from him by any but his chief or trusted persons of his household.

Toward morning Charles awoke and rekindled the fire, but did not lie down again. Perceiving that Skippie had likewise finished his slumber, he beckoned him to approach.

"Skippie," said he, "I have been dreaming of my Indian mother. I was too young to remember my white mother. What was she like?"

"Blue eyes, like the sky. Tall, straight, fair skin, and light hair. An angel."

"Enough, Skippie! I would not hear another word in regard to her form and beauty. But was she good?"

"An angel."

"True. She is in heaven. Was she not religious, Skippie?"

"An *angel*," he repeated.

"I forgot, Skippie. But, Skippie, I cannot help loving my Indian mother very, very much."

"She is an angel."

"Oh, true! you saw her."

"I found you. I lived in the woods five years, hunting for you."

"I did not know that, Skippie. And it may be the reason why you follow me and seem determined to watch over me."

"Right."

"You mean it is for that reason?"

"I do."

"I thank you, Skippie; but I am now old enough to take care of myself; and if any thing occurs during this visit which it would be desirable for them to know in the valley, I shall send you thither."

"So."

"And you will go?"

"Go," he replied, with one of his affirmative nods.

The sun arose in great splendour on the second morning, and after partaking of a hearty meal, which had been prepared by the skilful Skippie, the travellers pursued their journey toward the boundary-line of the State of New York, and passed it in the forenoon. Then, turning to the left, they followed the old war-path in the direction of the lakes which ran near the northeastern corner of Pennsylvania.

When the sun was midway in the heavens, Charles faintly heard a hallooing, and, as the sound appeared to be in the direction he was pursuing, his pace was quickened. The cry seemed to proceed from one in distress, and Charles knew it was not an Indian.

Presently he detected the recent footmarks of a man in a path that crossed the one he was following; and, as the halloo was still heard at intervals on the right, he dismounted, and, throwing the reins to Skippie, proceeded cautiously in that direction. The path, which followed the course of one of the small tributaries of the Delaware, soon emerged from the dense thicket of bushes and entered the dark woods. And here an unexpected scene awaited the young adventurer. On his right, and but a few paces distant, in the forks of a chestnut-tree, was a large panther, in the act of springing upon him. The animal was in a crouching attitude, its eyes glaring furiously, and the point of its tail oscillating rapidly, as is usual with carnivorous beasts when assailing an enemy or seizing their prey.

The practised eye and steady hand of Charles sufficed for the emergency. Almost as instantaneously as thought, the report of his rifle rang through the woods, and the panther lay struggling in its death-throes at his feet. And even then the animal might have inflicted a serious wound had he not been despatched by the dirk of Skippie, who bounded forward and stabbed him to the heart in the midst of his convulsive flounderings.

"Done that before!" said he; meaning that he had stabbed other panthers and escaped their claws.

"But it was not the voice of a panther we heard, Skippie," said Charles.

"No!" said a stranger; "but verily the voice of one crying in the wilderness!"

"Ha!" said Charles, descrying the form of a man in the same tree the panther had occupied, but upon a perpendicular branch some twenty feet above the forks, which he seemed to be hugging with desperate tenacity.

"How did you get up there?" asked Charles, seeing the limb, which was without lateral shoots, swaying backward and forward under its heavy burden.

"My son," said the stranger, who was a man of large dimensions, "I am uncomfortable here. Let me first contrive to get down, and then I will speak of the manner of my getting up."

"Slide down, sir," said Charles.

"You are sure he's dead?"

"Quite," replied Charles, lifting up one of the feet of the animal and displaying its enormous but harmless claws.

"That was not a pleasant descent," said the stranger, after descending more rapidly than he desired, and being slightly stunned by his collision with the earth; "but," he added, "it is the mode of the bear, and they say I am as hardy as one, if not as rough, sometimes."

"Now, will you tell me how one of your bulk and weight could ascend such a pole as that?"

"God aided me, and all things are possible with him. I know not the manner of it, my friend. I do not recollect climbing up there, but I suppose I must have done so. I remember being pursued by the animal, and mounting to the forks when she was at my heels. Many a panther have I seen in these wild woods, but never have I been pursued before. Yet it was my own fault or imprudence; I killed her young one on the wayside, not supposing its mother to be within hearing."

"The mother is never out of hearing," said Charles, "when her young are basking in the sunshine. But who are you? Let me see. The Rev. David Jones! I am glad to meet you, sir."

"And you have my solemn assurance, my friend, that I reciprocate the gladness, although I do not recognise your face."

"We have met several times, sir. Once at Princeton, when you disputed with the Presbyterians——"

"Exhorted—expostulated, my young Christian friend, as I do not doubt you are a convert from the pagans—a brand snatched from the fire."

"Again, at Burlington, where you denounced the doctrines of Mr. Odell, the Church-of-England minister."

"Denied—not denounced—universal election, and the indispensable necessity of the so-called apostolical succession in the ministry. God is quite as able now as ever to call labourers into the harvest-field. They might as well say that none but Jordan's waters would do for baptism. And I have heard of one of the bishops sending to Palestine for a bottle of it. The story goes, that, after he had used it, one of the officers of the ship declared that——and I believe it, my friend."

"We met again at the foot of the Jenny Jump Mountain, where you offered to preach to the Quakers if they would take their hats off."

"I did, indeed; and I intended to smite their god Mammon, but they would not listen."

"Again, I saw you commune with the Moravians."

"That is true. They are a good people, and they have the true religion, excepting their mode of baptism."

"And I saw you baptize two negroes in the trout-brook near the hut of my——"

"Ha! your what? Who are you?"

"One of the negroes—old Rose—would not go into the water until I killed a rattlesnake that was basking on the opposite side. And when I had done so, she said it was the devil, who had stationed himself there to keep her away from salvation."

"Now I recollect all that. Oh! you are the young white man who lived so long with the Indians. That is the reason you now dress like one. I thought your speech too good for a savage. And you are college-bred. Charles Cameron is your name. Give me your hand again!"

"And now farewell, Mr. Jones," said Charles. "I must not withhold you from your good work."

"Where are you journeying, my young friend?" asked the preacher, detaining him.

"To the village on the Chemung, where my Indian mother is spending the summer."

"We will go together. My route lies in the same direction. I go thence to the Seneca Lake, and along Seneca River to the Oneida. They receive the gospel messenger everywhere with kindness. With my staff and knapsack, I fear no man, civilized or savage."

"But only panthers."

"True—panthers, and sometimes a serpent that crosses my path. I have a pistol for them, but am apt to forget it until it is too late to use it."

"But why were you travelling in *this* direction?"

"I had turned aside to pray; and when I arose I found the panther's kitten playing with the string of my moccasin. I thought it right to destroy the animal; and when it cried under the edge of my knife, I thought only of the lambs it would have sacrificed if I had spared it, until roused by the furious scream of its dam as she came bounding toward me. Then, as I fled, I thought I had done wrong."

"Not so, sir; for we have destroyed them both, and

the skins will be trophies for me to exhibit to my red brethren."

Charles then removed the skins from the animals, while Mr. Jones informed him of all his recent peregrinations. Since the baptism in the pool of the trout-brook, he had seen General Washington, and sojourned with his particular friend, Colonel Wayne, from whom he received instructions to visit the different tribes in Pennsylvania, New York, and the West, preaching to them, and persuading them to remain neutral or else to take up arms in behalf of the colonies. And he stated, in a confidential tone, (for he remembered that Charles had organized a company on the right side,) that he bore, secreted on his person, a commission in the army as chaplain, and was then on duty— that which had been assigned him. He had passed through the Yankee settlement on the Wyoming, where, although the people were pretty good whigs, they treated the preacher with less respect than the Delaware Indians on the beautiful Wyalusing. They seemed to hate the Baptists and the Quakers, and the Baptists and the Quakers were as far asunder as the poles

The process of skinning the panthers completed, the journey was resumed. The Rev. Mr. Jones, at Charles's urgent solicitation, mounted the horse; while the agile young man, having had a taste of his old sport, and finding his appetite still unsatisfied, proposed making a short hunt through the woods for a fawn, or a fat young buck, which might be eaten at that season. And he strode away to gratify his inclination, promising to meet his companions at a noted spring about a mile distant.

"My son," said the bulky preacher, as he rode down the path toward the broader trail which he had crossed when turning aside to pray, and intently regarding the lithe form of Skippie, "will you not be very tired travelling on foot?"

"Tired?" said Skippie, with an abrupt shake of his head.

"It is a long path we are following, and if you desire it you may ride behind me."

The only reply Skippie made to this friendly offer was a quizzical glance over his shoulder, with a smile of derision.

"You are a modest lad," continued the benevolent Baptist. "But you need not fear to speak."

"Fear! The de'il!" at length exclaimed Skippie, without deigning to turn his head again.

"Boy! you sadly need baptizing to wash away your foulness, or the birch to teach you better manners."

"Dirk!" said Skippie, holding over his head the bright blade of the weapon named.

Mr. Jones could not exactly comprehend the meaning of the word and gesture; but he concluded that nothing could be accomplished with so impracticable a subject, and he ceased to notice him. The dirk, however, could give him no uneasiness, being incapable of fearing what man could do, and having really felt some flashes of compunction when flying from the panther. Finding the lad would not converse with him, he commenced singing one of his favourite psalms; and, as he had a musical voice, the woods soon resounded with his melody.

He continued to sing without interruption until startled by a frightened gobbler that flapped up from the whortleberry bushes near the path. It alighted on one of the lower boughs of a spreading oak, and, with its long neck stretched out, seemed desirous of listening to the spiritual song, so different from the sounds usually heard in the forest. But Mr. Jones was preparing to regale him with a sound more familiar to his ears. He had drawn forth a pistol from beneath his black buckskin coat, and was taking a steady aim, when the turkey fell headlong to the earth, his neck almost severed by the rifle-ball of Charles, who had approached Mr. Jones to request him to cease singing, as it frightened the deer.

"A capital shot, that!" said Mr. Jones, leaping from his horse and lifting up the gobbler. "I am glad to see you again," he added, as Charles stepped forward with a smile on his lip.

"Why do you call it a capital shot?" asked Charles; while Skippie sank down and rolled over in convulsions of suppressed merriment.

"I aimed at his body, I confess," said Mr. Jones, with gravity; "but the ball rose in a straight line and broke his neck. It was a good shot for a pistol, and the distance must have been fifty paces."

"At least," said Charles, comprehending the mistake of the Baptist, and having no disposition to undeceive him.

"Pistol!" said Skippie, through his tears of silent laughter.

"Certainly, a pistol, my lad. Why do you laugh at my capital shot?" demanded Mr. Jones.

"Is not your pistol cocked, Mr. Jones?" asked Charles, seeing the reverend gentleman replacing the weapon in his bosom.

"Bless my life! But there was no danger, it being empty."

"Empty!" reiterated Skippie.

"Yes, empty. Did I not just kill the turkey? What's this? No!" he continued, seeing the priming remained, and inserting the ramrod. "I don't remember reloading it. I am sure I did not. How can it be explained?"

"I can explain it, Mr. Jones," said Charles. "I have no doubt you would have struck the mark, but then you might have spoiled the breast of the turkey; so I fired at his neck, and killed him before you had time to complete your aim. You thought the report came from your pistol, and, on seeing the gobbler fall, it was natural to suppose you had killed it."

"It must have been so! Well, we shall have food, at all events. The circumstance reminds me of what occurred to one of our Pennsylvania volunteers at Braddock's defeat. Without observing that he had lost the flint from his gun, he kept on pulling the trigger and ramming down cartridges. Some of the men say he declared, as they retreated, that his shoulder was black and blue from the rebounds. But I don't believe that portion of the story."

As the shades of evening descended, the party encamped near the bank of the Delaware, on a level piece of ground, where a small rivulet flowed through a cleft in the hills toward the river. Here the turkey was dressed and cooked by Skippie, while Charles stretched and dried his panther-skins.

At supper a most ravenous appetite seemed to have seized upon them all, and the two youngest could not avoid evincing some anxiety for the termination of Jones's lengthy prayer. He not only invoked blessings on his young companions, but desired they might speedily return to a Christian community. He asked that the savages might be converted and baptized; that they might be inspired with a resolution never to shed the blood of their white brethren who had settled in their forests; and, finally, that the counsels of the Continental Congress might have the heavenly guidance, and the cause in which they were embarked be gloriously triumphant.

And, after his emphatic "Amen," he arose and silently gazed in every direction. He did not explain; but Charles attributed his conduct to the force of habit, knowing it to be unsafe in many places to utter such patriotic petitions.

"Now, fall to, boys, and help yourselves," said Mr. Jones, resuming his seat before the fire, and literally tearing the smoking turkey in two by the drumsticks; and in the course of ten minutes all that remained of the gobbler were his bones, his bill, and his toe-nails.

In the night, when the blazing fire made the scene cheerful, and when all were in a comfortable condition after their hearty meal, Mr. Jones would have given vent to his grateful feelings in songs of praise, had it been deemed prudent. If there should happen to be a war-party in the vicinity, on a nocturnal march,—a thing neither probable nor impossible,—they might be attracted thither; and so the tuneful inclination was repressed.

But Mr. Jones felt no hesitation in relating his adventures on the Ohio River the preceding year, when acting in the capacity of a missionary among the Western tribes. He was relating a scene of burning at the stake, a sentence sometimes executed on prisoners,—a proceeding which Mr. Jones did not consider so barbarous as the burning of Protestants in enlightened Old England or of Quakers in puritanical New England, on account of their religious belief,—when they were startled by the loud snorting of the horse as he ran toward the camp. In the moonlight it was perceivable that the faithful animal's ears were thrust forward, as he turned his head over his back; and his eyes, catching the rays of the fire, became illuminated like globules of glass at a white heat.

The object causing the alarm was evidently between the camp and the river; and perhaps an enemy might be crouching behind the slight embankment, not twenty paces distant, taking a deadly aim at the hitherto unconscious travellers.

Charles turned his face in the direction of the intruder, so unerringly indicated by the horse, and gazed steadfastly, while Skippie prostrated himself and applied his ear to the ground.

"As for my part," said Mr. Jones, taking from his pocket a worn Testament, bound in black leather, or leather blackened by time, "here is my defence, and it never failed me yet." So, turning over the leaves, he began to read such passages as he deemed the most appropriate on such an occasion.

"I see!" whispered Charles, raising his rifle noiselessly. "It is an Indian."

"One!" said Skippie, rising, and unsheathing his dirk.

"And we are three," said Mr. Jones, lifting his eyes from the page, and placing one hand on his pistol; "but do not be the first to fire; he may be a friend."

"I am only in readiness," said Charles, endeavouring to fix his aim. "If he raises his gun, then I will be justified in pulling trigger."

But he did not raise his gun. On the contrary, his head, scalp-lock and all, sank down and vanished behind the slight embankment, and the next moment his voice was heard, saying, in very good English—

"Don't shoot! I'm a friend."

"What friend?" asked Mr. Jones, in his full, loud voice, rendered strong by much preaching. "What nation, if you are an Indian?"

"I'm a white man," said the stranger.

"He is, at least, in Indian costume, like myself," said Charles.

"Yes, but I'm white, though," said the stranger, hearing the last speech, and now approaching boldly. "And you see I haven't got a gun. So there's no danger."

"Do you call yourself a white man, my friend?" asked the preacher, staring like the rest at the curious aspect of the stranger. He was one of those short fat men we sometimes see who have no necks, their heads growing out between their shoulders. He wore leggins, hunting-shirt, and blanket; his head had been shaved, the scalp-lock alone remaining; and his face, plump and round, with a scarcely-discernible point of a nose, had been fantastically painted—one side being red, with sundry black spots interspersed, and the other altogether black.

"Yes; I'm a white man," said he, "like two of you; but I've been living with the savages, and they painted me. I thought once or twice when I stooped down to drink that my face looked black. Is it very dark?"

"Black, my friend," said Mr. Jones, "on one side."

"I thought they were making sport of me!"

"Who are you? your name?" demanded Charles.

"I've a famous big name! One of their greatest chiefs is called Cornplanter, or Cornstalk—I disremember which; and so they called me POPCORN."

"What was your name before you lived among the Indians?" asked Mr. Jones, seeing Charles's diversion.

"Oh, I'm Peter Shaver, among the whites.'

"True!" said Charles. "I thought I knew your voice, Peter; but they have so disguised you that your own mother wouldn't recognise you. Here, look in this small mirror."

Peter looked and stood aghast, while the rest could not refrain from hearty laughter.

"I'll take his sculp for it!" cried he. "I'll be revenged, if I have to lose my life! The tarnationed, rascally savage! If I ever meet him—and I've a notion to go back—I'll have his sculp or his sculp-lock! And if I can't find him, I'll give some other red devil a terrible thrashing!"

"Suppose you begin with me," said Charles.

"I don't care!" said the indignant Peter. "If these gentlemen will see fair play, and you won't use any thing but your fists——"

"Stranger," said Mr. Jones, rising to his feet and placing his hand on Popcorn's shoulder, "if you are a friend, and come in peace, sit down and eat such as we can spare you, or else depart. This is our camp, and you are our guest; but you will be thrust out if you do not behave yourself. Know that Charles Cameron is no blackguard, to fight with his fists like the degraded bullies of the ring."

"Charles Cameron! It is, by jingo! Oh, I beg your pardon a million times! And you are no Indian, no more nor me! Don't you know me?—Peter Shaver?"

"I know you very well, Peter, and have been merely jesting when perhaps I should have been very serious. Sit down and eat. You are too late for the turkey, but the jerked beef may suffice. Eat and smoke, and then tell us your adventures;—why you left your employer's service, and how you came to be dwelling among the Indians."

Peter, having a most voracious appetite, as he had a most capacious stomach, without further parley assailed the viands set before him.

When he had finished his meal he related his story substantially as follows. On the day he set out from Mr. Schooley's house to visit the mill he was seized by two Indians. They threatened to tomahawk him if he made any resistance or attempted to escape. He was compelled to dismount. One of them led the way on foot, while the other followed on his iron-gray pony. When any one approached they plunged into the inaccessible recesses of the forest, and remained silent and still until the way was clear, and then ventured forth again, avoiding the most frequented paths. Peter strove in vain to ascertain their purpose. He could not learn to what nation his captors belonged, nor why they had made him their prisoner. The only name he could understand—which they pronounced in the usual way—was Girty's; and he came to the conclusion that the noted leader of the British and Indian borderers might have discovered some great merit in him, or military qualification, which had superinduced his arrest.

When encamped for the night, Peter was permitted to recline before the fire in dignified silence, while the Indians prepared his food and filled his pipe, and manifested other indications of a high appreciation of his importance.

The second day the journey was prosecuted with less caution, and at night his two captors signified to Peter that it was time for him to "be Indian too." So they shaved all his hair off but the scalp-lock, painted his face red, gave him a blanket, leggins, moccasins, &c. They laughed, however, at the manner of his carriage or the singularity of his attitudes, and seemed to make several animated speeches on the subject. They then addressed themselves to Peter, who, not understanding a word they had said, made no response, although they patiently awaited one. Then they gave vent to explosions of laughter, and jabbered more, while their stoical captive snored before the fire.

After several days of moderate travel, during which the Indians seemed to be mindful of the comfort of their captive, they arrived in the vicinity of Lake Cayuga. Here they were met by many people of the Mohawk and Oneida tribes. But most conspicuous among them were two squaws, one of middle age and the other quite young, and both, as Peter declared, very beautiful, with the exception of their pink skins. They came running toward him with their arms extended; and, Peter said, he also opened his. But they stopped abruptly when within a few paces of him, and, very impolitely turning up their noses, likewise turned upon their heels and walked away. They hung down their heads, as if ashamed of something, or disappointed in the man they had sent for.

A few moments after, and while hundreds were standing round, a chief stepped forward and made a fierce speech to Peter's captors, who stood in silent shame. Then such shouts were heard as never assailed his ears before. They were shouts of laughter, loud and prolonged. After which the chief, who had scolded his captors, approached Peter, and informed him, in very good English, that the stupid Minisinks had brought them the wrong man. But Peter's joy on hearing this was dashed a little when told that he had better return immediately, or the enraged Indians might do him an injury. Peter's experience among the Indians, however, had hitherto been so agreeable that he could not be apprehensive of a change of treatment, and so he wandered forward into the village in quest of something to eat. The eldest of the women whom he had seen sent him victuals, with a message to depart. He lingered, nevertheless, while occasional bursts of merriment still assailed his ears.

Finally, the chief seized him by the ear and led him out of the village, pointing to where the pony had been left, and shoving the indignant captive in that direction. But Peter's pony had been taken, and in its place was a jackass of similar color, but whose sides had been variegated by the brush of a savage artist; and the sullen animal now resembled the zebra,—a beast he had once seen at a show. They told Peter his pony had been "swapped" for the jackass, and that he must mount and ride away; and, after a moment's reflection, and concluding it might be a very good swap, and an acquisition in the Jenny Jump settlement, he leaped upon the beast. Then Popcorn, as they called him, was cheered by the multitude; and the ass, either guided by the thong or frightened by the deafening sounds, turned his head in a southeastern direction and trotted off, braying so loudly that all other noises were utterly obliterated.

"They had put some corn-cakes and dried meat in my bag," said Peter, "and swapped for my corn as well as my pony. But the consumed jackass kept trying to bite me, and every now and then roared like a lion. It took me two whole days to learn how to manage him. I found out I could only do it by knocking him down with a club. Then he was always gentle enough till next morning. But I lost the right path, and travelled in several wrong ones. And I can't tell how I got here at all, unless the jack came of his own accord and was raised by the whites. And now, gentlemen," continued he, "as I understand you are going to come back soon from the Indian country, I would be glad to travel with you, as I know I shall never find the way home by myself, and I want to whip the Indian who painted me."

"Not find the way home," said Mr. Jones, "when you are on the bank of the Delaware River! What better guide would you have?"

"But I can't keep on it," said Peter; "and I don't know which side I'm on."

"Not know which side you're on! Can't you see which way the current runs?"

"Yes, I can see that."

"Well, when you stand with your face down-stream, don't you know which hand the river is on?—your right or your left?"

"I'm terribly bewildered! I cannot tell, indeed, sir."

"Nonsense! Not know your right hand from your left?"

"But I'm left-handed, sir! Or, rather, I use one hand as well as the other, and never could tell which was right and which was wrong."

"This is my right hand," said Mr. Jones, "next to your left. You can remember that, can't you?"

"Yes, if you are always at hand to remind me."

The reverend gentleman could restrain his merriment no longer; and even the taciturn Skippie could hardly avoid giving vent to loud bursts of laughter.

Charles remained silent in troubled meditation. It was not to be doubted that Peter had been captured by the stupid messengers in the belief that it was himself. They had evidently seen him ride away from the house of Mr. Schooley, and, being strangers to the person of the one they had been employed to seize, the mistake had been committed. The kind treatment on the way, the assembling of the tribe,—among whom he had many acquaintances,—and the eagerness of the two women to meet him, who must have been Gentle Moonlight and Brown Thrush, rendered what was merely a conjecture as Peter proceeded with his story a certainty at its conclusion.

Without deciding whether Peter should accompany them back into the Indian country or continue his solitary journey, preparations were made for sleeping, by enlarging the shelter and widening the couch. But, before the eyes of the party were closed, they were roused by the braying of the ass at no great distance. The sounds of his voice reverberated through the great valley of the Delaware, and were re-echoed by every ledge of cliffs. The wolves and owls were silenced by the stupendous roar, far more hideous than any uttered by themselves.

"He's in a grass-swamp about a half mile up the bank," said Peter. "When I saw your fire, I didn't know but you might be savages, and so I crawled here alone. If you hadn't taken me in, I should have gone to bed without my supper, as my provisions gave out yesterday. But I made a pin-hook this morning, and caught two trouts. One of 'em was a foot long, and made a good breakfast. I had some salt left, but you know I couldn't eat that by itself. And I had a knife and flint, and struck a fire."

In this manner Peter's tongue ran on until the rest of the travellers were slumbering soundly.

The next morning it was left optional with Peter whether to return with the travellers to the Indian country or to pursue his solitary way across the Blue Mountain to the white settlements. He chose the former, repeating his determination to whip the two Minisink Indians who had captured and painted him.

Nothing further worthy of special notice occurred until the party arrived in the vicinity of the southern extremity of Lake Cayuga. They were approaching the village where the foster-mother of Charles often spent the summer, and in the neighbourhood of which she held a large tract of rich land inherited from her mother.

Charles paused, and, placing his hands over his mouth, uttered the loud halloo he had so often sounded in his youth when returning from distant expeditions with the sons of the chiefs and sachems. Soon there was a reply which produced an animated expression of pleasure on his handsome features; and, as they drew nearer the village, numbers of men were seen running toward them through the beautiful grove in which the town was situated.

The foremost of those who came out to receive the adopted son of Gentle Moonlight was Calvin, the young Delaware chief who had been educated with Charles at college. They embraced, and shed tears of joy, for they had always been very intimate friends.

"They had concluded you would not come," said Calvin.

"And then they sent the Minisinks to seize me: did they not?" demanded Charles.

"I think so," said the other; "but they do not confess it. Ha! I see you have Popcorn with you!"

"Yes, I'm back agin," said Peter; "and when I set eyes on those nasty Minisinks there'll be a fight."

"Let me advise you to be peaceable," said the other. "You may get into danger."

Peter, struck by his manner, remained silent. The Rev. Mr. Jones was surrounded and welcomed by many of his Indian acquaintances as they approached the town.

Very soon the news of the voluntary return of the White Eagle spread through the village; and, when led by his friends to one of the principal wigwams, he was clasped in the arms of his foster-mother, who held him long in silence, while the Brown Thrush, smiling and weeping alternately, sang one of the wild songs Charles had so often listened to with delight.

"My sister,' said Charles, when released from the embrace of his mother, and at the same time kissing her tearful cheek, "thou hast not forgotten the words of thy brother when we parted many moons ago. It is the song you promised to sing when he returned. And didst thou never forget thy brother?"

"How could I?" said she. "The ripples murmured in the bright sunlight, as they did when we played together on the margin of the merry brook, and the soft sound was like the low voice of my brother. The bright stars danced in gentle glimmers, as they had done when we wandered together in the silent night. The fawn you gave me followed my lonely steps and bleated for thee. The wild-roses blossomed, and withered, and fell, because thou wert away. And, oh, my brother, the Thrush was drooping her head, and would have died, if thou hadst remained with the Antelope! And thou dost ask if I did not sometimes forget my brother? How could I?"

"Thou couldst not—nor I thee, my sister! In my dreams we met again in the solitude of the great forest, where the birds sang in safety and no rude foot crushed the violets. We sat beneath the lofty arch of the giant trees, and the sparkling waters murmured their low melody at our feet. Ha-wen-no-yu, the great Father of all good spirits, looked down from the blue sky and smiled upon us. And he heard the prayer we uttered:—that, after age had crept over us and we had closed our eyes upon the scenes of this world, we might meet again in the great hunting-grounds, and still wander together as loving sister and brother."

"And what did he speak?"

"He seemed to smile upon my request."

"Then, oh, Kacha Manito, I pray thee bring age upon us soon, so that we may close our eyes and depart for that happy land! My brother, thy sister too has dreamed. She thought thou wert separated from her by a great chasm, over which neither of us could pass. And when you attempted to leap over, the Antelope ran before thee; and when I strove to come to thee, she frowned and bade me remain; so there was no more happiness in this life, and I prayed the good Kacha Manito to remove us both to that happy land!"

"But these were merely dreams, my sister, and we should not be troubled by them. You see I can come to thee, and thou canst come to me. The Antelope will smile when she beholds you, and beckon you over the chasm. And thou must smile, too. The Thrush will love the Antelope; and soon, when I return to my father, both you and my mother must go with me."

"My son," said his foster-mother, after a short silence, during which the musing maiden made no reply, "the warriors of the nations are assembling at the Great Island, between the broad lakes, (Ontario and Erie,) where the council-fire is burning. From the shores of the salt water, where the sun rises from the blue deep, to the rolling prairies, where it sets, the chiefs are coming. They are digging up their tomahawks and sharpening their arrows for war. It was for this reason I sent thee word to come. I longed to behold thee once more. And I desired that thy voice might be heard in the council. Thou art my representative, and they will listen to thy words. I will go with thee, and the sweet Thrush shall sing the song of peace on the way; and, when we see the smoke of the council-fire ascending, it may charm the ear of the fierce Thayendanegea, thy brother and her brother. And then, if the hatchet be buried again, we will go with thee to thy white-haired father, and behold the beautiful eyes of the Antelope."

"My mother," said Charles, "your words sound like music in my ear, and I will obey thee."

Then, while a sumptuous repast was in preparation, Charles regarded his Indian mother and sister in silent admiration. They were fairer than most families of the Iroquois, and, unlike the majority of them, had oval faces and regular features of delicacy and beauty.

Bartholomew Calvin, the young Delaware chief, who sat beside Charles, had lingered among the lakes much longer than had been anticipated; and the Thrush was the magnet which attracted him. Charles could not avoid perceiving it, and he knew not whether to be angry or pleased with his friend for presuming to love his sister. But there were no indications of his passion being reciprocated; and it was not to be supposed that either Gentle Moonlight or the passionate Brandt would promote the alliance, unless the "Tamed Terrapin," as they called him, or the degenerate son of the Algonquins, would throw away his Christianity or his civilization and take up his abode among them in the forest.

CHAPTER IX.

NIAGARA—THE CAPTIVES—POPCORN—THE JOURNEY WESTWARD.

THE next day they set out for the Great Council-Fire, between the broad lakes, where the earth was shaken by the roar of mighty waters, and where Heno, the Spirit of Thunder, sat in his majesty and hurled his bolts at the enemies of heaven.

The cavalcade (all now being mounted) consisted of some twenty warriors, with their sisters and mothers,—the latter always having a voice in the ratification of treaties; and it was understood that, as usual, the pale-faces would strive to negotiate for more of their land. They had been preceded the day before by a very large delegation of Senecas, who were, with the exception of Red Jacket, (whose father was a Cayuga) in favour of war—war against the Colonies.

The Rev. Mr. Jones gladly availed himself of this opportunity of meeting the representatives of so many tribes. And Peter Shaver, having not yet succeeded in finding his enemies, vowed his purpose to look for them around the Great Council-Fire, and to chastise them wherever he might see them. The young Delaware chief, melancholy and sighing, followed in silence.

As Peter endeavoured to urge his long-eared charger forward, there was a very boisterous explosion of laughter. Some of the boys had inserted pepper under the tongue of the jackass, and as he trotted along he kept up for some distance an incessant braying; and while the boys yelled, and the men uttered every conceivable sound and some that were certainly inconceivable, poor Peter could only gesticulate with his clenched fists and threaten vengeance.

This amused his tormentors the more, even while they admitted "Popcorn," as they called him, was a brave man; and he was no coward, as the sequel will show.

Our party were welcomed to the Great Council by Brandt himself; and a vast number of Charles's old play mates, now chiefs and warriors, crowded round him and renewed their professions of friendship and attachment.

But Charles perceived with regret the greater number of white men mingling with the Indians were British agents. Sir John Johnston, John Butler and his son Walter, Girty, and McKee, as well as the implacable Queen Esther, were there.

The chiefs were the first to speak. White Eyes, an aged chief of the Western Delawares, had the precedence, and he was in favour of peace and alliance with the Americans; but Captain Pipe, another chief of the same band, declared for the British.

The Caugnawagas all spoke in favour of the British; while, the only Cherokee who spoke at all took the opposite side. The Shawnees were inclined to join the Colonies, but could never do so, so long as the death of Cornstalk, a great chief, and his son, Elenipsico, remained unavenged. They had been killed in a Western fort because the whites believed some of the Shawnees had murdered a Mr. Gilmore. Mr. Gilmore had been shot and scalped by Elliot, an English agent, *for the purpose* of producing such a result.

The chiefs of the Five Nations permitted the chiefs of other tribes to be heard first, because they had come a great distance to meet them there; and when the representatives of the various Western tribes had uttered their sentiments, Thayendanegea rose and spoke in favour of war—war against the Americans. He said, "States are ungrateful, like men. The first pale-faces that landed on our soil were poor, and we pitied them. We gave them land, and they grew rich. Then they despised us, and sought our destruction. So with the Colonies. When they were weak, and the people few in number, we were termed the lords of this broad continent, and their humble petitions were addressed to us. Now they consider themselves the lords, and would drive us from our inheritance. Let us conquer them or die. Death in battle is preferable to degradation in life. Such is my judgment. But we will have the warriors of our great father over the broad water to aid us, and we shall be victorious. If we do not embrace this opportunity, we shall never have another. If we remain neutral, who will assist when the victor in the present contest shall assail us? No matter which party is beaten, the other will some day drive us from our fathers' graves. Rather let us be buried in them!"

Charles was then permitted by the aged chiefs, as a special act of courtesy, to follow his foster-brother. He said he could not agree with his brother. The Americans were not to be dreaded so much as the British. The oppression came from the government beyond the ocean; and, if they oppressed their own people, how could it be supposed they would spare the Indians? He was in favour of a strict neutrality, unless the Indians should be unanimously inclined to join the Colonies—a thing he did not look for.

Sir John Johnston ridiculed the idea of permitting boys to speak in council, but admitted that the mother of Charles had a right to send him there. He controverted what had been said with indignant warmth.

Simon Girty next spoke in behalf of the royal cause. He made a very great impression by means of ingenious falsehood. Professing to be quite conversant with the purposes of the Americans, he announced that they intended to exterminate the Indians as the shortest way to possess their lands. And this declaration was substantiated by McKee and Elliot, all renegade tories.

Red Jacket replied to Girty, and said he derived no right from his mother to speak in the council, and especially to utter lies. He was in favour of neutrality. If they participated in the war at all, many of their brethren would fall. That was inevitable. And they would be weakened. If they kept aloof, the victor, whether America or England, would be weakened from losses and weary from suffering, while the Indians would be strong and more numerous than ever. That was their best security.

Young Bald Eagle, of the Pottawatomies, called Red Jacket a coward,—all words and no blows.

A Wyandot chief did the same.

A Mingo chief sustained the last two speakers, and declared for war against the Americans.

A Shawnee chief said his nation was divided, one-half agreeing with the Western Delawares to remain neutral.

The Oneidas, influenced by the Rev. Samuel Kirkland, who was present, announced their determination to remain at peace with the Americans.

The British officers then proposed to expel the missionaries from the council, and an intense excitement prevailed. Many tomahawks, which had been concealed, were brandished, and the utmost efforts of the sachems and chiefs were required to prevent the white men from desecrating the council-house with blood. They arrived at no other definite result than an agreement of those favourable to the British to meet again at Oswego.

Then a general dispersion took place, and our party prepared to return to the village they had set out from, near the head-waters of the Susquehanna.

The friendly Shawnees, Delawares, Cherokees, and Oneidas, were encamped on the same ground; while the tribes committed to the British cause kept aloof, and regarded them with looks of anger and aversion. The two missionaries, and the foster-mother and sister of Charles, as well as Charles himself and the redoubtable "Popcorn," were in the midst of the former.

In the evening Brandt came alone to the tent of his aunt, and sat down in gloomy silence between Charles and his sister.

"Oh, my brother," said his sister, "do not go with them to Oswego. Come with us to the peaceful vale where the south winds are sighing sweetly through the quivering leaves."

"No, sister," said he, sadly. "The war-whoop is heard on the shores of the northern lake. The war-paths are open. The tomahawks have been dug up. Thy red brother must lead the van of the battle. He must not kill his white brother."

"No!" cried the Thrush. "He would not do it if he met him in battle!"

"But Thayendanegea's people might kill him. The White Eagle must remain with his brother."

"The White Eagle is free," said Charles, "and may soar whithersoever he chooses."

"No!" said Brandt.

"What does my brother mean?"

"The White Eagle must not be pierced by the arrows of his red brother. He must not, then, stand before the bow. He must remain with his sister, among the women, if he will not fight the American pale-faces. Then the White Eagle must have some other name. He will no longer be a chief. They will call him the Frightened Hare!"

"Never!" said Charles. "I will lead my white people against the British. Let my red brother keep from before our rifles!"

"The Thrush will go with the White Eagle," said the maiden, "and sing him to sleep, so that he shall not harm his red brother."

"The Brown Thrush must go with Thayendanegea," said the chief.

"No!" said his aunt, speaking for the first time, although she had been an attentive listener. "My sister's daughter now has no mother but me. My sister is dead. My sister's son, listen to my command. The Thrush shall not go with you."

"My mother's sister, my ears are open. What you have said has entered them, and you must be obeyed."

"My sister's son," she continued, with deliberation, "the Brown Thrush shall go with the White Eagle."

"You command it. It must be so. But whither will they go? You cannot command the three thousand warriors whose chiefs have decided that my white brother shall not return to the pale-faces until the war is ended."

"False, treacherous, perfidious Thayendanegea!" said Charles. "And this is the cowardly work of the one I have loved and trusted! No more my brother! Henceforth we are foes!"

"My brother, do not make my blood boil over. Another had died ere the speech were finished. Thayendanegea did nothing. He knew it not until the chiefs had decided. He did not approve it, but he could not oppose it. He loves his brother still. He waits to hear his brother's next words."

"Forgive me, my brother!" said Charles, with tears in his eyes. "I ask my brother's pardon."

"It was the Malcha Manito, and not my brother. But what can my brother do? The warriors surrounding him, who will not declare war against his white brothers, will not oppose the decree of the chiefs. They are not ready to fight their red brothers."

"I will escape. You know the White Eagle can soar above his enemies."

"But whither will he direct his flight? He will not find the Antelope in the peaceful vale."

"My brother speaks no fables," said Charles, pale, and deeply moved.

"No. Thayendanegea cannot say what is not true. His brother's white sister has been, ere this, conveyed away. It was the decree of the chiefs, solicited by the Queen of the Senecas; but she cannot be injured. You are unhappy?"

"Oh," cried the Indian maiden, "let her be brought hither, or go where we go, and I will kiss away her tears and sing her to sleep!"

"Sister's son," said the aunt, "let it be so."

"It will be so," he replied. "Such is the purpose of the one who decided every thing, and whose decision was merely ratified by the chiefs."

"And that was old Esther," said Charles.

"Queen Esther," said Brandt.

"My brother," said the Delaware chief, Calvin, who had hitherto remained a silent listener, addressing Charles, "I will remain with you, or we will go together, whithersoever the great Ha-wen-no-yu, or our Holy Father, may direct our steps."

"Farewell!" said Brandt, rising. "The maple-leaf is red. It has been painted by the first frosts. Ere it falls we may meet again. Our lodges must be replenished with meat, and our women must gather the corn. And before the war-trail winds toward the sea we may hunt the buffalo in the West."

And he was gone before his mother's sister could interrogate him further. And not many minutes afterward the approach of Queen Esther was announced by fife and drum, which had been presented her by the British.

Queen Esther, or Catharine Montour, decked in gaudy habiliments, entered, and sat in their midst, upon a large scarlet robe spread for her by one of the attendants.

This woman—who had acquired an almost despotic influence over the Senecas, the most powerful of the Six Nations, by her incantations and superior intellect—was herself a white woman, or the daughter of the half-Indian wife of one of the noble French governors of Canada—Frontenac, it has been said. She had been stolen by the Indians when an infant, and raised among them. She married a chief, and never could be induced to return to her white kindred.

She was now in the eightieth year of her age, and her face was but a concentration of wrinkles, although she had once been handsome and accomplished.

"Ha, Gentle Moonlight," said she, with a sardonic smile, "there is a cloud upon thy face! Oh, yes! I did it; it was me. War, war to the hilt! My work. Blood must flow. Brandt shall be the Grand Sachem at Oswego. He shall be king; but he shall be the head-warrior, too. And why don't you *command* this young Eagle to marry the poor Thrush? and then we would make him a great prince. Oh that he was a Seneca! I would *order* him to marry; and no one disobeys me. What! dost frown at me? Tut, boy! But you won't escape. I have too wise a head for that. You will not leave your darling Antelope? Oh, no! Well, then, you shan't. She will come to you. That was Queen Esther's wit! Adieu! Go peaceably and submissively to the West, on the Scioto, or cross over to the 'Dark and Bloody Ground,' as some call it,—but it is neutral now,—and hunt the deer and buffalo. But do not destroy the Antelope!"

Without permitting any one to reply, she arose and departed, preceded by her martial music.

Shortly afterward, Charles was roused from his abstraction by the quiet entrance of Skippie, who stood before him and said—

"Going!"

"Going, Skippie?"

"I."

"I understand. Tell my father——"

"All. Know all."

POPCORN'S FIGHT WITH THE INDIAN.—P. 115.

And before Charles could utter another word Skippie was gone.

Shortly after this, Charles was again startled by a tremendous uproar among the boys. It appeared that, in imitation of their fathers, they had been holding a council. They had their interpreter, who rendered every thing in plain English to Peter Shaver, who was present. Very soon Peter was informed that he had been elected king. And, upon desiring to know where his subjects were to be found, they informed him he should be ruler over all the Capitanasses. There had been a tribe of that name in Jersey, although Peter was not aware of it. Peter, therefore, supposing he had been made the laughing-stock of the boys, being called King of the Capitanasses because he rode an ass, indignantly withdrew. They followed, whooping and crying, "Popcorn, King of the Capitanasses!" The men laughed heartily as Peter strode over the ground toward the camp of Gentle Moonlight. And, as he approached, he espied the Minisink Indian who had put the dark stains on his face, and which no process of washing and rubbing he could employ had yet removed. Finding the Indian merry at his expense, he threw aside his blanket and charged upon him with his fists. Now, although Peter was short and fat, and rather short-winded, he was somewhat scientific in the use of his fists. A ring was instantly formed around the combatants, with shouts and cries of merriment. The Minisink strove in vain to get the "Indian hug" on Peter. Peter planted his blows with such precision and rapidity that his adversary was forced back, and, as he retreated, dodging from one side to another, Peter was applauded by the spectators. Finally, Peter succeeded in planting a blow on the stomach of the Indian, which laid him on the ground, and then the victor would have been content to drop the quarrel. Not so the Indian. Incensed and suffering, he drew his knife and made several desperate lunges, which were warded off with difficulty. The spectators interfered, and disarmed the Indian, who threatened to be revenged on some future occasion, while the boys conducted their new chief and champion in triumph to his tent.

But the bruised Minisink soon found sympathizers; and as the British agents, under the guise of peddlers, had distributed no small quantity of rum among the men, there soon arose a cry for the scalps of the American pale-faces. When this reached the ears of the foster-mother of Charles, she had her tent removed to a place of greater security, where it was surrounded and guarded by a number of Delaware warriors; and early in the morning our party set out, in a southern direction, toward the head-waters of the Alleghany.

Gentle Moonlight, Brown Thrush, Charles, the young Delaware chief, the Rev. David Jones, and Peter, formed the party. Although a prisoner, Charles was permitted to retain his arms, having given his word that he would not attempt an escape for the space of seven days. This he did the more readily, as he knew it would require that length of time to convey Julia to the place in the West designated by Queen Esther, and where he hoped to be permitted to see her.

Although our party were granted the privilege of encamping as often as they pleased on the route, to make long or short marches as might suit the convenience of the sister of the mother of Brandt, yet it was soon apparent that they were followed and observed by seven of the guards of Queen Esther, whose duty it was to prevent any communication with the settlements of the white people. But they were also preceded by seven Oneida warriors friendly to the American cause. These warriors shot an abundance of game, as they proceeded, for the use of the travellers.

The weather was fine, and the journey, although easy and pleasant, (for the foster-mother of Charles was rich, and had been lavish in expenditure when providing for the comfort of her children,) was devoid of special incident until the party crossed the dividing-line between New York and Pennsylvania. Here they rested while canoes were sought in which to descend the Alleghany River; and here they were informed by a runner of the approach of Julia, guarded by two Mingo chiefs, who could speak the English language, and who had been charged, as the runner assured Charles, to provide for all her wants, and to prevent her from suffering the slightest bodily inconvenience on the journey. Runners likewise came from Oswego, confirming the rumour that Brandt had been made grand-sachem of the Five Nations. It was also understood that the Indians would not go upon the war-path until the next spring; and in the mean time they were to disperse in hunting-parties, and secure a large supply of buffalo-meat.

The camp of the travellers, or captives, (for it appeared they were still subject to the direction of Queen Esther,) was situated in one of the wildest, and at the same time one of the most lovely and romantic, spots in nature. It was on a small delta of the Alleghany. The bright water flowed at their feet on the south, and upon its surface the golden beams of the sun danced in ever-varying splendour. Behind, they were defended from the chilling winds of the north by a high mountain, whose sides were clothed with evergreens.

The camp was sheltered from the dews and the noon-day sun by a grove of sugar-maples, upon whose boughs, ever and anon, rested myriads of wild-pigeons, pausing in their migratory flight. Charles and Bartholomew Calvin explored the mountains and streams in the vicinity, and admired the bold features of the country. And it was during one of these excursions with gun and angling-rod, that Calvin confessed—what Charles had already suspected —his passion for the sister of Brandt; and at the same time expressed the sad conviction—which was evident to all— that the Thrush was deeply, blindly in love with the Eagle. Charles said every thing in his power to encourage and comfort his friend, assuring him that, whatever might be his affection for his foster-sister, or her attachment to him, they could never be united.

And the poor Thrush and her aunt devoted themselves to the generous task of providing for the comfort of the captive maiden, whose arrival was now daily looked for. She was the Antelope, loved by Charles, whom they loved, and therefore they must love her too. The jealousy and hatred that might have poisoned more civilized women under similar circumstances found no place in their bosoms. It is true, according to their code of morals, a chief might have more than one wife; but they were not ignorant that Charles, during the process of his education, had adopted the Christian faith, and would be governed by the laws of the race from which he was descended. And, likewise, Mr. Jones had made some progress in their own conversion to Christianity. Nevertheless, the devoted Thrush sang joyously as she prepared soft furs and fashioned robes of fine cloth and hoods and moccasins for the Antelope.

It was while thus engaged in the deep solitude of the silent grove that Charles once encountered her. He had left Calvin and Peter fishing up the stream, near the camp of the seven guards of Queen Esther.

"My sister," said he, sitting down at her side on the bleached trunk of a fallen tree, then checkered by the straggling rays of the morning sun, "you will be kind to your white sister, will you not?"

"My brother loves his white sister. I love my brother."

"But will the Thrush always love the Antelope when she sees her brother gather the sweetest flowers for her nosegays?"

"Why not? Cannot my brother love us both? And why should we not love one another?"

"I fear, my poor sister, that you are incapable of comprehending me."

"Oh, never fear. My brother Thayendanegea used to say the White Eagle would forget his wild Thrush and remain away. But it was not so. I did not believe it. And did he not return? He used to tell her, also, that her white brother would love his white Antelope and forsake the Thrush. I did not believe that either. He was mistaken in the one, and will be in the other."

"But, my sister, suppose it had been as Brandt said?"

"The Thrush would still have sung. She would never have blamed and hated the Eagle. But it would have been a mournful song,—her own death-song. She would have folded her wings and died."

"Do you not know, my sister, that among the whites it is unlawful for a man to love two maidens at the same time?"

"Oh, yes! Mr. Jones has told me. That is among courts and cities, and where the country is torn by the iron ploughs. I do not doubt it. But we will not go thither. The Antelope will remain with us in the warm sunlight, near the edge of the bright, leaping waters at the foot of the mountain. She will see the antlered buck followed by two does, and the birds of fairest plumage attended by two mates. She will forget the white people and their cruel customs."

Charles despaired of convincing her of the superiority of the customs of the white people; and, after a protracted silence on his part, while the Indian maiden resumed her song and plied her delicate fingers in the fabrication of an exquisitely-ornamented pair of moccasins for Julia, he resumed:—

"But, my sister, hast thou not seen that thy brother's friend, the young Delaware chief, was fascinated by the song of the Thrush?"

'He would not wrong his friend. He would rather perish."

"I know it. But I would not have him die. I love him too. We were brothers at the college."

"And did he not hear thee speak of me? Did he not know thy sister loved thee? Let him return to his people in the East, or wed among the Delawares of the West. The Brown Thrush knows her mate!"

"My sister," continued Charles, "I say these things to thee that thou mayest be prepared for the events of the future. Once I loved thee only, and I love thee yet. But I could not avoid loving the Antelope of my own race, when she was so kind to me. What thy brother says is the truth. A Christian is not allowed to have two wives. And the Antelope is a Christian. Her husband must have but one wife!"

"Be it so!" said the maiden, lifting her confiding eyes to those of the young man. "We will not marry. We will build no nests. The Antelope and the Thrush will only love and charm the White Eagle. And when we go to the great hunting-grounds together, Ha-wen-no-yu may not have such bad laws as the white men."

Charles, half amused and half vexed at the argument and devotion of the child of nature, ceased the discussion. He was startled, however, soon after, by the arrival of Peter Shaver, bearing in his arms a very young bear-cub, which kept up a piteous crying for its dam.

The Indian maiden leaped up in terror, and asked if the dam had been killed; but Peter, not understanding her language, only offered her the "pretty pet," as he called it. Then, in reply to the same question from Charles, he said he had not seen the dam.

The Indian girl, upon learning that the dam had not

been destroyed, gathered up her work and fled toward the camp, not doubting the men would soon have to use their rifles.

"Yonder she comes now!" said Peter, as he beheld the infuriated animal plunging down the side of the mountain, attracted by the cries of her offspring.

"Stop the cub's cries, Peter," said Charles, "or else you may feel the weight of the mother's claws before we can kill her."

"It wont stop!" said Peter. "And if I shoot it, its mamma may catch me with an empty gun! I'll let it go!" he continued, and instantly threw it down. But, instead of running away, the cub followed Peter as he retreated behind the fallen trunk. "Oh, what shall I do?" cried he, now stricken with terror; for the creature would not leave him, and the dam was coming with fearful strides.

"Climb a tree," said Charles, amused at the efforts of Peter to shake off the cub, "or else kill it."

"Oh!" cried Peter, "he's biting my hand! Help me, Mr. Cameron!" And as the poor man glared fearfully at the old bear, now within fifty paces of him, his knees trembled so violently he was unable to climb the tree he ran to. But the Delaware youth, who had followed to see the result of the experiment, and Charles, who did not relish a closer proximity to the old bear, fired their rifles nearly at the same moment, from opposite sides, and both with effect. Nevertheless, she was not killed, though mortally wounded, and rolled and ran together to the foot of the tree behind which Peter Shaver was endeavouring to conceal himself; and there she fell, but not before striking one blow at Peter, which merely caught the skirt of his buckskin coat as he fled round the trunk. He was held fast, however, though the bear was dead, her teeth being desperately sunk in a root of the tree, upon which Peter's cap had fallen. Peter continued to make violent struggles to extricate himself, and still called lustily for help.

"Why don't you turn and fight, Peter?" asked Charles, advancing carelessly.

"Shoot, Popcorn!" said Calvin.

"Oh! he'll tear me all to pieces! I've lost my gun!" cried Peter, who had dropped his rifle when the bear sprang toward him.

"Take your tomahawk or knife," continued Charles, seeing the bear was quite dead. One arm clasped her cub, while the other nailed Peter's hunting-shirt to the tree.

"I can't! I tremble so!" said Peter; "kill him, if you please!"

"No," said Charles; "you must distinguish yourself before you can become a great Indian. If we were to dispatch the bear, the Indians would call you a woman."

"Dad burn the Indians and the women," cried Peter, "when a savage bear has hold of my shirt-tail! Get out of the way, if you won't help me!" and, extricating himself by a violent effort, he sank his tomahawk in Bruin's head.

"That finished her!" said Calvin.

"You have conquered," said Charles.

"You dealt such a deadly blow," continued Calvin, "that she never moved afterward."

Just then Peter's ass, which was browsing near, began to bray.

"Your steed, even, is cheering you, Peter. Well done, great Popcorn!" added Charles.

"Gentlemen," said Peter, who soon began to suspect they were quizzing him, of all offences the most unpardonable, "I guess you're not in earnest, for I believe the bear was dead before I struck her. But I don't like to be made sport of. If you doubt my courage, just strip and let us fight it out!"

But this was not agreed to. Boxing was not one of their accomplishments; and they declined the honour, assuring Peter they did not doubt his superiority in the mode of combat proposed.

The braying of the ass was caused by the smell of the blood of the bear. Charles had been informed by the Indian who had made the exchange with Peter, that it was his startling braying, whenever he got the scent of blood, which rendered it necessary to part with him.

CHAPTER X.

ENCAMPMENT ON THE ALLEGHANY—ARRIVAL OF JULIA.—
THE WARWHOOP—QUEEN ESTHER.

AT the first wail of the whippoorwill perched on the trunk of the fallen tree where the Indian maiden sang in the daytime, and just when the last glimmer of twilight was succeeded by the silvery rays of the rising moon, our temporary sojourners at the foot of the mountain were startled by the hailing halloo of an Indian, which they immediately understood to be the announcement of the approach of Julia, the captive maiden.

The only direction by which horses could approach the small area in the midst of which stood the encampment was by following the course of the river, along the right bank of which was an old Indian path. Up this path Charles and the Indian maiden ran, hand-in-hand, to meet the captive; and when they turned an acute point of one of the ridges, round which wound the path, meandering with the stream, they beheld the object of their solicitude. Rushing forward, Charles clasped his affianced in his arms, and, when relinquished by him, she was as heartily embraced by the Indian maiden.

Silence prevailed for many moments, during which their tears could not be restrained. But their throbbing hearts were relieved.

"Oh, Julia," said Charles, "I did not think, when we parted, we should meet again in such a place as this! I, too, am a prisoner. They detained me in hopes I would unite with them in the war against the Colonists. And they brought thee hither to remove one of the motives I might have to escape. I fear you have suffered very much!"

"Indeed, I have not!" replied Julia, with a slight smile and a blush. "It has been like a dream—a repetition in my slumbers of some of the fireside stories I have listened to of long winter evenings. The two chiefs who captured me could speak our language very well, and provided every convenience for me in their power. Their first care was to assure me I should sustain no injury; their next, that I should meet with thee. After that, all was pleasing novelty and romantic adventure."

"Her voice is like the warbling of the robin or the sound of dancing waters," said the Indian girl; and Charles rendered it into English.

"How beautiful!" said Julia, gazing at the face of the child of the forest.

"Let us now hasten to the tent of my Indian mother," said Charles, leading the way. "But who is that?" he continued, seeing a white man following, the two chiefs having halted with Queen Esther's guard.

"That is our gardener, Paddy Pence," said Julia. "You may come now, Paddy," she continued.

Paddy ran forward and prostrated himself before Charles, whom he had not recognised; for Julia, with maiden modesty, not wishing him to hear that which might be uttered on her meeting with her lover, had directed him to remain some distance behind.

"Oh, Misther Indian chafe," cried he, "if you have kilt Mr. Charles, do plase send me and Miss Julia back to the Jenny Jump, and Mr. Schooley will pay you a thousand pounds; I know he will, for he said he would!"

"When did he say that, Paddy?" asked Julia.

"I mane I know he would naturally say sich a thing afther he found out we had both been captivated!"

"Paddy!" said Charles.

"You know me name, Misther Indian; and I hope you don't mane to take the sculp of a frind."

"Paddy, don't you know me?"

"Are you one of the great and noble and ginerous chafes who used to ate and smoke at Misther Schooley's table? I thought I knew yer voice. And do you know I always thought you the handsomest one of them all?"

"Be done, now, Paddy; none of your nonsense, or by the patron saint of all the Paddies of ould Ireland——"

"Wha! I know you now, Mr. Charles, by your poor brogue!" cried Paddy, leaping up. "And, as sure as the moon is shining over us, I had forgotten your hunting-shirt, and leggins, and breech-clout, on the day you left us. And here I've been mistaking you for one of them blackguard savages!"

"Paddy," said Julia, as they moved slowly toward the fire at the hut, "you must not abuse the Indians. If Charles is not one, this lady is."

"I beg yer pardon, miss," said he, addressing the Thrush; "it was only an Irish slape o' the tongue."

After interpreting the speech, Charles informed Paddy that the Indian lady did not understand English.

"Then, be the powers," said Paddy, "she wouldn't be likely to sculp me for me Irish."

They were met at the threshhold of the encampment by the foster-mother of Charles, who tenderly folded Julia in her arms, and placed her on the seat of furs which had been provided for her. She gazed long in admiration of the features and form of the white maiden; and then, turning to Charles, said she was very lovely, but that he must not permit her to estrange him from his forest sister.

Every delicacy the camp afforded was produced for the captives; and Paddy had just a sufficient recollection of his position and his duty to forbear the gratification of his ravenous appetite until his mistress bade him eat.

The Rev. Mr. Jones, who had been making the woods vocal with his spiritual songs, came in and shared the smiles of Julia. Calvin, too, paid his devoirs in his usual melancholy way.

"Murther!" said Paddy, at the end of his repast, when, lifting up his eyes, he saw, standing before him, a tomahawk in one hand and a scalping-knife in the other, the redoubtable rotundity of the chief of the Capitanasses,—Popcorn.

"I hope you couldn't be so cruel, Mr. Indian, as to sthrike a man wid a full stomach, and when he's in sich a good humour that he wouldn't bate the worst inemy in the world."

"Paddy!" said Peter Shaver, hardly able to maintain his composure, although still conscious of the presence of the dark blotches painted on his face by the Minisink artist.

"Paddy!" iterated the gardener. "The divil take me if me name isn't pat in the mouths of all the black—— Misther Charles, can this chafe understand English?"

"Perfectly; and Irish too," said Charles.

"I mane," continued Paddy, "in the mouths of all the picturesquely-painted chafes of the magnificent natural forests and mossy strames and gliding rocks."

"Paddy Pence," continued Peter, approaching a step nearer, "don't you know me?"

"No doubt of it, yer noble honour; but I can't jist call yer name at prisent, though it was on the ind of me tongue a minute since. You came to Misther Schooley's wid the rest of the tall majestic chafes and———"

"Paddy Pence," said the other, "you are the first man who ever called Peter Shaver tall and majestic, and I thank you for it."

"Peter Shaver? What! Peter Shaver, our little pot-bellied overseer? It is! Och, forgive me, St. Pater! Why, you nasty little blackguard, to come wid your disguises and impose yerself on gintlemen as a natural chafe of these eternal wildernesses! Begone, ye spalpeen, and larn betther manners!"

"Come! Foller me, and I'll teach *you* better manners, you Irish cur, you!" said Peter, rolling up his sleeves, and stepping out under the spreading maples.

"I won't fight ye," said Paddy, "wid sich savage instruments as them," gazing at the tomahawk and knife. "But find a good hickory cudgel, and I'll soon paint yer bald head the original colour of yer hair."

Charles and Mr. Jones interposed, and after a few words of peace and explanation the two old acquaintances became reconciled, and sat by the fire the remainder of the evening relating their marvellous adventures.

And Julia, declaring she felt no fatigue, as her progress through the wilderness had been by easy though tortuous marches, readily consented to narrate the manner of her capture.

"Every afternoon," said she, "since the forest-leaves have been variegated by the early frosts, it has been my habit to ride over the grounds we used to visit together. It was not considered prudent to walk alone in the paths, for a number of large rattlesnakes had been seen by Mr. Green every year at that season, seeking, as he says, their dens in the rocks where they pass the winter. Nor would my guardian permit me to go unattended. Richard, you know, could not spare the time to accompany me. And so Paddy, armed with the French fowling-piece given to Mr. Schooley by Governor Franklin, followed my steps, and kept my erratic person in view, as much as I saw proper to permit him. But my chief reliance was on Solo, my poor, faithful companion.

"It was upon the gentle slope where Richard, you know, had girdled the noble forest-trees for the purpose of enclosing another field, that I paused and listened to the dirge-like sound of the breeze as it murmured through the boughs of the stricken oaks. And I sang a mournful ditty,—tho requiem you composed for the night of the conflagration of the grove devoted to destruction by the civilized Vandals. Leaning on my elbow,—no doubt the picture of dejection,—and my sympathetic palfrey as motionless as a monument, I was startled by the sudden cry of poor Solo; and, turning, I saw him rolling in agony on the ground, transfixed by an arrow which had passed through the points of his shoulders. Paddy came running toward me with great swiftness, but when he saw the arrow he fired his gun at random, and, without pausing to recharge it, threw it down and took to his heels. But he was instantly confronted in the path by one of the Mingo chiefs, who laughed very heartily at his panic-stricken face. He seized him and bound his hands.

"The other chief arose from the tall grass near my horse, and, taking the reins in his hand, assured me, in very good English, that it was not their intention to injure either of us, although we must submit to be their prisoners and promise not to utter any cries. He said he was employed to convey me to the West, where I would meet the White Eagle. That assurance, Charles, bereft me of half my terrors. And yet a painful thought flashed through my mind——"

That I had, perhaps, resolved to become an Indian again, and might be violently tearing thee away from thy home," said Charles, smiling.

"Something of that nature, I admit," said Julia; "but it flitted away like the gleam of the lightning, and the Mingo assured me you knew nothing of his proceeding. The object of his employer was to prevent you from returning and bearing arms against your red brethren. Then I signified

THE CAPTURE OF JULIA AND PADDY BY THE
MINGO CHIEFS.—P. 136

my readiness to accompany them, if they would also take my poor wounded Solo. This they could not agree to. But they assured me his wound would not prove fatal, though it had been their intention to kill him. They said the report of Paddy's gun would soon attract the people thither, and the dog would be taken care of. And so they hastened us away to the old sycamore, where their horses were concealed. Paddy was made to get up behind one of the chiefs, and then we plunged into hidden paths, whose existence I had no knowledge of before, and rode, I suppose, many miles without halting. They spread a shelter toward morning in a deep valley, and wrapped me in furs, so tnat neither the chill of the night-wind nor the dew of the leaves could reach me. I could not eat the food they offered; but I recollect seeing Paddy's jaws in motion. I fell asleep and dreamed of thee, Charles, and the Indian maiden, and a scene like this.

"When daylight appeared, we resumed the journey. Supposing they might be pursued, our captors frequently deviated from the usual paths, for the purpose of misleading those who might attempt to follow us.

"After the second day, the chiefs were less apprehensive of being overtaken. They now suffered poor Paddy to go unbound, but warned him not to attempt an escape. This he pledged himself not to do, assuring them, upon his honour, that, if liberated, he would not know which course to take, and would starve in the woods. In short, to their infinite amusement, he begged them not to leave him behind. They killed various birds and other tender game for me; and, my appetite returning, I could partake of them with a good relish.

"In this manner, the weather being very beautiful all the time, we completed the journey. Paddy and I were delivered into the hands of the seven warriors—Senecas, I think—encamped a few miles from this place up the stream. One of their party guided us hither, and uttered the halloo which apprised you of our approach. He then vanished, and I saw him no more."

When Julia concluded her recital, Paddy, who had been listening to Peter, was seen to spring upright.

"And you mane to tell me that that is the prant of the

bear's nails on yer leather shirt?" cried he, when Topcorn recounted his recent adventure.

"I do, Paddy, and hang me if I can't prove it!"

"And so you must be afther having a vulgar set-to at boxing wid the filthy crature, instead of using a shelalah! I m astonished at yer taste!"

"But I killed him with my tomahawk, Paddy," added Peter, in a low tone, "and he never hurt a hair of my head."

"A precious small dale ye have left at all! If it wasn't for the shaving of the hair, and painting of wan's countenance in that blackguard fashion, I would have no objections to be an Indian meself for the trifle of a week or two. But what do they lave that plume of a tuft on the top o' yer head for?"

"That's the scalp-lock, Paddy."

"The sculp-lock! Divil the bit shall they have to sculp me by! I'll have ivery blade taken off the top o' my head! I'll be as bald as a shaven monk to morrow morning, if there's a razor to be had! They shall find no sculp-lock on Paddy's head! And now, what in nature is that horrid roar I hear?"

"That's my—my horse, Paddy," said Peter, hesitating, and recognising the sound.

"And I'd like to saa that same horse o' yours. I hope you don't fade him in the ear."

"In the ear?"

"Yes; hasn't he ears?"

"Oh, very large ones. But I don't know what he can be smelling now. Didn't you hear something?"

Shouts and the reports of guns were indeed heard. Charles and Calvin sprang up and listened attentively.

"McSwine!" said Charles. "It is the voice of McSwine! Julia, your captors were pursued, and have been overtaken. My father permitted McSwine to go upon the trail, and he is an experienced woodsman. Listen! Did you not hear that? The Senecas cry, OONAH! It is for us to fly. We will not move! My mother, let Queen Esther's guards hide from the fatal aim of McSwine. He is our friend, and will deliver us. We will remain!"

"My son," said the Gentle Moonlight, "there are more than a hundred Seneca warriors encamped behind us, and others are on the march. They have been sent to kill buffalo, and merely await our motions, for they have been charged to see that no one escapes before we reach Chilicothe. Such was the speech of a runner who passed this morning."

"Queen Esther," said Calvin, "cannot have given orders to restrain *my* actions. I will go to the Oneidas, and then to the faithful band of Delawares remaining in their wigwams. I will return with as many as will accompany me, and we will defend the sister of Brandt's mother, and his own sister."

Calvin started away, and was soon lost to sight in the intricacies of the woods. Meantime an occasional shot was heard, followed by the yells of the savages, which seemed to grow fainter in the distance.

Charles went forth alone in the direction from which the yells at first proceeded, and sounded a horn his father had given him. It was replied to immediately by McSwine, who was standing but a few hundred paces distant. The next moment the rescuing party advanced, and were soon greeted with the animated congratulations of Charles.

"Hoot, mon! Our blude's up! Where's the lassie?" said McSwine.

"Safe, safe!" cried Charles. "She is yonder, where the fire is glimmering, in the camp of my foster-mother. And she is safe for the night. The Senecas, though wolves by day, do not often prowl in the night. Come in and eat. And you are here, Will?" he continued, heartily welcoming Van Wiggens, and patting the head of his frisky, stump-tailed dog.

"Yes, tam dem!" said he. "Dey steal te goot and te peautiful Miss Lane, and leave te scolding Mrs. Wan Viggens!"

Charles cordially grasped the hands of the rest of the party—some five or six in all—who had accompanied McSwine.

But the Indians knew McSwine's Scotch accent, and recollected his herculean frame, which, years before, had been terribly familiar. Hence their flight before they knew exactly the numerical strength of the rescuers.

Charles led his friends into the tent of his Indian mother, where Julia gave utterance to the thanks she felt for the pursuit, and where the Indian maiden and her aunt had already prepared for them a plentiful repast.

They ate like half-starved wolves, having fasted for several days. And, as they masticated the bear, Peter Shaver was heard to say he had killed him.

"Tam! Who's dat tere?" cried Van Wiggens, pointing at the chief of the Capitanasses.

"I'm Peter Shaver, Will," said he. "Don't you know me?"

"Peter Shaver? Warn't he drownded at te Gap? Dey saw a pig fat round ting floating town te river, which some said was a swelt hog, and some said it vas like Peter Shaver. Most of us dought it vas Peter, and it vas more like him tan you."

"Bill Van Wiggens," said Peter, quivering with anger, "you once felt Peter Shaver's fist on your fat paunch. If you'll step out, you may feel it again, and then you'll know him!"

"Tat's his voice, I'll swear to it!" said Van Wiggens. "I pelieve you now, Peter. You needn't prove it any more. And you look more like a man as an Indian tan you did before. Peter," he continued, in a half whisper, "tam if I don't turn Indian myself! Mrs. Wan Viggens will be afraid of me den!"

Peter Shaver, Paddy Pence, and Will Van Wiggens, surrounded by the three or four clansmen of the Cameron who had followed McSwine, formed a separate group some paces apart, and entertained each other with the recital of their exploits.

"Now, Hugh," said Charles, when the last bone had been picked, "you will tell me the news of the valley, and first of my father."

"Well, mon, well. The laird was never sick in his life, since we carried him over the hills of Scotland, his breast and shoulders shot to pieces by the English cannon. He reads and studies in his castle, watching for his bonny laddie's return, but not impatiently. He waits the Lord's time, who holds us all in the hollow of his hand."

"God bless my good father!" said Charles; and McSwine uttered a hearty Amen.

The faithful Scot informed Charles that the capture of Julia had produced great consternation in the neighbour hood, and for several days after the occurrence it seemed doubtful whether a party could be formed to go in pursuit. Mr. Schooley, almost distracted, did nothing but write letters to all the chiefs and sachems he had ever known; but there were no messengers to deliver them. Richard rode from one house to another, offering insignificant pecuniary rewards for the rescue and restitution of the lady. His tears flowed incessantly, but he was religiously averse to bearing arms himself. Yet he ran and brought the French gun that had been dropped by Paddy, and, putting it in the hands of Van Wiggens, proposed supplying the whole party with horses and ammunition."

"Poor Solo!" cried Julia, at this point. "Tell me, good Hugh: what was my poor dog's condition when you left? Say no more of Richard, or his honest scruples."

McSwine informed her that he had himself withdrawn the arrow, and that the faithful animal could use his legs immediately, for he evinced his gratitude by leaping up with his paws against his breast; and, when they started in the pursuit, Solo had to be locked up, else he would have followed them, and might have died on the way.

"Let us pray!" said Mr. Jones, suddenly returning from one of his solitary nocturnal rambles, during which he had been forgotten by the rest of the party. "I have heard the signals of the wolves of Queen Esther. They are rallying in the mountains, and after they have buried their dead they will come upon us with howls and gnashing teeth."

"You've got my French gun, Mr. Van Wiggens," said Paddy, "and I can't fight."

"You shall have one of my pistols, Paddy," said Charles.

"And one of mine," said Mr. Jones. "My voice will intimidate them more than my arms. But, alas! blood has been spilled. I heard their death-halloo."

"True, mon!" said Hugh, "we fired bock at 'em. And when Hugh McSwine fires his rifle at mortal mon he becomes immortal."

"Let us pray, then!" repeated David Jones, falling down on his knees. The whole party, excepting the Presbyterians, followed his example; the Indian maiden and her aunt with as little hesitation as the rest. And the Indians, unlike many of the civilized Christians, never experience any feeling of shame or degradation in bowing before the Great Spirit in humble adoration. They care not who sees them worship the Creator, any more than to be seen admiring a beautiful flower, or when charmed by a sublime spectacle of natural scenery.

The eccentric Baptist uttered a long petition to the Supreme Ruler. He prayed that the party then kneeling in the solitude of the wilderness might be delivered from their enemies; and, next, that the Sons of Liberty, led into battle by George Washington, might triumph over the legions of the tyrant.

Then he admonished his hearers that to merit the aid of their Maker it was indispensable that they should be eager to help themselves, which was the best proof of their worthiness to be assisted.

And after this, Mr. Jones, by the permission of the party, retired a few paces apart, and sang one of the martial psalms of David, in which all the honour of victory was ascribed to the Lord. And as the savage orgies of the Senecas in the distant hills could be distinctly heard, constantly borne on the gentle night-breezes, the mighty sound of Mr. Jones's voice must have penetrated the ears of the enemy.

After their defeat, the guard of Senecas bore their dead —two of their number having fallen—to a place of security, and buried them with all the ceremonies usual on such occasions. They then sent a runner to the large hunting-party of their nation encamped in the vicinity. Just before the messenger reached the encampment, Queen Esther arrived; and when the runner delivered his message, and made known the fact that two of the guard had fallen, an intense excitement ensued. Queen Esther, who had been accompanied by several of the principal chiefs recently returned from Oswego, immediately summoned a council of warriors, at which it was resolved to surround the camp on the Alleghany at early dawn and demand the delivery of the offending whites into their hands. This project had the hearty approval of the Queen, and she anticipated with delight the torture she meant to inflict on her captives.

But Bartholomew Calvin had not been idle. He collected the party of Delawares who still acknowledged his authority, and also a number of Cherokees from the South, who were passing toward the neutral hunting-grounds beyond the Ohio. A small band of Shawnees, being assured they had no cause of complaint against the Colonists for the murder of Cornstalk at Fort Point Pleasant, as that deed had been done by the agents of Lord Dunmore, likewise consented to join him, but with no promise to make war against the Senecas. These, together with the seven Oneidas granted as a special protection to Gentle Moonlight and Brown Thrush, numbered altogether, including the party at the camp, some seventy men; and, apprehending an early assault, Calvin lost no time in leading his succours to the scene of action. They arrived late in the night, and, to avoid disturbing the slumber of our party, sought a few hours' repose under shelter of the surrounding trees.

As they had foreseen, the warwhoop of the Senecas rang down the valley of the Alleghany at early twilight. Charles, and Calvin, and Hugh, followed by the rescuing party of Scots, rushed at once to the narrow pass above, which, if successfully defended, closed the principal avenue of access to the encampment; for it was defended in other places by almost precipitous cliffs.

The Indians who had followed Calvin still lay concealed, in obedience to his instructions.

At the pass Queen Esther herself came forward and demanded the delivery of the party who had fired on her guard. This request was refused by Charles, because the guard had been the first to fire, and because the whites were his friends, and were pursuing the Indians who had captured the unoffending maiden.

"You see I have the means of compelling obedience," said Esther, pointing to the long array of painted warriors behind.

"I see you have many brave men," said Charles, "but we have warriors quite as bold to meet them."

"But not so many, On-yit-hah," (bird of the strong wing.) "And why should the White Eagle defend the accursed palefaces? Ay, he is a pale-face, too! And am not I a pale-face? But we have dwelt among the sons of the forest, to whom the great Ha-wen-no-yu gave the whole of the woods and the prairies. America's rivers, mines, minerals, fishings, hawkings, huntings, and fowlings,—as enumerated in the impudent grant of James, Duke of York, to Berkeley, Baron of Stratton,—and all other royalties, profits, commodities, and hereditaments, have ever belonged, and ever should in justice belong, to the noble Indians, who have spared and adopted us. You and I are bound in honour to be the foes of their foes, the friends of their friends. Speak, On-yit-hah!"

"Queen Esther, it is too late to reverse the doom of the Indians. They now stand but as the trunks of the trees of the forest, while the pale-faces are as innumerable as the leaves or the stars of heaven. The leaves may fall; they return again in the spring; but the oak, once uprooted or felled, rises no more. It is in vain to speak of exterminating the white race on these shores. And whether King George succeeds in subjugating the people, or the people in throwing off their allegiance, the result will be the same to the doomed Indian. I will weep with you and mourn their sad destiny; but it would be worse than useless to contend for them in battle, and criminal to engage them on either side in the strife between the Colonies and the crown. Let us unite in preserving them from the danger on every hand, and thus we may contribute to prolong their existence."

"Enough, ungrateful boy! But you and I must perish with the doomed Indian! Know you not it is better to die nobly and quickly amid the smoke and slaughter of battle, than to ignominiously drag out a miserable existence and finally sink into contempt? Better that you, and the white maiden, and your Indian mother, and Thayendanegea's infatuated sister, should all perish, than breed divisions among the warriors of the scattered nations. And you, degenerate son of the Lenni Lenappé," she continued, addressing Calvin, "why dost thou not sigh at the feet of some high-born white damsel?"

"Queen Esther!" replied the enraged youth, "whoever accepts me for a husband must be virtuous and contented with her lot. And such was not the case with thee."

"Fool! coward! wretch!" cried the exasperated old hag. "I will have you a prisoner and burn you at the stake!"

"Not so fast, madam, if you please!" said Calvin.

"There are warriors of my nation now crouching within call. Let your wolves but once more sound the warwhoop, and thou shalt be my prisoner!"

"Ha! ha! ha! The poor silly youth! Boasting of his Delawares when there are not two hundred of them capable of bearing arms if they were all collected from the four quarters of the earth!"

"We have Oneidas, Cherokees, and Shawnees in our camp," said Charles.

"Not seventy, all told, On-yit-hah. I learned at the council the numbers and probable localities of every nation. But Indians should not shed each other's blood. We came hither to fight the white men who slew our warriors. Will you give them up?"

"Not while there is an arm among us strong enough to raise a tomahawk!"

Queen Esther, seeing the pass could be defended by the small party already posted in the commanding positions, drew back, announcing her purpose to consult her chiefs once more before giving the signal for the attack.

And while Charles awaited the result of the consultation, Paddy Pence came running toward him, nearly out of breath, and very pale.

"Mr. Charles! Mr. Charles!" said he, "there's Indians in the bushes under the trays. I stepped aside, niver draming of sich a thing, and when I cast me eyes downward, sure enough I beheld an Indian fornents me toes. And he was winking and making mouths, and screwing about in his slape! I turned as soon as I could convaniently, and tried to stale softly away. But, as St. Pater's my witness, the logs I thought I was stipping over iverywhere were slaping Indians! And I sat down on one, and he drew up his fut and struck me behind such a powerful blow that me head, before I could stop it, went against a tree siven yards away."

"Nonsense! Don't trouble me now with your idle dreams," said Charles, making an effort to assume a severe gravity.

"Drames! Och, murther! An' I hope the savage will think it a drame when he wakes up! Och, Paddy Pence, Paddy Pence! It's coming to be the very thing they said would happen to ye in the wild country of America!"

Leaving the Highlanders under McSwine posted in positions to command the pass, Charles, who had been beckoned away by his foster-mother, slowly walked toward the tent. She lifted the curtain of dressed skins, and revealed a spectacle that caused the young man's bosom to swell with tender emotions. At the extremity of the pavilion he beheld Julia partly habited in the Indian costume, profusely and richly ornamented. At her feet sat the Indian maiden, her head reclining on the captive's knee and her lustrous eyes fixed in admiration on her lovely face.

"The Brown Thrush is very kind to her pale sister," said Charles, advancing in obedience to the desire of his foster-mother.

"Oh, yes!" said Julia, smiling sadly. "She has been kind and loving. And what return can I make for such affection? To carry her into the habitations of our people would be to deprive her of happiness."

"Kacha Manito dwells in the air," said the Indian maiden, who had learned many English words. "He likes trees, flowers, rocks, and streams. He would not stay in strong houses."

"And I could not dwell in tents," said Julia.

"Unless detained as a prisoner," said Charles.

"Oh, then there would be no remedy," said she.

"Would the Antelope escape?" asked the Thrush. "If so, she shall return to her people; and, if she desires her Indian sister to go with her, she will do so. And then the White Eagle will put down his tomahawk and rifle, and no one will watch to take away his life. His sisters would be very happy."

"But the Thrush would droop and die if taken from her native woods," said Julia.

"Then she would go to the Spirit-land and sing until her white sister and the White Eagle came. In that hunting-ground there are no rains to wet, no frosts to chill us. The good Manito makes all happy. No more dying, no more pain here," she added, placing her hand on her breast

"And hast thou any pain there?" asked Julia.

"Oh, yes! The Malcha Manito keeps saying I must kill the Antelope, or On-yit-hah (bird of the strong wing) will fly away and return no more. But the Good Spirit whispers that when the Antelope dies the White Eagle will fold his wings on some high rock and close his eyes. I could not bear to see him so."

After a long silence, during which both Charles and Julia scanned with amazement the ingenuous features of the Indian girl, the latter asked the Thrush if she had not said she loved her white sister, and if she could really be induced to take her life if assured it would not grieve the White Eagle.

The Indian maiden said the Thrush never sang falsely. She did love her white sister dearly. She loved her before she ever saw her face, from the description her brother (Brandt) had given, and because the White Eagle loved her. But she said it would not be an unfriendly act to send her sister to the eternal flowers and fruits of the Spirit-land. She would be very happy there, and the Thrush would be very happy here with the White Eagle.

Charles and Julia only gazed in astonishment, mingled with painful forebodings. And the Indian maiden continued substantially as follows:—

"But her white brother might mourn, and never smile again. Then his forest-sister would do nothing but shed tears. No; she would not kill her sister. Her word was spoken. But her white sister might kill her. She would dig up a root for the Antelope to give her. She would take it from her snow-white hand and swallow it. She would be happy in the Spirit-land, and her pale-face sister would be happy with the White Eagle in the house of his white-haired father."

"No!" said Charles, with emphasis. "The White Eagle would be as miserable if his red sister died as he would to lose his Antelope. Neither must die. But if one of them were to kill the other, On-yit-hah would dart up into the clouds and never alight upon the earth again. His sisters must live and love each other."

The Indian girl, smiling through her tears, wound her arms round the form of Julia, and kissed her repeatedly.

Charles, being informed by his Indian mother that a messenger from Queen Esther awaited him at the pass, hastened in that direction.

Julia's tears were wiped away by the long silken hair of the forest-maiden, and they ate together the delicious viands placed before them by the Gentle Moonlight.

CHAPTER XI.

THE COMPACT—PADDY AND THE SOW—ARRIVAL AT CHILLI-COTHE—THE BAPTISM OF BOONE AND ST. TAMMANY, ETC.—RESOLUTION TO ESCAPE.

WHEN Charles approached the pass where the messenger from the Senecas awaited him, Hugh McSwine whispered to him, as he passed,—

"Be watchful, my laddie. Dinna' trust him further than you can see; for it's Girty!"

"Girty!" said Van Wiggens, hearing the name. "He's a tam rascal."

"I know him well," said Charles. "Never fear; but keep your rifles ready."

He then walked boldly forward, and accepted the hand which Girty offered him.

"I suppose, Mr. Girty," said Charles, "you are prepared to announce the decision of Esther's council."

Girty hesitated a moment as if disconcerted. He had arrived upon the ground after the withdrawal of the Queen from the pass, and, as he was carefully painted and costumed like an Indian, it had been his wish to remain unrecognised.

"The eye of the White Eagle is clear," said Girty, not denying his identity; "and no doubt his wisdom has foreseen the result of the deliberations of the warriors."

"We have at least conjectured what might be the decision of our enemies," said Charles, "and we are prepared for any contingency."

"Be assured you are not prepared for battle," said Girty. "Five hundred Seneca warriors have arrived since daybreak."

"The few we have to oppose them," said Charles, "are prepared to die in defence of the white maiden and those who pursued her captors. We have warriors of several tribes; yours are all Senecas. We have Delawares, Oneidas, Cherokees, and Shawnees; and, if you attack us, you must abide the consequences. An eternal enmity will ensue between these nations and the Senecas. And the Indian maiden is the sister of Brandt, and her foster-mother his aunt. Queen Esther durst not attack us!"

"It is true!" said Girty, admiring the bold confidence of the young-man.

"Then what can you do?" demanded Charles.

"We will tell the Shawnees that the garrison at Point Pleasant, although subject to the orders of Lord Dunmore, when Cornstalk and his son were murdered, now refuse to obey him, and that the men who performed the butchery are among the rebels. And they will leave your camp."

The facts, as stated by Girty, were undeniable, and Charles did not attempt to controvert them.

"Then what song," he asked, "has Girty to charm the ears of the Cherokees?"

"Did they not sell their lands in Kentucky to a North Carolina company, and has not Virginia decided that the title of the North Carolinians is invalid, because Kentucky lay within her limits?"

"Then I suppose there was no sale," replied Charles, "if the company had no right to buy."

"But," said Girty, with a malicious smile, "Virginia says the Cherokees had a right to sell, and, as they have relinquished their title, she becomes the owner, and is preparing to take possession. This will charm the ears of the Cherokees."

Charles had not heard of these transactions, and they might be as Girty said; and, if so, the hostility of the Southern Indians would certainly follow.

"Then there are the Delawares and the Oneidas," said Charles.

"Among the Delawares whose voice is strongest?—the Garden Terrapin, Bartholomew Calvin, or the Great Mingo chief, Logan, whose family were slaughtered by the bloody Cresap? And the Oneidas will follow the rest. Time will array them all against the Colonies."

"I did not come hither, Girty," said Charles, "to listen to your speeches. Let us act. Shall we fight, or part in peace?"

"This is the decision, my young friend, as I would call thee:—The white maiden, and the party that pursued her captors, to return to their homes in Jersey, if you will remain and wed the Brown Thrush, and swear never to lift hand or voice against the Indians; or——"

"Let me hear the alternative!" said Charles, seeing Girty hesitated; "for that will be the sentence."

"Or else," said Girty, his penetrating eye fixed upon the countenance of the young man, "the whole party—rescuers and maiden, the recreant Calvin and yourself, Gentle Moonlight and the Thrush—must depart immediately for Chillicothe and await the determination of a grand council."

"Will Thayendanegea be there?" asked Charles.

"He will."

"And Red Jacket?"

"He will."

"Then we will go to Chillicothe. Let the chiefs meet around the council-fire which has been burning for ages, and I will speak to them. But I warn you, Girty, not to molest us as we descend the river!"

"You are not to descend the Ohio. The Queen says you might escape into Virginia. Your course will be southwest until you strike the head-waters of the Scioto, down which you can float in canoes to Chillicothe. The Seneca warriors will follow in your rear; the rest of the Five Nations will proceed along the southern shore of Lake Erie, on your right, while the Tuscarawas will be on your left."

'I care not!" said Charles, "so they do not molest us. My word is passed to meet you at Chillicothe."

"The Queen has no confidence in the big Scotchman who has slain so many of her subjects. She recollects him well when he fought on the Conococheague."

"Then let her beware of him, for I know not whether he will be a party to the compact. If not, you may prevent his escape if you can. And I must also consult the white maiden before the agreement is ratified. If she will not go——"

"She will go!" exclaimed Julia herself, who had besought the Indian girl to conduct her to the scene of conference, and had been led noiselessly round the cliff to where Charles and Girty stood. "Yes, she will go with you to the grand council-fire at Chillicothe, and she will not depart from the wilderness until all her white friends may accompany her."

Charles signified his approbation by a proud smile. He knew not whether Julia had heard the first proposition; but, if she had, it was quite apparent she would not accept her enfranchisement on the terms proposed.

The announcement in camp that they were in effect the prisoners of Queen Esther was variously received, and perhaps by none with more secret satisfaction than poor Van Wiggens. Even his little mongrel cur, that had accompanied him, seemed to wag his blunt tail in delight; for he had generally received as many blows from Mrs. Van Wiggens's broomstick as his master got wounds from her tongue.

The aunt and sister of Brandt, now the Great Sachem of the Five Nations, did not doubt that his influence would be exerted in behalf of themselves and their friends. And David Jones thought he would have an excellent opportunity of being heard by the representatives of all the tribes. But neither he nor Charles had correctly estimated the powers of Girty, McKee, and Elliot, who represented in the wild woods the military chest of Great Britain.

The Indians whom Calvin had induced to consent to aid in the defence of the camp, upon being advised of the agreement, rose from their lurking-places, and, after uttering several halloos, dispersed in pursuit of game. In vain the Delawares pleaded with Calvin to accompany them. He could not be torn away from the Indian maiden.

Charles and the Rev. Mr. Jones, desirous of hastening to the place designated for the meeting of the grand council, urged forward the preparations for departure. The horses were packed without delay, and, as the aunt of Thayendanegea had quite a number of extra ones, the whole party were well mounted. But it was in vain that the Indian women strove to persuade Julia to ride as they did—astride like the men. She preferred the English custom.

The first day some forty miles were accomplished, and they encamped on the Shenango River, selecting a position susceptible of defence. But there was no molestation. Mr. Jones uttered a long prayer in the deep solitude of the forest, and after a hearty meal the travellers, all excepting the sentry, were hushed in profound repose. But the stillness of the night was once broken by the fierce barking of Van Wiggens's dog, who snuffed the prowling wolves. Hugh McSwine wished to kill him, as he might betray them if an enemy should be lurking in the vicinity. But this the honest Dutchman would not listen to. He took his "Vatch" in his arms, and, whenever he manifested an inclination to bark or whine, he choked him into silence.

Fortunately there were no enemies lurking in the vicinity; and the next morning, after a hearty breakfast, they resumed the journey. But, as the meat had been consumed, several of the most skilful woodsmen were sent forward to kill game for their next meal. A buffalo they found afforded some sport. It ran in view of the main body of the travellers for more than a mile, and finally fell in their rear within a few paces of Peter Shaver, whose ass, scenting the blood, brayed, as usual, most vociferously.

"And what sort of a baste is that?" asked Paddy Pence, who had been lagging in company with Peter, and listening to a narrative of his exciting adventures among the Indians.

"It's a buffalo," said Peter. "And a fine fat cow."

"A cow, you say! And I wonder if it gives any milk! And who'd milk such an ugly monster? But the mate is good, for I tasted some in the camp."

"It's mate was a bull, Paddy. There are no wild steers in these woods; and the beef of a bull even an Indian won't eat unless he's half starved."

"And who was saying any thing about its swatcheart? You must be hard of hearing, though you and your baste have ears enough for four men and sax horses. Mate!—I said mate!"

"Oh, you mean meat, I guess. But here they come to skin the cow."

During the day several deer were slaughtered, and subsequently there was no scarcity of provisions in the camp.

And Paddy became familiar with the rattle of venomous snakes, and, after repeatedly flying from them, learned to kill them like the rest,—an operation of easy performance when one has the nerve to do it, for they are very inactive.

One day Paddy, emboldened by his continued escape from the dangers of the wilderness, borrowed Van Wiggens's rifle and sallied forth with the hunters, to enjoy some of the forest sports which were described every night to admiring listeners. There was no danger of being lost, as they were now following one of the small tributaries of the Scioto, and he had only to keep in view of the stream to guard against the possibility of wandering from the right direction.

But he soon returned to leave his horse in charge of Peter, saying he would try it on foot, as his "baste" made so much noise dragging its "fut" through the dry "laves" the deer all ran away before he could see enough of them to fire at. But Paddy strove in vain to kill a deer. He started several, whose snorting he could hear very distinctly as they sprang up from their beds, and once or twice he had glimpses of the whites of their tails as they leaped over the bushes; but they were gone before he could take aim and pull trigger. After bestowing some abusive epithets on them for not standing, like "dacent bastes," to be shot at, he contemptuously abandoned the pursuit, and confined his attention to the turkeys which every now and then crossed his path near the stream, within the narrow valley of which he still confined his wanderings.

But Paddy grew weary at last, and had not a single trophy to exhibit. The turkeys wouldn't stand fire either; and he thought it very singular that a gobbler up in a tree should be able to see him first, inasmuch as he was larger than the bird, and had larger eyes.

He sat down on a log beside the path. It was growing late, and the last rays of the setting sun bathed in gold the tree-tops and summits of the distant hills. A squirrel chattered on a bough above, with its tail curved over its back. He looked at Paddy, and Paddy looked at him.

"The little baste is poking his jokes at me!" said Paddy "And if I should kill him, wouldn't the boys laugh? Joke away, my little crature; I don't understand yer lingo, and I'm sure I shouldn't take offence at it. But what's that same?"

Paddy was attracted by a rustling among the leaves in a dense thicket within a dozen yards of him. He thought he heard also a sound like the crushing of acorns under the giant oak that overspread the thicket. But he could see nothing animate, although the chopping of nuts continued at intervals. With his eyes fixed in the direction from whence the sound proceeded, he remained perfectly motionless, his gun in readiness to fire, and his legs prepared to run, if any imminent danger became apparent.

He knew not how long he sat and watched. But he could hear the men fixing the tent-poles near a bend of the stream some two hundred paces back; and, seeing he was not likely to be relieved from his perilous situation, if he were really in danger, by the nearer approach of his comrades, he began to experience an uncomfortable sensation of fear creeping up his back and gradually lifting his cap from his head. But still he could see nothing likely to do him injury. The saucy squirrel only mocked him; and the huge owl that flapped through the dusky recesses of the forest, where the rays of the sun rarely penetrated, never ventured to assail a man. It could not be a panther he heard, for that dreadful animal did not feed on acorns. A bear was not dangerous, as he learned from Peter Shaver, unless one seized her cub. Paddy had no cub, and he resolved not to touch one if they should come around him as abundantly as the fallen leaves.

It would not do, however, to remain thus inactive, and so he stooped down and peered under the bushes.

"Be jabers!" said he, after gazing some time in silence, "I'm not afraid o' the likes of you! I've twisted the tails of too many pigs in ould Ireland to run away from one in America, and with a gun in my hand to boot!"

It was a large white sow, apparently of great age, which had strayed from the settlements of the white man, escaped the knives of the Indian and repelled the assaults of the wolf. It now ceased to crack the acorns, and lay quite still in its bed of leaves, for it had likewise become conscious of the presence of Paddy. It lay with its fierce eyes fixed upon the intruder, as if partaking of the fearful and repellent nature of the wild beasts of the forest with whom alone it had been long associated. But, if it had forgotten the friendly form of man, Paddy had not forgotten the usually harmless capabilities of the pig, and so he resolved to have it for a victim, and as a unique trophy in the wilderness.

He raised his gun and fired before getting a steady aim, and the ball, striking too high, glanced along from the top of the animal's head, cutting a furrow through the roots of the bristles and covering its back with blood. For a moment it was stunned, and Paddy, supposing it dead, approached with confidence. But, before he could seize it, the recovered animal rushed toward him with open mouth. Paddy, however, was in his element in a contest with a pig, and so, throwing down his gun, was in readiness for the assault. He sprang up with his feet apart and descended on the back of the sow, with his head toward her tail. He clasped his arms tightly round her body, and hugged her neck with his legs, so she could not turn and bite him. But she could open her mouth, and did so, and squealed and squeaked terrifically, running along the path toward the encampment. All were anxious to see the beast making such horrific sounds; and when the sow plunged in the midst of the men she was so much concealed or disfigured by the body of Paddy that none of the spectators could conjecture for several minutes what sort of an animal it was. The squealing was not strange to their ears; but they did not suppose a hog could be found in a region so far from the dwellings of white men.

And soon the ass, getting the scent of blood, began to bray with all the power of his lungs; and Van Wiggens's mongrel cur, being the first to perceive the true nature of the beast, and true to his instincts, rushed forward in the midst of the *mêlée*, (for the sow was now exhausted, and only turned and squalled, surrounded by the crowd of travellers,) but, instead of seizing the animal's ear, as he intended, got hold of Paddy's calf by mistake.

"Och, murther!" cried Paddy. "Take away the dog! He's tearing me leg! Two on one is foul play, and fair play's a jewel. Take away your baste of a cur, Mr. Van Wiggens, or I'll worry you when I'm done with this chap. I'd thank you for the loan of a knife, Mr. Shaver," he continued; "for mine has dhropt out of me hilt in the tussell." And, being accommodated by Peter, Paddy succeeded in cutting the throat of the sow, and so put an end to its squealing.

The sow, being very fat, was highly relished by the men; and there was great abundance of deer and turkeys killed by the hunters. Paddy's knife and Van Wiggens's gun were found where they had been dropped; and the affair of the sow caused much merriment when referred to during the remainder of the journey, which was accomplished without further difficulty or remarkable event.

When the party reached Chillicothe they were in advance of the Eastern Indians; but quite a number of Western chiefs and their families were present. Chillicothe was an old Indian town, and consisted of many huts of a more substantial character than those generally inhabited by the roving children of the forest. Gentle Moonlight possessed several of these houses, of which her deceased husband had been the proprietor, as well as a large body of land adjacent to the village. These she took possession of, and the whole party were soon comfortably domiciled in huts and tents.

But, as runners were constantly arriving from various directions, the place was continually agitated with news, sometimes encouraging to the captives, but often the reverse.

The Cherokees and Shawnees, as well as other Western Indians sojourning at Chillicothe, although they were very kind to the aunt and sister of Brandt, and friendly to Charles, Calvin, and the missionary, Mr. Jones, did not seem to regard the other captives with the respect which had been hoped for. There were, besides, a number of prisoners from Pennsylvania, Virginia, and Kentucky, and they were so carefully watched and securely guarded that even the obtuse Peter Shaver could not avoid the inference that peace was not to be "calculated" upon.

Among the prisoners met with in the town was a tall, straight man, with broad shoulders and muscular limbs, denoting extraordinary strength. He generally sat apart, smiling composedly at the diverting conduct or amusing anecdotes of the Indians; or, if not addressed by any of them or the object of their notice, his eyes were fixed abstractedly on the dark woods down the right bank of the Scioto; and one beholding his countenance would suppose he longed to be again a free rover in the boundless wilderness.

This was Daniel Boone, then in the prime of manhood; and it was the second or third time he had fallen into the hands of the Indians. He was a brave man, and the Indians loved him. He was as good a woodsman as any of their own chiefs, and they respected him so highly that extraordinary exertions were made to induce him to live among them and become the head of a great family. But he had already a wife and children in Kentucky; and, besides, he loved the solitudes of the forest rather than the boisterous society of his fellow-men, whether savage or civilized.

The Rev. Mr. Jones and Boone had often met before; and the latter had promised the preacher that when they encountered again, if there should be water, he would desire to be baptized. And now the preacher claimed the fulfilment of his promise, declaring to the Indians who listened that the ceremony would afford him more pleasure and be a greater honour in the sight of the Good Spirit than the taking of scalps in time of war. And Boone did not object. His wife was a Baptist. He had reached the meridian of life, and would no longer postpone the performance of a sacred duty.

And so, on the third day after the arrival of the party at Chillicothe, the banks of the Scioto were lined with Indians, men, (old men mostly,) women, and children, to witness the baptism by immersion of "Captain Boone." But Mr. Jones had not usually been in the habit of going down into the water with a solitary convert, nor was he under the necessity of doing so on that occasion. The aged TAMMANY, a chief of the Western Delawares, who had ever been his friend, stood beside him on the margin of the water, prepared to submit to the ordinance prescribed for the salvation of sinners. Priests of other denominations had proposed other modes of baptism; but the plan of Mr. Jones, who had been most instrumental in his conversion, seemed appropriate to the Indian, and very similar to a ceremony of their own in washing away the blood of another race.

Nor were the enthusiastic Baptist's labours to end with Tammany—who subsequently became a saint; but Gentle Moonlight and Brown Thrush likewise consented to go down with him into the water and take upon themselves the Christian's vows. Mr. Jones did not require any extraordinary sacrifices. Their great Ha-wen-no-yu, he said, was but another name for the Christian's God, their Kacha Manito the Christian's Holy Spirit, and Malcha Manito the devil. The latter they must cease praying to to punish their enemies, as the God of the Christians could destroy as well as preserve. Although with them this was not quite an admitted axiom, yet they promised to follow the instructions of their Christian guide. And Boone himself stipulated that he was not to be turned out of the church for the occasional epithets—called oaths—which sometimes escaped him, and of which he might be unconscious. It was a fixed habit, and he was too old to correct it. In short, Mr. Jones did not require of his Indian converts any other change of life than to believe in the plan of redemption he taught, and to conform to the few precepts he strove to impress upon their minds. They might be great warriors and chiefs and at the same time very good Christians. And Boone might go on killing game and scalping his enemies as usual.

Charles and Julia were silent spectators of the scene, which was solemn and impressive. The Sabbath day was unclouded, and not a breeze ruffled the surface of the water. With a becoming gravity of face, a dignified step, and the song of praise issuing from his mouth, the preacher went down into the water; and, the requisite responses being uttered, and no one forbidding, the ceremony of baptism by immersion was duly performed.

"Now, Charles," said Julia, "what good effect will that produce?"

"They believe," said Charles. "They rely implicitly upon the truth of what Mr. Jones has spoken. He has said there can be no salvation without baptism, according to the Scriptures. They believe it, and are baptized. There will be no important change in their conduct. My forest mother and sister were ever good and guileless."

"And now, Charles, the Thrush is a Christian!"

"Yes, but still an Indian. Why do you seem distressed?"

"These terrible rumours!" said she, as they slowly followed the dripping converts returning to their wigwams. "What is to become of us? I might have escaped from my captors, but I thought you would soon return with me, and I was impelled by a love of romantic adventure. I thought it would soon be over, and never dreamed of actual danger and real vexations. But they have brought me still farther into the boundless forest, I know not how many hundreds of miles away from——"

"From whom, Julia? You have no kindred on earth that you know of, and no better friend than myself."

"True. But will I not lose my best friend? Is he not surrounded by enemies?"

"We will escape, Julia," said he, in a low tone, (for James Girty, the brother of Simon, was, as usual, standing near them, and probably endeavouring to learn the subject of their conversation.) "Mr. Boone," he added, "has planned it, and will accompany us. He has learned that the Indians intend making a hostile visit to Kentucky, and we will be there to receive them."

"Kentucky! still farther into the Western wilds!" said Julia, with a sigh, which indicated that her love of forest adventure, of which she had often boasted in her letters to Kate Livingston, was rapidly abating.

"Once there, Julia, we will be free. We will be no longer subjected to the tyrannical caprices of Queen Esther, who, I learn from the Seneca that came in this morning, declares I must either wed my Indian sister or else remain a prisoner."

"Will not the Indian maiden and her aunt go with us?"

"No. At least such is not the intention. If war ensues, as I fear it will,—for the British agent here has arms, ammunition, trinkets, and money, to distribute gratuitously, and the Americans, not being similarly represented, are looked upon by my silly red brethren with contempt,—they would not be permitted to dwell among us."

"Then let us go! I fear your forest sister will do some dreadful deed."

"Why?"

"She speaks fiercely and gesticulates violently in her dreams."

"She dreamed of war,—of her brother, no doubt, and thought he was slaughtering her Christian friends. No; she will never injure you. She might have committed violence on her own life, had not Mr. Jones told her it would be a fatal crime and bar her entrance into the perennial paradise."

"Let us depart immediately!" continued Julia. "Oh, let us go before the grand council of warriors assemble! I know they will declare war. Indeed, as Mr. Jones said last night, when the party came in from the Monongahela, their approach announced by the terrible scalp-halloo, which still sounds in my ears, war has already begun! And the horrid spectacle of human scalps, stretched on hoops, drying in view of our tent! It is too dreadful!"

"I know it. But control your emotions, Julia. Do not seem agitated and shocked by such exhibitions during the next few days. I did not like to announce the startling tidings that have reached us, for fear we might be betrayed by our feelings. But it is too true that the tomahawk has fallen on the heads of our people in some of the frontier settlements, and Mr. Boone is convinced that the Five Nations will carry the Western tribes with them to the British. We must be discreet, and apparently indifferent to the occurrences around us; and soon we will be beyond the reach of our enemies. Be in readiness to fly at any hour of the night. Boone will plan every thing."

"And will they not pursue us?"

"Certainly. But our party will number some twenty-five well-armed men, as other prisoners will go with us; and we will be able to keep the foe at bay until we cross the Ohio. Most of the warriors here are, as you see, old men. Boone is advised of the movements of those more active, now lingering on the Little Miami, where they have fallen in with a large herd of buffalo. We will have the start of them, as their runners will give notice of their approach and announce their success. In the mean time we must do nothing to excite suspicion."

"But why not go at once?—to-night?"

"Some of our men are unarmed. We must contrive to supply the deficiency from the British depôt, and Boone will devise the means. We must employ stratagem, and keep the boys and old men in good humour. They are, as you may have observed, exceedingly fond of diverting scenes; and Boone, though seemingly incapable of smiling himself, is preparing an exhibition for this afternoon which will amuse them. He has had Paddy Pence and Peter Shaver looking at the bloody scalps, and informed them (confidentially) that the only sure method of avoiding a similar fate is to be adopted into an Indian family. They have most eagerly consented, and an old squaw, the widow of a Choctaw warrior, has agreed to receive one of them as her husband and the other as a son. The ceremony of initiation will take place this evening before the assembled population of the village. Boone will be more popular than ever, and they will cause the Englishman to give the adopted couple two good rifles. And Hugh McSwine, though so silent and grave, is heartily co-operating. His Scots will assume the Indian costume, indicating a purpose to undergo the ceremony of initiation as soon as Indians can be found to adopt them. Poor Van Wiggens would, I believe, prefer living among them to returning to his scolding wife. He, too, will probably be adopted to-day. Go now and cheer my poor sister. Tell her I am much pleased with her, and that I hope our heavenly Father will permit us to dwell together in paradise, never to be separated more."

Julia had scarcely entered the house of Gentle Moonlight when Charles heard the halloo of a small party of warriors returning from the South. From the sounds, he understood they had a prisoner and one scalp.

He soon after saw a young man of herculean frame led into the town. He was not made to run the gauntlet, for as yet war had not been formally declared, although it certainly existed. The prisoner's name was Simon Kenton, who, on subsequent occasions, suffered much harsh usage at the hands of the Indians, and has since figured in several romances. But, as this is a plain narrative of facts, we will not make any draughts on the imagination. He was a young man without education, an excellent shot, a good woodsman, a brave scout, honest and generous. But he deemed it no disgrace to steal horses from the Indians, and had just been taken in the act.

CHAPTER XII.

THE CEREMONY OF ADOPTION.

THE procession approached the river, passing by the skin tents and log houses on its line of march, the route having been planned to please the greatest possible number. The head of the column was led by Diving Duck, (the meaning of her Indian name, its orthography forgotten,) who was to adopt Paddy and Peter into her family. This old squaw was a worthless creature, having never lived happily with her husband, and had always been addicted to immoderate drinking.

Next to Diving Duck came Peter Shaver, mounted on his jackass and surrounded by all the boys. Every now and then some one would hold a piece of raw meat to the ass's nose, and then he brayed. This was succeeded by prolonged laughter, which, beginning with the boys, spread like an epidemic through all classes up to the most stoical octogenarian.

Paddy followed immediately behind the ass, and was accompanied by Van Wiggens and his dog. The Scots and other white prisoners were farther in the rear, serving to lengthen the procession.

When they arrived on the bank of the river, Peter dismounted, and his ass was led away braying by one of the boys having raw meat or pepper-corns.

"And now," said Paddy, "before we go any furder in this family bisness, I wud like to be towld what I am to be."

"You are to be an Indian," said Charles, who acted as interpreter.

"I know that, Misther Charles," said Paddy. "But, I mane, what am I to be in the family? Am I to be the black old Didapper's son or husband?"

Charles, after speaking to the squaw, said she was not yet prepared to announce the lucky man of her choice.

"She manes," said Paddy, musing painfully, "to take us both on trial. Tell her, Mr. Charles, I won't go into her family until I know what futting I am to go on."

"Paddy, she wishes to know the position you would prefer."

"Position? Och, she manes sitiation! Say son, by all manes, and board and mending; I'll saa after the wages widout her assistance."

"And what would you be, Peter?" asked Charles.

"I guess any thing rather than be sculped," said Peter. "But you will please make the best bargain for me you can. Although I'd rather be her husband than die at the stake, I rather think I would prefer dying any easy way than to marry such an ugly infernal old——."

"Howld yer tongue!" cried Paddy, furiously. "Would ye be afther having that translated till her? Would ye have her to be scratching yer nasty piebald face here in this company? To be sure ye would! And thin you think she wouldn't have ye, and be afther taking me, do ye? And that would be one of yer Yankee tricks, would it? It's dishonest! it's ungintlemanly! it's——rascality! to take advantage of a rival in that fashion! And, if ye was to succeed, I'd pound yer head to a jelly with me two fists. And then to talk about dying in any aisy way! I would like to know the difference atwane dying by having the breath burnt out, bled out, drownded out, or physicked out? Dying aisy, is it?"

Now, Charles had rapidly translated such portions of this speech as best suited his purpose, which, together with Paddy's menacing attitude and gestures, produced a prodigious burst of merriment. Even the young prisoner, Simon Kenton, whose arms were stretched asunder and made fast by thongs to a strong stake that ran across his breast, laughed so heartily (for he had a sound pair of lungs) as to attract general attention. Boone, taking advantage of this, and seeming to be an entire stranger to the tall captive, (although they were intimate friends,) remarked to one of the warriors that no man could laugh without pain when bound in that manner; and, the good-humour of the latter preponderating over his prudence, he drew his knife and liberated the captive's arms.

Diving Duck, comprehending what had passed between Paddy and Peter, turned her ugly face toward the latter and uttered a torrent of vituperation which it would have been difficult for Charles to render into intelligible English; but the purport of it could hardly have been mistaken even by a dog. And Van Wiggens's little mongrel cur retreated a few paces and barked at the virago, no doubt detecting some resemblance between her and Mrs. Van Wiggens.

"And that's the reward you get for blabbing in that undacent way," said Paddy. "Och! you ought to be ashamed of yerself!"

This little speech being made known to the squaw, she approached Paddy with a ghastly grin, meant, no doubt, for a grateful smile, and, taking his hand, called him her husband.

"What does she mane by that?" asked Paddy.

"She says," continued Charles, "that she thanks you for resenting the vile aspersions of the Yankee Popcorn, the chief of the asses, and a thousand other pleasant things I am unable to translate in this modest company. And, as a slight manifestation of her gratitude, she is determined to bestow her hand upon you."

"Murther! how am I to get out of this scrape? I'll give you a broken head, Misther Pater Shaver, for yer foul play. You're a vile chating rival, and, be the sowl of St. Patrick, ye shall not succade! Be the powers, ye shall marry her or burn! Misther Charles, tell 'em to tie me to the stake; for I'm ready to die, aisy or hard, jist as they plase. I wont be a blackguard savage and the towl of a little fat nose-talking Yankee! Let us both burn together at the same stake, as me Catholic ancestors did in the time of Elizabeth, who was nicknamed the Vargin Quane. The Holy Vargin presarve us! It sames that the whole family of Pences are to be the victims of the women! Tell 'em to pile up their fagots! Grane ones will do. The grase of my fat companion will make 'em burn. And when we are both wrapped in the flames, Pater," he continued, doubling his fists and assuming a boxing attitude, "I'll give you a taste of the science by way of dessert to the fry!"

This, too, when interpreted to the Indians, produced peals of laughter, and the old chiefs patted Paddy's back, calling him a brave man.

"I would have been a dutiful son to ye," continued Paddy, moved to tears, "and maintained ye at yer aise; and, instead of being grateful, you must be calling me mother names. No! I won't be the father of any sich a vile varmint!"

"Paddy!" said Peter, moved by the tears, for they convinced him he was in earnest, "oh, Paddy, say no more about burning! I'll save you from that. I'll marry her rather than die. I guess I can manage her. I'll marry her, Paddy!"

"Then I shall be bound to pay you riverence. And, in the first place, I beg yer pardon for what I have said to your disparagement, and take it all back agin."

This being rendered into the Indian tongue, Diving Duck

became more furious than ever, and said they should both burn, as she would not marry either of them.

Then Peter, amid shouts of laughter, got down on his knees and humbly begged her to pardon him and accept his hand.

"You see what it is," said Paddy, kneeling behind Peter, "for a woman to have two strings to her bow. Kape at her, Pater; she'll yeald prisently. Depind upon it, she'll not let ye die if she's to lose a husband by it."

And Peter, persisting, received a blow on the side of his face which sent him sprawling on the earth.

"What do ye mane by trating me rispicted father in that ungintlemanly manner?" cried Paddy, springing up and seizing the old squaw, whom he held securely by the arms in despite of her kicks and cries, to the infinite amusement of the crowd. "If you are to be me mother I must tache ye betther manners. And is this an example to sit before the face of yer childer? Is this the sort of brading ye would bring yer darlint son up to? Ye ought to be ashamed of yerself!"

And the Didapper uttered two words to Paddy's one. But, when he relinquished his hold, Charles announced to the disappointed multitude that the ceremony of fire would have to be substituted for that of water, as Diving Duck would have neither of them for her husband.

At this juncture Van Wiggens, who had been a contemplative spectator of the scene, stepped forward and whispered to Charles that, although he did not fear burning at the stake half so much as he did the scathing tongue of Mrs. "Wan Viggens," if it would not be bigamy and subject him to the penalty of the law, he was willing to save his two friends from death by becoming himself their father and the husband of the furious squaw.

When this was announced to Diving Duck, she scrutinized the Dutchman very carefully, and, after walking round him as if examining the limbs of a horse, signified her willingness to accept him as a substitute, provided he would whip both of his sons after the wedding.

To this condition both Paddy and Peter readily consented, and the squaw then grasped the hand of her affianced lord. But the little stump-tailed mongrel cur of Van Wiggens seemed to have some objection to the arrangement, and flew round, barking fiercely at the squaw, who paid no further attention to his violence than to seize him by the back of his neck and cast him over the bank into the river, whence he speedily swam ashore, cowed into submission.

"Tam her! he thought it was Mrs. Wan Viggens!" said the Dutchman.

All the preliminaries being adjusted, six young Indian girls, supposed from their stature to be about midway in their teens, came gliding forward. Each of them grasped a hand of the three candidates for adoption, and led them down the river-bank and along the edge of the water to a gigantic sycamore, whose broad leaves, though deeply reddened by the early frosts, yet hung over the stream and intercepted the rays of the descending sun. The great crowd of Indians posted themselves a short distance apart, where they could see the operation of initiation to the greatest advantage. Boone and Charles, however, attended the candidates under the tree.

"You must submit without resistance," said Boone, addressing the men; "for, if you do not comply with their demands, you will not be considered perfect Indians."

"Be the powers," said Paddy, looking to his right and his left, "such cratures as these don't same as if they meant to do us any harm. But, if ye plase, Misther Bone, I'd take it as a favour if you'd tell me what they mane to do wid us in the wather."

"No matter what: all you have to do is to obey them in every particular," was the reply.

"And they mane to go in wid us?" continued Paddy.

"Certainly," said Charles; "don't you see they are prepared to do so?"

Paddy examined the costume of the girls, which consisted merely of blankets and narrow breech-cloths. Their leggins and moccasins had been left behind.

The Indian maids proceeded, according to the usual custom with candidates for adoption, to disencumber the men of their clothing.

Peter Shaver, being in Indian costume, was easily disrobed,—one of the girls removing his blanket, while the other undid his moccasins and leggins, leaving nothing but his breech-cloth,—a sort of apron going round the body above the hips and reaching nearly to the knees.

The girls were exceedingly amused and interested. Peter's corpulency, and his very white skin where the sun had not shone upon it and where the dust of travel had not accumulated, particularly arrested their attention.

Peter had been so much among the Indians of late, assimilating with their habits, that he did not think of blushing at the exposure of his neck, shoulders, breast, and knees.

It was different with Paddy and Van Wiggens. They submitted in silence to the removal of their coats, and even their shirts, and stood with all the indifference they could command, like pugilists prepared for encounter in the lists.

"Mr. Bone! Mr. Bone!" whispered Paddy at this stage of the proceedings, "plase tell 'em we haven't got any breech-clouts on."

They seemed to be aware of this, and proceeded to remove only the moccasins and leggins, rolling up their breeches, however, and exposing their legs as much as possible.

"You must submit without complaining," remarked Charles, with a seriousness well affected, when the girls again seized their hands and led them toward the edge of the water.

"Complainin', did ye say?" responded Paddy; "and if it's killing they're going to do, ye may be sure we'll die an aisy death. Mr. Bone, if you are acquainted wid the parents of these girls, you'd do me a favour to bespake one of 'em—and be me faith you may include both—for me, as soon as we are turned to savages. And if there are no praists to marry us, Mr. Jones might do till we could find one."

"The Indians will let you have as many wives as you can support," said Mr. Boone; "but the priest would ban you if you had more than one."

"I know it! But do ye think he'd curse a man afther he'd turned Indian? He would marry me to one and I'd marry meself to the other. Like a good Christian, I'd have one lawfully-wedded wife, and, like an Indian, I'd have anither which the praist'd have no business to meddle wid. It's forward, is it, me darlints? On wid ye! I can stand in as dape water as any o' ye," he continued, as he was led into the stream.

They waded out until the water rose to the shoulders of

the girls, and then commenced the process of scrubbing. Each of the maidens had taken into the water the cob of an ear of Indian corn, with which they rasped the breasts and limbs of the white men.

"Mr. Bone," cried Paddy, "what d'ye think they're rubbing us for? There's no flays under the water to bite us."

"But dere's a tam crawfish biting my leg," said Van Wiggens, "and I wish dey'd rub furder down."

"You needn't rub me so hard," said Peter to his attendants. "I'm almost an Indian now. Don't you know they made me a chief?"

"Popcorn! chief!" said one of his girls, who could speak a few English words.

"Murther!" cried Paddy.

"Are they hurting you?" asked Charles.

"Hurting, is it? It's tackling one to death! What are they rubbing us for?"

"Ask them," said Boone; "they can answer in English, and have been taught our language for the purpose of explaining such things."

"My most lovely and beautiful miss,— and there's a charming pair o' ye, as much alike as two cherries,—be plased to tell me what're ye rubbing the small of me back for?"

"Wash white blood away," was the answer.

"White blood, is it? Be my sowl, ye're mistaken, for it's as red as a rose."

"White man's blood—wash away—Indian's blood come."

"Now I understhand! And ye're a charming one to do it! And she spakes as good English as Paddy himself! And won't you be me swate little wife? Och, murther!" cried he, turning to the other, "you naadn't tear me flesh away, for I meant to take both of ye."

"Dey ton't know enough of English to scold," said the contemplative Van Wiggens, "and I'll marry one too. Do you scold?" he asked of one of his scrubbers.

"Me no talk. Diving Duck talk much," she replied, smiling mischievously.

"Tam te old Titapper!" said Van Wiggens; "I forgot her. She's an old granny of sixty. I'm only dirty, and Mrs. Wan Viggens is dirty-two. I vant a young vife."

"Why are *you* so silent, Peter?" asked Charles, observing the Connecticut man plunged in deep abstraction.

"I guess I'll stop at that," said Peter, endeavouring to thrust aside his attendants. "Maybe there's more in this operation than we are aware of. By water our sins are washed away, and we are made Christians. This may be an invention of the devil to wash away Christianity and make us hisn."

"Och, murther!" cried Paddy. "Begone, ye divil's imps! 'scat, ye witches!" continued he, and by a powerful effort succeeded in thrusting the girls momentarily away from him, to the great diversion of the spectators on the bank, whose silence hitherto indicated that they were awaiting some such scene.

"Me wash good! Hold still!" said one of the girls, returning.

"No! 'scat! Begone! or I'll drownd ye like blind puppies. It's a contrivance to sell our sowls for the price of our bodies! And I wont be a savage widout I can be a civilized Catholic Christian too."

"Oh, you may be a Christian," said Charles, "if you can be content to put up with one wife."

"I'll do it, and defy the divil!" said Paddy; "and I'll draw lots betwixt 'em. Hillo!" he continued, seeing the girls dragging him and his companions into still deeper water. "Don't do that! It's up to me breast now, and it'll soon be over yer heads. It wouldn't be safe, me darlints, to go in ony daaper. Hillo, I say! It's up to me chin, and the divil's daughters are swamming like bavers. Stop, I tell ye! Would ye drownd yer future husband? I can't swame! I tell ye I can't swame!" And when Paddy uttered this earnest protestation he had to hold back his head to keep his nose above water.

"Wash all white blood out! Wash head too!" said the girls; and, making a simultaneous effort, they succeeded at the same moment in pushing the heads of all three beneath the surface. Then, springing nimbly aside, (for they were skilful swimmers,) they laughed very heartily, while the spectators on the shore made the welkin ring with their plaudits.

"I guess that'll do, won't it?" cried Peter, popping up again and expelling a stream of water from his mouth.

"Murther!" cried Paddy, rising, puffing and floundering like a porpoise. "Me swate lovely gals!" said he, after succeeding in fixing his toes in the sand at the bottom, and keeping his mouth and nose an inch above the surface, but unable to see the shore, and incapable of proceeding in any direction without danger of submersion, "och, me swate cratures, I'll marry ayther of ye, or both thegither, as soon as ye plase, if ye'll only pull me out o' this!"

"Tam dem!" roared the Dutchman, rising the last of the three, and, being able to swim, struck for the shore. But he was seized by his attendants and forcibly thrust under again.

"Tam der skins!" he continued, rising again and facing his tormentors. They seized his hands, and he endeavoured to kick them. But at every attempt to do so they thrust his head under, amid shouts from the whole population of the town assembled on the bank.

There was one witness to this struggle, however, who did not remain an idle spectator. This was Watch, Van Wiggens's faithful little mongrel cur. He leaped into the stream and swam to the rescue of his master. But, before he could reach him, he came near forfeiting his life; for a young brother of one of the girls aimed an arrow at his head, which grazed his nose; and he was fixing another to the string when one of the chiefs snatched the bow away. The girls themselves did not fear the dog.

"Make Indian dog too," said one of them, when Watch exposed his teeth.

"He'll bite!" said Van Wiggens.

"Wash white man's blood out of dog too," said the girl, and the next moment she dived beneath the surface. An instant after, Watch uttered a sharp cry and disappeared.

"Dey are de teiffle's taughters temselves!" said Van Wiggens.

"He's Indian dog now," said the girl, rising, after several moments of breathless suspense, during which it was generally feared poor Watch had descended too deeply and remained too long under the water ever to rise again. "He won't bite Indian now," she continued, holding the almost lifeless animal's nose above the surface. "He won't die," said she, reversing the body and causing the water to flow out of his mouth. And, when animation re

THE CEREMONY OF BAPTISM IN AN INDIAN FAMILY.—P. 161

turned, poor Watch, released, paddled back to the shore in piteous submission, and did not open his mouth again.

"Aha! me darlints!" cried Paddy, watching an opportunity, and seizing both of his girls round their waists, "I've got ye now! We'll sink or swame thegether! If you can howld your breaths the longest under the wather, you'll find Paddy Pence can squeeze the hardest above it, and he'll die with his death-grip upon ye!"

The Indians on the bank yelled with delight, and the girls begged to be released.

"Divil the bit!" cried Paddy. "I'll saa ye at the bottom first! Will ye be me squaws? Answer me that, my darlints."

"Must ask mother in a basket," was the reply. The mode of declaration among the Indians is to leave a present in a basket at the tent of the girl's mother.

"In a basket, is it? No! it's in the strame! And ye must answer for yerselves, and I'll fax the mother aftherward. Onyhow, ye can jist let me have a kiss or two to sale the bargain;" and Paddy, in despite of their cries and struggles, kissed them repeatedly, while the spectators greeted him with cheering shouts.

Van Wiggens, following the example of his dog and of Peter Shaver, submitted to the will and pleasure of his attendants, and was glad to find that when he ceased to make sport for them they ceased to torment him.

This ceremony lasted more than an hour, and was terminated by one of the old men, a sachem, who approached the water's edge, leading the old squaw into whose family the men were to be received. Some words of investiture were uttered during the profound silence that ensued when the girls led the washed candidates to the shore. They were to the effect that the adopted Indians must forget that they ever were white men, and love and honour none but Indians. They were to hunt game in time of peace, and to steal horses and scalp their enemies in time of war. Van Wiggens's dog was to watch at the door of his wigwam while Diving Duck hoed the corn in the garden; and he besought his new brother not to beat his squaw so much as her first husband had done.

The Dutchman, who had looked with dread and aversion on his second Mrs. Van Wiggens, plucked new spirits upon learning that among the Indians husbands were allowed to whip their wives and be masters of their own households. And without the least delay he ordered his wife to prepare a dozen roasting-cars for his dinner, which being translated by Charles, the old squaw went away grumbling, doubtless to obey the command.

Then the next thing to be done was the assuming of the Indian costume by Paddy and the Dutchman. The latter objected to having any of his hair cut off, while Paddy was for having his head entirely denuded. He had a deadly aversion to scalp-locks. Boone and Charles superintended that portion of the ceremony, and in a very short time the two new Indians—one Dutch and the other Irish—were strutting proudly through the streets.

But Paddy and Peter saw no more of the girls that day. Nor could they form a matrimonial alliance, according to the *lex non scripta* of the tribe, without the concurrence of their mothers. Nor could Van Wiggens, in his capacity of the head of a family, cede away lands without the sanction of his spouse. Thus, in civil transactions, and particularly in hereditary matters, such as successions to titles and estates, the squaws performed a most important part. But, if the husband could do nothing without the permission of his wife, he might beat her if she displeased him,—that is, if he possessed the physical ability to do so; if not, she might beat him.

During the dusk of the deepening twilight, Boone and Charles, who still lingered on the margin of the river, espied a slight movement in a tuft of blackberry-bushes at the edge of the embankment and not exceeding six paces from where they sat. A moment after, they beheld a man slowly and noiselessly lift his head and gaze toward the village. They grasped their knives, for they had been talking of their meditated escape, determined, if it were an Indian who had been listening, to prevent him from frustrating their plans by taking his life, as they considered such a sacrifice justifiable when necessary for their own salvation. But they were relieved on seeing the man approach them. It was Kenton, who had succeeded in secreting himself while the Indians were enjoying their sport, with the intention to effect his escape as soon as it grew dark; but, fortunately, hearing the project of Boone and Charles, he wisely and nobly relinquished his purpose of immediate flight. He knew his disappearance would subject the rest of the prisoners to a stricter vigilance, and might cause the death of some of them.

"You are a noble fellow!" said Charles, upon learning his motive.

"And you shall escape with us," said Boone.

"Yes—never fear me!" said Kenton. "I'm harder to hold than an eel. They're in a good humour now. I didn't want any of 'em to see I had hid, though! The devil can soon get into 'em."

"And now, when you return voluntarily with us," said Boone, "their suspicion will be lulled."

"I thought of that," said Kenton, sitting on the root of the sycamore beside them. "Let's wait till they miss me and give the yell. There it is now! I knew it! They'd've given me a hard race! They're coming! Now let us meet them."

They did so, and the warriors patted Simon on the back, and said, "You honest man; but mustn't steal Indian's hoss. Don't be hoss-steal; don't be dam white man."

The Indians generally can speak enough of our language to make themselves understood; and they first learn how to swear. They have no oaths in their own language.

CHAPTER XIII.

THE FLIGHT—THE BATTLE—PADDY'S EXPLOITS.

BARTHOLOMEW CALVIN, after sitting some time gazing in silence at the handsome features of the Indian maiden who had innocently captured his heart and surrendered her own to another, rose up moodily and strode with melancholy aspect into the wigwam of his relative, the ancient Tammany.

The old chief beckoned him to be seated, and pointed toward the pipe and tobacco. To his surprise, the young man declined smoking. He then ordered one of his wives to set some bear's-meat and honey before his nephew.

These he merely tasted, and then, sitting at his uncle's feet, said he had come thither to receive his counsel. He explained to him the painful condition of his heart and his sentiments regarding the war.

"Listen!" said the old chief, leaning his feeble form against the wall of his house, which was hung with skins, and scanning his attenuated limbs, shrunken with age and palsied with debility. "I have not many words to speak; but my sister's son shall have them all. I am old. Yet the days of my youth seem as yesterday. So the life of an old man is but short. I look at my skin-covered bones and laugh" (and his wrinkled face was then beaming with bright smiles) "with the children that mock at me. They will soon be placed away, and then I will tread the great hunting-grounds, where there is no age, no disease, no dying. Listen, sister's son! We pass like a feather blown away. Why should we wound and kill those people whom the Great Spirit sent to our shores? Can we kill them all and drive them hence? No; it is the voice of God. The Christian's God is the Indian's God. The Indian cannot oppose him. The Indian may fight for his lands and die with honour; but he must lose his lands, and then what is the honour of this world to him when he dwells in another? You sigh for the Brown Thrush. It is well. When the White Eagle spreads his wings and passes the mountain, she will charm thee with her song. Then Brandt will come, fierce as the wolf-dog and as bloody. Go not with him. Obey the voice of God. It speaks in the acts of the white men. They are like the leaves of the trees or the stars of the heavens. They cannot be counted. She will go with you. She was baptized because she loved the Christian youth. She will follow him. But he will have another, fairer to behold than the Wild Thrush. He cannot have two. Then you may have one. Go to Sagorighwi-yogstha," (Jersey, Doer of Justice.) "Die there in peace. Eat, wear warm clothes, sleep well, and be as happy as you can, and ever true and honest during life's short day. Then die. Death is only sleep. Awake in paradise. Meet me there. My sister's son, I have no more to say."

Calvin had listened intently, and every word of his ancient relative seemed engraven on his mind.

He withdrew and strode into the camp of the white people. Charles led him into his own tent, where none could intrude.

"You will not betray me, I know," said Charles; "and therefore I have brought you hither to make known our secret. The white prisoners will escape to-morrow night, and I shall go with them. Will you remain?"

"Does the Thrush go?"

"No."

"Then I will remain."

"Not, I hope, to follow Brandt?"

"No. But I shall probably follow thee with his sister."

"Alas! what will be her feelings when she learns I have fled from her? Calvin, I have never loved her as you do. My affection for her is strong, but it is only that of a brother. I shall pass many sleepless nights thinking of my poor devoted forest sister. She loves me as you would have her love you. She is very beautiful and good, Calvin. And when I am gone, and married to another, my friend, watch over my forest sister! Do not let her be destroyed. Bring her to the Jerseys, and, when she sees that men there never have two wives, she will love thee."

For an instant the fire of a long line of noble chieftains glimmered in the dark eye of the Indian youth and was then engulfed forever in darkness. The words of his uncle still sounded in his ears, and the haughty reply another might have uttered died within him. Without speaking, he pressed the hand of Charles and withdrew.

During the following day quite a number of the Eastern chiefs arrived, and a great many skins were placed round the council-fire, (always kept burning,) to be in readiness for the assembling of the representatives of the nations.

Logan, the great Mingo chief, strode through the village in sullen gloom, and once paused before the tent of Gentle Moonlight and gazed steadily at the fair face of Julia. She grasped his hand with tears in her eyes, for the sad tale of the murder of his family—wife and children, even his little pet pappoose, two years old—had often been repeated in her presence. And he did not speak. His tongue could not find utterance. But he pointed toward the East, and turned away. Julia understood him, and became more impatient than ever to depart.

In the afternoon Queen Esther's drum was heard. The

blood of the prisoners ran cold in their veins. Preceded by the music, and followed by her guards, the implacable old woman first visited the grand-council-chamber, and upon every skin she placed small pictures of the massacre of Cornstalk and his son Elenipsico, and Red Hawk, and the wife and babes of Logan. These had been engraved in Canada, under the direction of the Johnstons and Butlers, for distribution among the Indians. Then she walked round the council-fire three times, chanting one of her infernal songs, and casting brimstone into the flame.

Withdrawing from the council-chamber, she hastened to the house which had been prepared for her reception, and summoned the ancient chiefs of the Senecas to appear before her.

"My children," said she, "why have I seen the paleface prisoners walking about with guns in their hands? Are we not at war? Do they permit their Indian prisoners to go at large? Where are the chiefs that were betrayed at Point Pleasant? Who knows that before another sun we shall not be attacked in our wigwams?"

Ughs, shrugs, and grimaces, followed this interrogation.

"What shall we do?" she continued. "We are to have war. The Great Spirit has told me so in the council-house. Then we shall kill our prisoners. But, before that time, suppose our prisoners kill us?"

The Senecas brandished their tomahawks and uttered fierce threats.

"We will not permit them, my children. To-morrow morning, at early dawn, we will kill them all! That will be war! Then let the Oneidas, and Delawares, and Shawnees, and Cherokees, smoke the peace-pipe with the Americans, if they will!"

"Warriors!" said Red Jacket, who had followed Queen Esther, and anticipated some such sanguinary proposition, "hear what I have to say. Wait till all the chiefs and sachems, and the grand-sachem of the Five Nations, have met together and deliberated. That is all I advise." And he sat down.

"The Eastern prisoners are mine," said the old Queen, "and I may decide their fate."

"The sister and aunt of Thayendanegea are among them," said Red Jacket.

"They shall live," said the other.

"The White Eagle, Thayendanegea's white brother, is among them."

"If he will not wed Brandt's sister, Brandt will not mourn for him. He must die, if he will not marry and live with us."

"The Delaware youth, the son of Tammany's sister, is among them."

"He shall live, and marry Brandt's sister, when White Eagle is dead."

"I have spoken," said Red Jacket. "I have no more to say. Let my words be remembered."

The old Queen then dismissed the chiefs, without giving them any further directions. She relied upon their desire of vengeance for the loss of their brothers on the Alleghany.

It was near midnight. The fires in the wigwams had ceased to cast up their flames, and the smouldering embers threw a deep red glare over the sleeping forms of the Indians. They sleep as heartily as they eat, and repose is as necessary to them as food. Like the fowls of the air, when darkness comes their eyelids grow heavy. They do not have sentinels. Nor do they often attack in the night.

It was different with the whites. They were lying very still, it is true, with their fires burning low. But their eyes were open, and each impatient to rise at the signal and be gone.

Boone, Kenton, and Hugh McSwine were with Charles in his little tent communicating with the large one which contained the rest of the male prisoners. They were lying on their buffalo robes, speaking in whispers. The horses which were to convey them to the Ohio River were in readiness, a few hundred paces from the village, held by one of the faithful Scots, whose absence from the prisoners' wigwam had not been observed by the Indian who hastily counted the captives at night. And Julia had assured them that she would be able to rise and leave her tent without awaking her companions.

It was now near the time of departure, and Charles grew impatient for the signal Julia was to give. The curtain of buffalo-skins hanging between them and the large wigwam containing the rest was slightly agitated.

Charles started up, but instantly resumed his recumbent position, knowing that Julia would not come from that direction, stepping over the bodies of the men.

Again the skin was moved, followed by a low sound, like the chirp of a cricket, and Hugh McSwine sprang up hastily.

"I dinna' think it can be him," said Hugh, "but it's like the chiel's midnight-signal. If it be you, Skippie," he continued, "come in, mon!"

The skin was thrust aside, and the whole party rose to their feet, with the bright blades of their brandished knives reflecting the dim red glare of the sinking embers. The form which stood before them was in the Seneca costume.

"Whisper low!" said Boone, grasping the intruder by the neck with his left hand, "or I'll let out your blood in the ashes."

"Loosen your gripe, mon," said Hugh; "don't you see his eyes are popping out? He's strangled, mon, and can't speak."

"He may give the alarm-halloo," said Boone, staring at his unresisting victim.

"No," said Charles. "A spy would not have obtruded upon us in this manner. Release him, Mr. Boone."

Boone did so, and the poor fellow sank down and breathed heavily, for he had been nearly suffocated.

"Skippie!" at length was uttered by him, as he placed a number of letters in Charles's hand.

"It is Skippie!" said Charles. "Never was any one so perfectly disguised! And he comes from my father. But I have no time now to read the letters," he added, thrusting them in his bosom.

"Bundle outside," said Skippie, pointing in the direction.

"What is it? Who is it for?" demanded Charles.

"Miss Julia," was the reply.

"Return and take charge of it, Skippie. And follow us when we leave here to-night."

"Leave to-night?" asked Skippie, with unwonted energy.

"Yes."

"Good!" he said, with apparent satisfaction.

"Why?" asked Charles.

"Dead to-morrow!"

This announcement produced, as was natural, great internal commotion; and Hugh, knowing the shortest method of obtaining information from his unique countryman, soon learned that Skippie had been an auditor at the brief conference held in Queen Esther's wigwam. The intelligence of her diabolical design filled the breasts of the prisoners with fierce indignation. Hugh proposed taking her life before departing; but this was objected to as hazardous and unnecessary. Hugh, however, was permitted to watch the sleeping guards of Queen Esther who had been stationed near the wigwam in readiness for the bloody work in the morning. They were wrapped in bear-skins, and lay under a persimmon-tree, and Skippie had been compelled to step over some of their bodies to reach the tent. There was, however, another place of egress prepared for such a contingency. Nevertheless, Skippie's information was well-timed, for the presence of the savages under the tree had not been discovered, and the escaping party would have stumbled upon them.

A handful of sand thrown against the tent was the joyful signal Charles had been waiting for, and the moment he heard it his keen knife glided noiselessly down the canvas. He stepped out, followed by Kenton, who was to precede him to the place where the horses had been concealed. It was a starlight night, and the form of Julia, easily discernible, was encircled by the arm of Charles, who led her softly away in the direction the guide was pursuing.

Boone brought up the rear, leading the prisoners, while Hugh and Skippie lingered behind to watch the sleeping Senecas.

They moved in silence, or spoke in low whispers; and so still was the night that they could hear the occupants snoring within several of the houses they passed. They were just opposite the last house, and supposed there was no further danger of interruption and discovery, when a man ran out from the hut and stumbled against Charles and Julia. Boone's knife was uplifted, and in the act of descending, when his arm was arrested on recognising a well-known voice.

"Tam her! Trunk! Snoring all te time! Hello!" he continued, when jostling Charles; and, seeing Boone's raised arm, cried, "Ton't! I'm Vill Wan Viggens, and —where's my dog? Here, Vatch!"

"And, be the powers!" said Paddy, following, "do ye take me for yer falthy cur? But I don't wonder at it. You've been drinking. A pretty pass I've come to! A savage mother so drunk she can't stand up, and a Dutch daddy who don't know me from his dog! Here's yer dog behint me. He don't know ye when ye're disguised with sich abominable bad liquor."

"Hush! Be silent, Paddy!" said Charles, placing his hand on the amazed Indianized Hibernian's mouth.

"Howly Mother! Is it you, Misther Charles?" asked Paddy, in a half whisper. "And where are ye going? And mayn't I go wid ye?"

"Yes. Follow and be silent."

"I'll go mit you too," said Van Wiggens. "I'm sick of being te husband of tat drunken old squaw."

"Fall in and be silent," said Boone.

When they reached the horses (and Kenton had by some inscrutable means contrived to have not only the best animals of the Indians, but an extra number of them collected together) they all prepared to mount, being upward of twenty in number, which included several prisoners who had been captured in the West.

Simon Kenton, the tall, broad-shouldered young man, who had been often in the hands of the Indians, and who was beloved by them, because, like Boone, he was brave and generous, was quite as familiar with the country on both sides of the Ohio, and on the Scioto, as any of the red warriors themselves. He made Paddy and the Dutchman mount two of the supernumerary horses he had intended to lead. Much time was consumed in extricating some of the animals from the thicket, and Boone evinced a degree of impatience, fearing that Kenton's eagerness to secure horses might cost them dearly.

When every thing was properly adjusted, the cavalcade moved off in a brisk pace in the direction of Paint Creek. But before they had gone far they were startled by the awful voice of Peter Shaver's jackass in the Indian town. He brayed most discordantly, and the hills reverberated the sound.

"Somebody's been kilt," said Paddy; "for Pater's ass

niver brays widout smelling blood. I hope, Misther Charles," he continued, in a lower tone, "it was none of us."

"It was not you, Paddy, nor I," said Julia, smiling.

"Och, Blessed Vargin! and it's you, is it, Miss Julia? I'd know yer voice the darkest night that iver shone! And where's the t'other little swatcheart?"

"One is enough, Paddy," said Charles.

"Enough, is it? Yes, and, be the powers, it's often one too many. And Van Waggens had one too many at home, and he must get another! But it's glad I am to saa you have got rid of one, and she a wild savage!"

"Hush, Paddy!" said Julia, sharply. "She is a gentle creature, whom I love as a sister."

"Thrue enough for you, Miss Julia! and was she not Misther Charles's Indian sister, and won't she be yours when you are——"

Paddy's words were arrested by a sudden commotion behind, caused by the arrival of Hugh McSwine and Skippie, who came up at a gallop.

"Hugh!" said Charles, gazing steadily at the excited countenance of the Scot, for they were now crossing a small prairie, and the stars were shining brightly, "you remained behind. Is that not the solution of the loud braying?"

"I did not see the ass," said Hugh, equivocating.

"Let me see your hand, Hugh."

Hugh held it out silently. It was covered with blood, as was also the sleeve of his buckskin hunting-shirt.

"It was wrong, I fear!—very wrong; and we may repent it. There can be no peace now. And they will all join the British. I'm glad Mr. Jones determined to escape with us. If he had remained, as was his intention yesterday, he would have been lost. To-morrow, the first white man they see, if it be not one of the infamous renegades, will be tomahawked or burned at the stake. How did you accomplish it? Who did you strike?"

"I dinna' ken their names," said Hugh. "But my dirk——"

"*Their* names. More than one, then?"

"Three. Skippie led the way. They were to fall upon us in the morning with tomahawk and scalping-knife.

That heated my blude. The guard set over us will never see the dawn of day!"

"Terrible!" said Julia, leaning forward on her horse, and striving to shut out the horrible picture from her imagination.

"Did they alarm the village?" asked Boone, whose quick ear had caught the purport of Hugh's words.

"They never spoke a word, mon! There was only a whizzing gushing noise about their throats, a kick or two, and they were as still as ever. When Hugh McSwine has one hand on a foeman's neck, and his dirk in the other, there are never any words or screams."

"But the ass?"

"De'il tak the ass! I vowed to cut his throat if I met wi' him again! But I didn't see him. He was biting the hazel-bushes round the tent, and when he smelt the blude he ran away squalling as if the de'il were at his heels!"

"And did he not rouse the Indians?" asked Charles.

"Skippie and I waited to see. Some did come out and gaze in the dark. But the ass had moved some distance from the dead men, who could tell no tales."

"Then why should we hasten so fast?" asked Julia.

"We heard the women screaming," said Hugh.

"Enough!" cried Charles. "Our escape has been discovered! We cannot conceal our trail. We must fly with the utmost speed. There can be no rest for you, my Julia, until we pass the Ohio. I hope you can bear the fatigue!"

"Oh yes, I can bear it," said she.

They increased their pace to the utmost, and the unerring guidance of Kenton kept them in the right direction. Boone was silent during the remainder of the night, riding by the side of Hugh and just behind Charles and Julia.

Charles, being familiar with the habits of the savages, informed Julia that their pursuers would not start on their trail until daylight, and could not possibly overtake them before they reached the Ohio River, some fifty miles distant, if they met with no delay and could keep their horses going until the next day at noon. And Kenton, keeping a little in advance, but within speaking distance, informed them with a chuckle that the fleetest horses had been taken from the Indians, and those they could not take had been let loose in the woods, and might perhaps follow them without riders.

Neither Boone nor Charles, however, seemed to attach so much importance to the agency of horses as Kenton did. They were aware that the Indian himself could run for days without apparent fatigue, and that he could cross ravines which equestrians must pass round, and traverse swamps in the direct line of march where horses, if they did not deviate, would stick fast in the mud. Yet they did not suppose they could be overtaken if their flight met with no interruption. But was it not likely they would fall in with some of the hunting-parties continually going into and returning from Kentucky? They were certainly beset with dangers on every hand, and it was not a proper time to be counting gains in the item of stolen horses.

The first interruption was caused by Van Wiggens's dog, which barked piteously at every leap, and began to lose ground. His master said he could not leave him behind, nor did he believe he could follow their trail. Boone reined in his steed and fell back to where the dog was yelping, and, leaning over the side of his horse, succeeded in grasping poor Watch by the tail, and lifted him up before him. The dog licked his hand in gratitude.

At early dawn Paddy begged them to stop and have something to eat. He said Miss Julia must be suffering with hunger, being unwilling to confess his own weakness. But Julia declared she could not and would not take any meat until they had reached a place of safety.

Charles, however, snatched some wild fruit as they rode through the thickets, which sufficed both for the maiden and himself. But Van Wiggens had an intolerable thirst, for he had been induced to drink some of his squaw's miserable fire-water, furnished by the British sutler. This, too, was partially allayed by Boone, who, throwing himself under the neck of his horse, dipped up water from the small streams they were occasionally dashing through. The poor Dutch Indian drank a little of this while in motion, and spilled more, which he wept over.

About the middle of the forenoon, and when Kenton was promising in a few hours more to show them the cliffs of the Ohio, the party halted abruptly, most of them with painfully-throbbing hearts. On an eminence in the prairie through which they were passing, and in the line of march directly before them, they beheld a company of some forty Indians. They seemed to be returning from a hunting expedition, as their horses were laden with buffalo-meat.

"Will they attack us?" asked Julia.

"I think they will!" said Kenton, whose quick eye had instantly computed their superior number. "But we can whip 'em! I'll have a scalp for every horse they take!"

Charles perceived that the Indians were astonished at the apparition of such a cavalcade. Most of the whites—and they seemed themselves to have forgotten it—were not only habited as Indians, but painted like them also. But their mode of sitting on horseback and manner of riding, even at the distance of several hundred yards, could not long deceive the hunting-party as to the true nature of their quality. Himself, however, and Kenton and Boone, might counterfeit the Indian without liability to detection; and so the three, after giving certain directions to Hugh, advanced toward the opposite party.

Three of the Indians came at full gallop to meet them. They were Senecas. In answer to their inquiry, Charles said his men were a party of adopted prisoners going to Kentucky to hunt buffalo.

The chief who had addressed him said all that was very good, and asked if all the prisoners had been adopted without running the gauntlet.

Charles said he believed some were retained for the torture, and had been taken to Sandusky, where they would probably be burned at the stake, as their captors had painted them black.

The chief asked if they had not scalped and burned "Captain Kenton, a horse-steal rascal, d—— white man!"

Kenton made an involuntary movement, as if to cock his gun, but was checked by Boone.

Charles said they had not yet decided his fate, nor Boone's.

"Captain Boone! honest man!" said the Indian, while Boone's grave features relaxed into a smile. "What horse?" continued the speaker, staring in astonishment at the noble black animal Kenton bestrode.

"One he borrowed," said Charles, in the Seneca tongue.

The Indian flew into a violent passion, and accused them

of lying. He said the horse was his own,—one he had left at home for his squaw to keep in good condition. He intended to ride him the next spring, when they invaded the white settlements in Pennsylvania. He then ordered Kenton to dismount.

This Kenton of course refused to do, although Boone advised a compliance, as the only possible means of avoiding a battle. But the next moment it was quite obvious the surrendering of the horse would not have sufficed; for one of the Indians had recognised Kenton, notwithstanding his paint, as well as Boone, and, uttering the warwhoop, wheeled away and sped round in circles. The other two did the same, to avoid the bullets of the white men, whose rifles were instantly thrown up to their faces. The Indians were the first to fire, but did no injury, as they were in rapid motion and some eighty paces distant. But Boone and Kenton (Charles did not fire at all) were more fortunate. The first brought his man to the ground, and the other, as was supposed, wounded the claimant of the horse, for he fell forward on his horse's neck and did not rise again. The third seized his companion, who fell to the ground, and dragged him away by the hand while his horse was in a gallop.

The party came down from the hill at a furious pace, yelling terribly, and the whites retreated under cover of the sumach-bushes at the edge of the prairie.

"I've got no gun. I can't fight!" said Paddy, when they had dismounted in the bushes.

"You can fight with your knife, mon," said Hugh.

"And wouldn't they be sure to kill me?"

"No surer than if you were to sit down without resisting and be scalped."

"Murther! And I didn't have the sculp-lock taken off!"

"Here's one of my pistols," said the Rev. Mr. Jones, coming up from the rear. "And let us all pray for protection and aid from above, and especially that this tender virgin may not be harmed. Get up, you silly coward!" he continued, bestowing a smart kick on the back of Paddy, who had fallen on his knees. "There's no time to be kneeling now. Pray standing at your post or lying down with your finger on the trigger and your eye upon the enemy. Let your hearts pray, my brethren; this is no time for lip-service. And remember that if the Lord of Hosts be on our side ten thousand foes cannot prevail against us. Be valiant, men, obedient to your leaders, and take a steady aim!"

The Indians, seeing the effect of the fire of the whites, and knowing Boone and Kenton were among them, although superior in number, became very circumspect. They immediately abandoned the prairie and plunged into the woods bordering the opening. Their women and children were sent out of the way or hidden in the grass, and preparations made for an immediate assault.

Our party likewise made preparations. Boone led them a short distance to the left, where there was the fallen trunk of a gigantic tree, charred by the camp-fires of many a hunting and war-party. Behind this the horses were tied and fed, and a guard set over them, concealed in the long grass which grew among the larger branches of the prostrate oak. And here, too, Julia was deposited in charge of Mr. Jones. The remainder of the party were then skilfully disposed by their experienced leaders, so as to make the place of Julia's concealment (the horses being likely to tempt the Indians) a sort of ambushment, and the most dangerous point for the enemy to approach.

When thus posted, our party, with a few exceptions, felt impatient for the battle to begin. They knew that pursuers were approaching, and dreaded being exposed between two fires. The Indians, however, were not inclined to accommodate them. They, too, were well aware that pursuit must have been made, and by delaying the attack their number would be augmented to an irresistible force.

An hour, which seemed half a day, thus passed, an occasional shot only being fired by the advanced scouts, from their places of concealment, when any portions of the bodies of their opponents were exposed.

"Why, Mr. Kenton," said Paddy, who had been placed behind a beech-tree, with directions to keep his body concealed, and fire his pistol as fast as he could load if any of the Indians came in sight, "I say, Misther Kenton, this ain't sic a terrible fight afther all. And this is a rigular battle, is it? Be the powers, I'll turn Indian-fighter meself! Be Jabers! what's that?"

Paddy having slightly exposed his coon-skin cap, the tail

(which had been left on it for a plume) fell at his feet, and at the same moment the sharp report of a rifle was heard in the bushes some sixty paces distant.

Kenton motioned Paddy to fall down and pretend to be dead. This Paddy did without hesitation, as soon as he comprehended the fact that the Indian's ball had grazed his head and carried away the tail of which he had been so proud.

The Indian sprang forward to scalp his supposed victim, and received the fire of Kenton. He fell in an open space, clear of bushes, as he ran toward Paddy, pierced through the brain.

"I brought him, Paddy!" whispered Kenton.

"Oh, plase don't bring him here, Misther Kenton!" said Paddy, who lay with his face against the ground and could see nothing.

"No, he's lying yonder in full view. He didn't kick; he jest quivered a little and then was limber. I've seen 'em do it before, when I got a good bead on 'em. But the others mustn't drag him off. Now, Paddy, if you want to show your bravery and be a great man, run there and scalp him. I'll watch, and keep the others away till you're done."

"What! gore my hands wid human blood?" said Paddy, spreading out his trembling fingers.

"No, he'll not bloody you much. Make a ring round the scalp-lock with your knife, take the head between your knees, and pull off the skin with your teeth."

"Taath? Me taath?"

"Yes, that's the way they do it. I've seen it done often."

"Och, Mr. Kenton, I'm sick! It's a faver-and-ager counthry. I've got a chale, and——"

"Hush!" said Kenton. "They're coming to drag him away."

"And ye'd 'a had poor Paddy to run right into their jaws!"

Again Kenton's rifle spoke the doom of an Indian, and the two lay together. Charles and Boone and Hugh McSwine, seeing what had passed, concentrated the most of their men near that point, knowing the Indians would make a desperate effort to bear away their dead.

But, as they approached, it was apparent that the enemy had been beforehand with them. Two of the faithful Scots, incautiously exposing themselves, were fired upon from the little bramble-swamp beyond the fallen Indians and killed. This success of the foe was followed by yells of exultation. Several of them darted forward to scalp the Scots, but were driven back by the fire of Boone and Charles, one of them borne off by his comrades mortally wounded.

The fire now became incessant on both sides in the immediate vicinity of the dead Indians. The Indians, however, were the greatest sufferers. The briery thicket in which they had collected having no trees to resist the balls of the white men, their death-yells were heard at short intervals. The whites were defended by trees, Paddy alone being exposed; but, as he lay perfectly still, he was supposed to be dead, and of course the enemy would not throw away their fire on him.

"Don't you move, Paddy, or you're a dead man!" said Kenton, reloading his rifle, which he had just discharged with effect at an enormous savage who betrayed his locality in endeavouring to aim at Boone.

"Lord!" cried Paddy, though careful not to move hand or foot. "I hear the bullets whazzing about like bumble-baas! That wasn't the rale battle we had at first! Now we are fighting in earnest. Och, murther! I shall be kilt! I'm a dead man!"

"They won't shoot a dead man, I tell you," said Kenton. "Be perfectly still, and you're safe. They think you're dead."

"And do you mane to insinuate that they can saa me here?"

"To be sure they can—every one of 'em. And if you try to jump behind the tree again a dozen bullets will go through your body."

"Murther! And if they bate us they'll sculp me for a dead man! And my sculp-lock wasn't shaved off!"

"Be quiet!" said Kenton, having again added a victim to his list. The last one fell in attempting to bear off the first he had slain, who, no doubt, was a chief. "Paddy," he continued, ramming down his ball, "they'll hear your voice, or see your cap move when you speak, and then you'll be killed, sure enough. Don't you see how they are barking my tree?"

"No; I don't want to see it," said Paddy, in a low tone.

"Tam dem!" said Will Van Wiggens. "Here dey all come togedder!"

After something like a simultaneous discharge from behind the trees, which the enemy had drawn forth by a stratagem,—placing their blankets on poles and moving them to and fro in the bushes,—the whole body of savages rushed out with brandished tomahawks, and, yelling terrifically, charged upon the white men before they could reload their rifles.

Some of them fortunately had pistols, and, although they could do but little execution with them, they served to intimidate the foremost of the enemy.

"Stand fast to your trees!" cried Boone. "If one man runs away we shall all perish. Fight with your tomahawks and knives—man to man, and we will conquer!"

"Give me your pistol, Paddy," said Kenton, whose tree was the nearest to the advancing savages.

"I can't move," said Paddy. "Och, murther! are they coming?"

At that moment the foremost Indian, some twenty paces in advance of the rest, sprang forward, unconscious of the close vicinity of Kenton, and, bestriding Paddy, stooped down to scalp him. Just when the knife touched the skin, and when Paddy yelled out "Murther!" the breech of Kenton's gun descended, and the savage fell upon his intended victim.

The rest of the Indians rushed past, Kenton himself being forced to fly before them, until they were opposed by Boone, McSwine, Charles, and their brave comrades, who sprang from their trees and offered battle hand-to-hand. The Indians faltered a moment and then retreated. They snatched up their fallen chief who lay across Paddy's body and bore him along. One of them strove to drag the supposed dead Irishman by the leg, not having time to scalp him there. But this was resisted by Paddy with all his might. He kicked and yelled so astoundingly that the Indian relinquished his hold and fled with the rest. And Paddy, knowing it would be useless to counterfeit death any longer, sprang up and valorously fired his pistol. He then jumped behind Kenton's tree. It was all the work of an instant. Moments were precious when men were loading their rifles and foes were exposed to view. But the Indians soon vanished, bearing away their dead.

"Come on, my brave comrades!" cried Paddy, now in advance of all the whites. "We've defated 'em. They're retrating, the savage blackguards! And one of 'em was astraddle of Paddy Pence! But Paddy pistholed him, the impident blackguard! Charge, men, charge! They're retrating!"

Paddy was not mistaken. Charles understood the purport of the yells and whoops of the discomfited savages. Content to recover the bodies of their slain, they were retreating precipitately.

"Now let us make tracks ourselves," said Kenton, leading the way toward the horses.

"Yes," said Boone; "we cannot be gone too soon. Our pursuers will come up quickly, and the attack will be renewed if we tarry."

"Mr. Bone," said Paddy, "did you saa ony one fall when I fired me pisthol?"

Boone made no reply.

"He's jealous!" said Paddy. "But, Misther Kenton, you can bear witness that I fired the last gun, and that I was the foremost man afther the inemy when they retrated."

Kenton, too, paid no attention to Paddy, but hurried toward the horses, now the object of his solicitude, for he could not be induced to leave any of them (even the supernumerary ones) behind.

"And did ye not saa it, Mr. Charles?" persisted Paddy.

"This is no time for nonsense!" said Charles. "Assist me in placing Julia on her horse."

And Hugh McSwine likewise turned his back on Paddy as he approached him, and, aided by Van Wiggens, who had behaved with perfect coolness during the conflict, succeeded in placing the dead Scotchmen on horses before their comrades.

CHAPTER XIV.

THE AMBUSCADE—THE NIGHT SURPRISE—CROSSING THE OHIO—LETTERS FROM HOME.

The party were soon remounted, and resumed the flight at a brisker pace than ever. Charles rode at the side of Julia, a little in advance of the rest, and their course was over the eminence in the plain where they had at first discovered the Indians.

Julia was very pale, for she had seen the dead Scots placed on the horses; and, as they still bled quite freely, Charles directed them to be kept behind, that no traces of their gore might be seen in their path.

"Miss Julia," said Paddy, who had been riding just behind, expatiating on his feats to Mr. Jones, who listened carelessly, singing one of the thanksgiving psalms of David, "I was the last man who shot an Indian. I was before all the rest of our men when the savages fled away. I was down on me face——"

"Down, Paddy?" asked Julia, in surprise.

"Yes, be jabers! down, and almost sculped! A dead chafe was lying across me——"

"Paddy, are you really in earnest?"

"Arnest, is it? Raal arnest! Isn't it, Misther Charles?"

"That part is true," said Charles, with a slight smile. "Kenton had broken the Indian's head as he stooped down to scalp Paddy, whom he supposed to be dead. And I, too, at first supposed you were gone, Paddy, and am rejoiced to find it was a mistake."

"And so am I, upon me sowl! But it was me who caused the blackguard savage to make the mistake, and that was the raison of his death; and I may dacently say I killed him. Yes, Miss Julia, he fell upon me, and he lay on my stomach as heavy as a nightmare. I couldn't move hand or fut. Then prisently the others came and lifted him off; and one of the blackguards had the impidence to saze me by the fut, and pull me toward the bushes to sculp me---och, murther!" cried Paddy, placing his hand on his head. "But I sent him sprawling in the laves with a kick, and he let go his holt; and I'm sure he was as pale as ashes at the thought of a dead man kicking him. Then I pulled up my pisthol and fired at the whole crowd o' 'em, and that was the last gun shot off in the battle."

"And so you were the last to fire, Paddy," said Julia.

"The last to fire, is it? Yes—that is,—I mane,—och, now, Miss Julia, don't be afther saying that same! And, if it's true I didn't shoot before, I was down flat on me face, wid no tra before me and in full view of the whole army of savages. And didn't Mr. Kenton tell me to lie still, and if I budged they'd raddle me with their bullets?"

"What caused you to fall, Paddy?" asked Julia, her curiosity somewhat excited.

"Och, murther! And to-be-sure it was one of their ondacent bullets. I was jist paaping from behint the root of the tra, and one of the blackguards had the ill-manners to aim his rifle at me head. The bullet, I suppose, would have hit me atwane the eyes if I hadn't dodged. As it was, it struck the top o' me cap, and cut off me cone-tail be the roots!"

"And did that make you fall?"

"Didn't it? Miss Julia, you were niver shot in that way, I know, or you wouldn't ask the question. I was stunned, and fell down and rolled over. And the savage who kilt me, not saaing Mr. Kenton near by, ran out to snatch me sculp. Then Mr. Kenton missed cutting his tail away and struck him in the forehead. Down he fell as dead as a door-nail. And then the battle began in arnest, fighting over his worthless corpse and over Paddy's body! And that's the truth of it, Miss Julia, and I hope it'll be in the London papers. I'm covered all over wid blood, and I've jist come out of the thickest of the fight. And here's the hill where we first saw the inemy. Murther! Och, Lord!" cried he, darting past Charles and Julia, and evincing the greatest terror on beholding an Indian child crouching in the tall grass near the path.

"The poor infant," said Charles, pausing, "has been placed there by its mother, not supposing we would pass in this direction."

"Poor thing!" said Julia. "See how still it is. Paddy's

horse has thrown dust in its face, and yet it does not cry."

"No," said Charles. "Like the young partridge, it remains in silence where its mother placed it. It is not two years old, and yet would bite your finger if you attempted to seize it. We will pass on. But I will assure its mother of its safety." And he did so, in a loud voice, in the Indian dialect. A moment after, the mother, who had been lying concealed only a few paces apart, in a small chasm, sprang forward, seized the child, and fled toward the woods.

"For shame, Paddy!" cried Julia, seeing the valorous Indian-fighter aim his pistol at the flying woman and pull the trigger.

"Och, it's not loaded, Miss Julia," said he. "I didn't know if there mightn't be others with guns and tomahawks all around us. Misther Charles knows they can bide in grass not an inch long. And sure you won't belave it was the baby that made me dodge. It was the twinty warriors I didn't know but there might be hid and aiming at us." And Paddy hastily rejoined the Rev. Mr. Jones, and listened in silence to the song he had never ceased to articulate during the incident of the Indian infant and its mother.

"This is a specimen of life in the wild woods, Julia," said Charles, "such as you have heard related during winter evenings before the cheerful fire. But you find it not so pleasant as you anticipated."

"If it were only relieved of its dangers—its butcheries!" said the pale girl, with a faint smile. "Still, it would be no sport that a poor maiden should voluntarily witness; but captives must submit to circumstances. I hope there will be no more slaughter. Do you think there will be more fighting?"

"It is probable. But we shall be able to repel any attack. I do not think they have exceeding twenty warriors at Chillicothe capable of pursuing us. They are still killing buffalo."

"And Mr. Kenton, I learn, has deprived them of their best horses. But, if twenty pursue, and unite with as many others on the battle-ground we are leaving, still they will greatly exceed us in number."

"But we shall surpass them in skill. Boone and Kenton are equal to twenty ordinary warriors. Then there is Hugh McSwine! Oh, Julia, he is terrible in battle, and slays his foe with the keenest delight. Some one dear to him must have been a victim: he seems actuated by an insatiable thirst for blood."

"And have you not killed some of them, Charles?" asked Julia.

"No. I am sure I did not; and I hope it may never be necessary for me to do so. They will follow us, however, and probably more blood will flow. If we had none of their horses, they might abandon the pursuit when they learn we have been the victors in the first battle."

"Then why not leave them?" asked Julia.

"I should have no objection. But the rest would never consent. Yet we shall reach the river in safety. We cannot conceal our trail; but there are many narrow ravines suited for ambuscades, and our foes will be very circumspect and tardy in the pursuit. And these exciting perils, Julia, will make our narrative the more interesting when, in old age, we sit by the blazing hearth, of winter evenings, and describe them. You must keep a journal, beginning with your capture and ending with our nuptials!"

The maiden blushed, but did not chide him; and she determined, if she escaped death in the wilderness, to preserve in writing a narrative of her adventures. This she did in letters to Kate Livingston and in a journal which we have been permitted to read and transcribe.

"Mercy on us! What is that?" asked Julia, hearing an awful sound, when they had proceeded only a mile or two from the scene of the recent conflict.

"Murther!" cried Paddy, spurring forward. "We shall have to fight agin. I know that voice!"

"Ah!" said Julia, "I recognise it too. It is Peter Shaver's ass, scenting the blood of the slain. Our pursuers have arrived!"

"They will be likely to pause at the scene of the recent action," said Charles, "when they learn its disastrous result. And Peter is among them. No doubt he had sense enough to escape killing by denouncing us and offering to join our enemies. But he will do no injury, and he must not be fired at if he appears within range of our rifles. He will desert to us the first opportunity."

A shot was heard fired by one of the party who had lingered behind. This attracted no especial notice at the time. But soon after Hugh McSwine and Skippie (the latter still having the bundle he had brought from New Jersey) came up at full gallop; and Skippie, pausing an instant near Charles, said—

"*He* did!"

"Who?" demanded Charles.

"Hugh."

"It was his gun, then. And Hugh never misses his mark."

"No. Got the scalp."

Charles turned his head and beheld Hugh, some few paces behind, stretching a scalp on a hazel-hoop as he rode along.

"This is horrible!" said Julia, pale and shrinking, for she comprehended all, and had even glanced at the bloody Hugh. And, besides, the ass of Peter Shaver was still faintly heard in the distance.

Boone came forward and pointed to some dim and distant heights before them, which were joyfully announced as the northern barriers of the Ohio River. There was, however, no assurance that they could elude their pursuers and pass the broad stream in safety. A raft would have to be constructed; the weather must be calm, and the water smooth, before they might venture to embark.

These difficulties and contingencies being apparent to Boone and Kenton, a hasty consultation was held, as they proceeded at a smart pace; and it was determined by the majority—and Hugh McSwine, of course, voted with the majority—that they would fight another battle. Charles saw the necessity of repelling their pursuers, but did not urge it.

They were now arrived at the beginning of a series of narrow ravines running between lofty hills, and here it was resolved to rebuke the foe. It was in the second of these ravines the first ambuscade was formed, it being deemed good policy to embolden their pursuers by permitting them to pass through the first in safety.

The men were stationed in places of concealment behind

detached rocks and under evergreen bushes, commanding the path through the narrow defile. The Rev. Mr. Jones, although he had no special objection to fighting the heathen in defence of his Christian friends, yet thought it proper, in view of his peaceful calling, to ride forward and remain with Julia during the carnage. But, before doing so, he made one of his characteristic prayers in presence of the assembled party, and the Scotchmen, particularly, responded with a loud "Amen!"

Not more than an hour had elapsed before the foremost of the savages came in view. They had passed through the first valley in safety, and did not seem to apprehend an ambush in the second one. Kenton recognised the owner of his steed in the foremost Indian, who seemed to be pointing at the foot-prints of his horse, which he could doubtless distinguish from the rest. They came in a long file, not more than two abreast, and the foremost of them were suffered to pass the concealed whites before the word was given to fire. Then a volley, consisting, by pre-arrangement, of but one-half the rifles, was discharged. Never were savages more completely surprised. They sprang in every direction, hoping to elude the aim of their foes. "Ugh! ho! yough!" were uttered by some, and by others the anglicism "Dern!" And yet, as Boone and Kenton were among those who had reserved their fire for the second discharge, only two or three fell under the aim of the Scots, and one, of course, by the fatal lead of Hugh McSwine. Most of the men had fired too high.

At the second discharge five or six fell, killed and wounded, and the rest fled precipitately, yelling terrifically, and without striking a blow.

The whites did not pursue them, nor even scalp their fallen victims, but resolved without delay to resume their march toward the Ohio River. One of the Indians, however, (whom Kenton recognised,) had sprung forward between them and the place where Julia had been deposited. They had not aimed at him, because he was the foremost of the party and separated from the rest.

This Indian soon came to where the horses had been placed, in a little nook out of range of the rifles. Paddy had charge of them, and, not scanning the savage closely, supposed him to be Kenton; and they really resembled each other in stature, and were costumed and painted similarly.

"Mr. Kenton," said Paddy, "and is it all over so soon? But what have ye done wid yer gun?" The Indian had thrown down his rifle, and his tomahawk had fallen from his belt as he plunged through the ravine.

"Dern!" said the Indian. "My hoss! Kenton d—— hoss-steal! A white-man tief!" and he proceeded, with all the haste in his power, to mount one of the horses ere Paddy could recover his presence of mind. Hearing the whites returning, the savage dashed away, and was no sooner out of sight, having turned an abrupt angle of rocks, than Paddy fired his pistol; and a few moments after the Rev. Mr. Jones's pistol was heard.

"Och, ye cowards!" cried Paddy, meeting the party returning. "Or did you mane to let that big blackguard savage come to me on purpose?"

"What have you done with him?" asked Hugh.

"Where's my horse?" shouted Kenton, seeing his best steed was no longer with the rest of the animals.

"The blackguard savage mounted him! And, as St. Pater is my judge, I thought it was you. But you naadn't fume and fret about it, Misther Kenton! Paddy's the boy to fax the prowling red thieves. Didn't ye hear me pisthol?"

"I heard two," said Charles.

"It was only the acho," said Paddy, "which desaved ye. I peppered him!"

"Where is he?" asked Boone.

"And where's my horse?" demanded Kenton.

"Be aisy, Misther Bone. If that is a spare rifle you have," (he had picked up the Indian's,) "plase let me have it. This pisthol won't kill at wanst. I shat the varmint through the lungs, but he won't fall for a few manutes, and thin we'll git yer horse agin, Misther Kenton."

Kenton uttered a fierce malediction, while the rest only vented peals of laughter, and the whole party hastened toward the jutting rock where the Indian had disappeared before Paddy fired.

"Good!" cried Kenton, his face wreathed in smiles, as he beheld his fine steed standing near the place where Julia had awaited the issue of the strife. "And there's the yellow rascal who stole him," he continued, seeing Mr. Jones gazing at the prostrate Indian, who lay perfectly motionless in the path, while the horse stood over him, snorting, with distended nostrils, arched neck, and eyes flashing fearfully.

"I told you so, be jabers!" cried Paddy, running forward. "Didn't I say me pisthol had done his basiness?"

"I have no taste for such exercises," said Mr. Jones; "and I would not be sorry if it could be made to appear that it was not my ball which smote the heathen."

"Yer ball? Did ye say yer bullet? And did ye shoot at him too, Mr. Jones?"

"I held out my weapon and pulled the trigger. He fell."

"And have you forgotten how it was when ye shot the turkey? And was not the report of yer pisthol but the revarberation of mine?"

"Unluckily, Paddy," said Charles, blowing the smoke from the barrel of the reverend gentleman's weapon, "Mr. Jones's pistol is empty this time, and yet warm from the recent discharge."

"And warm is it from the racent discharge? And mine is cowld, because it was discharged first. And are not our bullets of the same size? And would any blackguard Indian fall, afther being kilt by a pisthol, before riding some distance? I shall claim the credit of killing him meself, in spite of your inganious argyments. And I'll sculp him too!"

But when he laid hold of the Indian, finding he still breathed, he sprang back in alarm and begged the loan of a rifle or tomahawk to dispatch him.

"No!" said Julia, advancing, pale and tearful, "do not imitate the savages. Rather set them an example of forbearance and humanity!"

"He is not dead, and will immediately recover," said Boone, finding that the ball had glanced from his temple, having only stunned him. This proved true; and, after the lapse of a few minutes, the Indian was so far recovered as to be able to ride one of the horses—a silent, sullen captive.

The party now urged forward their steeds, and soon entered another narrow ravine. This they passed through without halting, and continued their journey toward the river.

They knew that considerable time would be consumed by their pursuers in burying their dead, and that they would hesitate long before plunging into the next defile. Hence they hoped to escape further molestation.

During the afternoon they arrived on the northern bank of the Ohio; and many of them cast longing looks at the opposite shore, which once attained, it was the general supposition they would be in a place of safety. But Boone and Kenton would not consent to the prevalent desire of the less experienced to halt and set about the construction of a raft. There were no natural defences at that point to enable them to keep a hostile party of superior numbers at bay during the preparations for the passage. And, besides, a strong wind prevailed, and the waves ran too high for any raft to ride in security. Nor would it answer to remain stationary until the subsidence of the gale, for the Indians would be upon them. Kenton had been captured once with a fine lot of horses, by thus remaining inactive until the foe, following his trail, surprised him.

Profiting by his experience on that melancholy occasion, Kenton led the way along the path down the river, so that the distance between them and their pursuers might not be diminished.

Mr. Jones expressed his fervent thanks that he had not been made an instrument of death in the hands of his heavenly Master, and often congratulated himself, as he rode along, during the pauses in his song, on the recovery of the savage.

Paddy was chagrined that he did not die, and die by his hand. He could no longer claim the credit of the stunning wound, as the effect of the concussion was evidently instantaneous. But he was consoled in some measure by receiving the Indian's rifle, which Boone loaned him, and by the loss of Van Wiggens's dog, which had not been seen since the battle, if battle it could be called. The latter incident afforded him a sort of malicious pleasure, inasmuch as the Dutchman insisted upon having seen the mark of Paddy's ball some twenty feet high on the face of the perpendicular cliff, and had otherwise depreciated the merits of the Irishman.

And, as they rode along the path, which sometimes diverged from the river where enormous masses of rocks had descended to the water's edge, the inquiry was passed along the line if any one had seen Peter Shaver in the ambuscade. No one had recognised him, but several had heard the familiar voice of his ass after the slaughter. Van Wiggens had no doubt Peter was among the savages, and seemed to think that Watch, his dog, had seen him and followed him. This was a source of hope, for he doubted not he should some day see Peter's face again.

Thus they continued without interruption until the autumnal sun, blood-red and magnified apparently to an enormous size, sank down before them; for their faces were toward the West. They now searched for one of those impregnable fastnesses in the hills, with its natural defences of rocks and fissures, in which to encamp for the night; and, when it was found, the tents were erected, the hungry permitted to eat and the weary to rest. The wind continuing somewhat boisterous, it was the opinion of Boone and Kenton that a passage over the river could not be effected until the following day.

A consultation was then held in regard to the fate of their prisoner; and as Boone and Kenton, as well as Julia, were in favour of liberating him, it was so determined. But he was compelled to swim across the river a few miles back, in full view of two of his captors. Pushing a dry log before him, he launched out in the stream, and was soon beyond the reach of rifles. Then he yelled like an enfranchised demon, and abused his enemies. It was feared their mercy would be productive of only evil, as is sometimes the case when extended to unworthy objects. However, they dismissed this Ground-Hog (for such was his name) from their minds.

After a hearty repast, Kenton and several of the most active men started back on their trail to discover, if possible, the camp-fire of their pursuers.

The scout proceeded several miles, and then ascended a high eminence, from which they could see eastward a still greater distance; but no fires were visible. It was possible the pursuit had been abandoned, and such was their report on returning.

And now a sense of comparative security pervaded the

encampment. Julia and Charles sent for Skippie, resolved to read the letters he had brought from their friends. But Skippie was nowhere to be found, although he had been seen since twilight. Doubtless, as Hugh McSwine asserted, he was out alone, reconnoitering the country in every direction.

Disappointed in this, Charles and Julia congratulated themselves upon the prospect of a speedy deliverance from their perils.

An hour after, Skippie came hastily into the tent, followed by Paddy.

"And you won't tell me what you've sane?" exclaimed Paddy. "But I'll hear it in spite o' ye, ye unfinished son of a sawny!"

"Dirk!" said Skippie, exposing the handle of his weapon, and darting a look of defiance at Paddy.

"Dirk, is it? Well, don't dirk me! I'm Misther Charles's friend, you know, and the deadly enemy of the blackguard savages."

"Your news, Skippie?" said Charles.

"Twenty!" said Skippie, pointing in a westerly direction and in the line of their march for the next day.

"Twenty Indians in front of us!" said Julia, in tones of sadness.

"They are not our pursuers, at all events," said Charles.

And, when Skippie had described them and the location of their camp in his laconic but graphic manner, Boone announced without hesitation that it was a party from Paint Creek going over into Kentucky on a predatory expedition; and, no doubt, the object of their attack was his station on the Kentucky River, called Boonsboro'. He had seen their trail, but did not mention it, as it was not fresh. They must have been encamped several days where Skippie discovered them, perhaps awaiting the arrival of reinforcements.

A council being held, it was resolved to attack them in the night. They occupied an important position in the line of march for the next day. The Indians had, no doubt, been making preparations for crossing over into Kentucky, and probably possessed canoes, which, if captured, would serve an excellent purpose.

Arrangements were made to set out immediately. Skippie, who could move with less noise than any one in camp, was despatched on their back trail to guard against any sudden surprise from that quarter. They did not apprehend immediate danger from their repulsed pursuers; but some other roving party, led by renegade white men, might possibly fall upon their camp.

Kenton was the guide selected to lead them against the warriors encamped near the river. Familiar with the features of the country, having often traversed every hill and ravine, the few words uttered by Skippie had made him sufficiently acquainted with the locality of the Indians. He nad himself encamped there repeatedly.

Paddy desired to guard the camp, and especially to protect Miss Julia. But this was objected to by Charles, and the Rev. Mr. Jones was designated for that purpose. Nor would Kenton suffer Paddy again to have the care of the horses. Therefore, much against his will, he had no alternative but to march.

They set out, treading noiselessly in each other's tracks, marching in single file, in the manner of the Indians. Boone had drilled them so well that the whole party stepped simultaneously, making but one sound, and that a low, dull one, the foremost man (Kenton) having carefully removed or softly crushed the leaves that lay in the path.

"Be jabers!" said Paddy, speaking to Van Wiggens, who was the next man in front of him, "it would be a good thing now to have your dog wid us."

"Tam dem!" said Van Wiggens; "if tey hurt a hair of my Vatch——"

"You must not speak so loudly," whispered Charles, who brought up the rear, stepping in the footprints of Paddy.

The moon was shining brightly, for there was not a cloud in the sky. A long silence ensued, interrupted only by the low sound of more than twenty feet falling softly to the earth. And, as they drew near the smouldering embers round which the slumbering Indians reposed in fancied security, their progress became very slow, and their scarcely-perceptible advance was no longer attended with any noise which might have been detected by the keenest ear at the distance of a dozen paces.

"Misther Charles," said Paddy, in a low whisper, "do you think there is gincrally as much fighting done by the tail of a line like this as the head o' it?" He asked this question when a curve in the path enabled him to see the men in front winding along like a huge serpent under the trees, through whose boughs the rays of the moon were streaming brightly.

"It is often the post of honour," said Charles.

Paddy thought he would prefer a post of safety; but he could not comprehend how the rear of the line would be exposed to as much danger as the head of it, and he so expressed himself. But he was informed that the whole line would glide silently round the sleeping Indians and be formed in the shape of a crescent.

"Plase, Misther Charles," said he, "have me put in the maddle,—in the bow of the moon."

"It cannot be done now, Paddy, without danger of discovery. You have the position you asked for, and you must keep it. Say no more, for yonder is the enemy's camp."

The camp of the Indians was situated near the mouth of a valley opening on the river. But a stream of water, emptying into the Ohio, with its steep alluvial embankments, was now between the sleeping Indians and their assailants, and the latter had to pass down the brook some twenty paces before there was any possibility of crossing over. Kenton and Boone stood several minutes in breathless silence opposite the slumbering Indians, the outlines of whose forms were dimly visible, and then moved on noiselessly toward the moss-covered trunk of an enormous tree that lay across the stream a few paces farther below. This tree, some eight feet in diameter, Kenton remembered distinctly, having often passed over it. It had been lying there, perhaps, for a century, and its damp moss and soft exterior afforded a sure and noiseless footing.

The head of the line passed over the tree and returned up the stream on the opposite side, diverging from it, however, so as to enclose the enemy. Paddy shivered with dread when he saw the foremost of the men thus countermarching and closely surrounding the unconscious savages. It was a moment of painful suspense. Charles could distinctly hear poor Paddy's heart palpitating violently when they were midway on the huge trunk and the word to halt was whispered back along the line. A wolf had crept up to the smouldering fire and snatched a bone, with which it sprang away growling. Several of the Indians moved and uttered some words, but did not lift their heads, for they recognised the sound and were familiar with the prowling habits of the animal. It is probable the consciousness of the proximity of the wolf served to lull them; for it was not likely an enemy could be near when the ravenous beast was in their midst. None but Boone and Kenton could have approached so noiselessly; and the Indians did not suppose those renowned and dangerous foes were in the vicinity.

The slumberers being composed, the sign was made for the men to resume their cautious approach. But, when a single additional step had been taken, another pause was ordered. An owl flapped up from the feet of Boone, where he had been assailing the eyes of a deer's head thrown aside in the bushes. It was one of the largest specimens of those birds of ill omen; and it now hooted loudly, perched on a bough immediately over the prostrate Indians.

"Och, murther!" said Paddy.

Charles reached forward and placed his hand on Paddy's mouth.

Several of the Indians stirred again and uttered incoherent words. But the owl was a familiar bird, and, supposing he had been alarmed by the wolf, they slept again.

Boone and Kenton, having reached the designated point, only awaited the closing up of the rear of the line to begin the slaughter. Their guns were at their shoulders, their knives loosened in their sheaths, and each had selected his victim for the supposed indispensable sacrifice.

But when Will Van Wiggens, who, from his corpulency, was the heaviest man of the party, made his next step midway of the tree, the huge rotten trunk sank down suddenly, precipitating the men, with a thundering sound and a mighty splash, into the water and mud beneath!

So sudden, so unlooked-for, so ludicrous, was this event, that the men who aimed their rifles, standing within a few feet of the heads of the Indians, became irresistibly convulsed with laughter, and fired without effect. The Indians escaped without injury. They disappeared in the bushes, their ears assailed only by the sounds of immoderate laughter! But they fled away, leaving their guns behind, amazed at such ill-timed merriment, and believing themselves beset by evil spirits.

"Murther!" cried Paddy.

"Tam it!" shouted Van Wiggens, floundering in the quicksand. The wolf howled from the summit of a cliff. The owl was mute, his glaring eyeballs fixed in astonishment.

"Oh Lord! Don't sculp me! I'll surrinder!" continued Paddy, as Charles succeeded in dragging him out of the stream by the heels.

"Open your eyes," said Charles, inexpressibly diverted.

"I can't saa wid 'em! They're full of mud! Oh, don't hit me on the head, brave Misther savage! I've been adopted meself, and belong to a dacent family. Me mither is Diving Duck, and—is it you, Misther Charles?" said he, opening his eyes. "Upon me sowl, I thought I was draming! Ye see, I was shocked by the fall, and me sinses was wandering. Don't mind me hasty words, if ye plase, Misther Charles. And I hope we have put to rout the nasty blackguards. Have we kilt 'em all?"

"Not one remains to hurt you, Paddy," said Charles, who still heard the distant yells of the flying enemy.

"And have we kilt 'em all?"

"Tam dem! Not a single von!" said Van Wiggens, who had extricated himself and learned the result.

After the prolonged laughter had in some measure subsided, a search was made for canoes, and several were found tied in the mouth of the creek. These they took possession of, and, placing the arms of the Indians in them, left a guard to watch until all the baggage could be removed thither from the camp. The wind had ceased its violence, and, as the surface of the Ohio was as smooth as a mirror, they determined to cross over early in the morning.

They were met, however, on their return to the camp, by Skippie, who, in unusual excitement, briefly informed them that their pursuers were advancing, led by Girty, who had joined them after the ambuscade. He said they were within three or four hours march of them, approaching cautiously, and apparently resolved to make a desperate struggle before permitting the fugitives to escape with their horses.

"I'll have all the horses in Kentucky in less than an hour!" said Kenton.

"And I'll see that the people get over," said Boone. "We are safe now, my young friend," he continued, addressing Charles, "at least for some days to come."

"True, sir," said Charles, quickening his pace, and with difficulty keeping at the side of Boone, whose giant strides usually impelled him forward beyond his companions; "and I am extremely thankful for it."

Julia seemed pleased to learn that the enterprise against the Indian encampment had resulted without bloodshed, and the patriotic Baptist gave thanks for the easy victory, not doubting the hand of Providence had shaped the expedition and produced the bloodless end. The great trunk over which multitudes had been passing from time immemorial, and upon which numbers had stood that night, seemed to have fallen precisely at a juncture admirably adapted to facilitate the escape of the Indians. A little sooner or later, and human lives would have been sacrificed.

Such were the deductions of Mr. Jones and the maiden. But Hugh McSwine and Will Van Wiggens ascribed the escape of the savages to the devil, who had first assumed the form of a wolf and then an owl.

No time, however, was lost in such idle speculations. The maiden was soon mounted, and the whole party pushed on toward the river with all the expedition in their power. And when Julia reached the scene of the recent accident Kenton's voice was heard urging the horses into the stream. It was a frosty night, though calm, and the animals, plunging and snorting, evinced their reluctance to swimming. They were nevertheless constrained to submit, and were soon gliding toward the Kentucky shore.

Julia was placed in one of the canoes and rowed over by Charles. At every stroke of his oar the poor girl's spirits rose, and her eyes sparkled in unison with the glittering drops that fell from the oars in the moonlight.

They spoke of their friends and homes in New Jersey,— of Charles's Indian mother and sister, whom they loved and pitied, but did not regret being separated from them,— of the beautiful country and pleasant climate they were about to enter,—and of the means of returning thence to their Eastern abode. Not one word was uttered of their deep and ineradicable love. It was too sacred for words— too manifest to be questioned.

The horses were soon landed in safety. The event was announced by three loud huzzas from Kenton; and, striking a light, his locality was marked by a great bonfire on the southern shore.

McSwine and Van Wiggens were the last to embark; and after entering their canoe they lingered under the clustering boughs of the trees that hung over the water,— the one hoping to add another victim to his catalogue and the other watching for his dog. Nor did they wait very long before the pursuing party came in view upon their trail, and Hugh had the satisfaction of putting an end to the existence of another human being. The one he had killed came to the bank, after the discovery that the fugitives were beyond his reach, and gazed in disappointment at Kenton's great fire, in the broad glare of which the smoking horses were plainly visible. He stood within six paces of Hugh's muzzle, and fell, without a groan, into the deep water.

But the discharge of McSwine's rifle was followed by a rush in that direction, and the bloodthirsty Scot became aware of his danger. He could not now leave the sheltering willows without being seen and fired upon; nor could he remain long concealed from their view where he was. So he recharged his gun, and determined to have another victim before he fell, if such was to be his end. But the Indians, fearing an ambush, kept themselves hidden, in readiness, however, to fire upon any canoes that might push out from under the clustering willows.

"Dere he is!" said Van Wiggens, in a whisper, hearing a dog yelp. "Dat's Vatch! I know his cry. Let me out, and I'll vistle for him."

"What, mon!" said McSwine, "lose your life for a dog? I dinna' ken how much your life is worth, but I value mine at a price aboon that."

"Dere he is! It's Vatch!" continued Van Wiggens, hearing a dog whining distressfully on the bank, and afterward seeing him indistinctly through the intercepting boughs.

"It won't do, mon!" said Hugh; "we maun awa' from

this. They're cooming down the creek. Lift your gun and we'll fire thegether." They did so, and under cover of the smoke from their rifles, which descended upon the water, and during the momentary consternation produced among the Indians, (for two more of them had fallen, one mortally and the other severely wounded,) McSwine made several vigorous strokes of the oars, which caused the canoe to glide out rapidly from the shore. "Noo fa' doon on yer face, mon!" he continued, setting the example to his companion, and knowing that the impetus he had given the light bark would soon carry it beyond the reach of the enemy's balls. But, before attaining that distance, the yelling savages sent a leaden shower after it. The water was ripped up around them, and the frail canoe was perforated in several places, but its occupants fortunately escaped without serious injury. Van Wiggens was slightly scratched on the most prominent portion of his body, his corpulency preventing an entire concealment of it.

McSwine and Van Wiggens, upon landing, were much applauded. But, when conducted to the great fire, upon which an enormous quantity of wood and brush had been piled, as if an illumination had been the design, poor Van Wiggens's spirits sunk again upon hearing the melancholy howl of his dog on the opposite side of the Ohio. He ran to the water's edge and called to "Vatch" to swim over; but in vain, as the dog either would not, or was not permitted to obey him.

Then the ears of the whole party were saluted with a familiar sound. This was the deep intonation of Peter Shaver's ass. Upon scenting the blood, he brayed forth his sense of the horrid deed upon the solemn midnight air; and the melancholy reverberations rumbled from shore to shore up and down the river.

This was succeeded by nine lusty cheers from the whites, while the furious savages made the night more hideous with their demoniac yells. The river was some six hundred paces wide, and at that distance Kenton could easily make himself heard and understood. And so he not only boasted of the number of horses he had captured, but ostentatiously paraded them in view of their recent owners. (Nevertheless, some of them had been stolen from the whites in Pennsylvania by the Indians.) He not only exhibited the horses, but descanted on their superior qualities, and pointed at the deep shoulders, the broad forehead, and clean limbs, of the steed which had belonged to Ground-Hog, whom he said he would scalp the next time he fell into his hands. Then an impromptu dance of victory followed, in imitation of one of the exultant ceremonies of the Indians, at which Charles smiled but faintly, for he thought no good could result from thus wantonly exasperating the enemy.

And when it was over, Simon Girty, standing on the opposite shore near a fire he had kindled, and in the light of which, under the shadow of an overhanging tree, he could be recognised, said, in a loud voice, "War is now declared! There are not one hundred white men in Kentucky. We'll see you again; you steal horses, and huzza over it before the faces of their owners!"

"Shut up, you renegade traitor!" answered Kenton. "The blackest nigger is a gentleman at the side of Simon Girty! I'll change my name from Simon to Sam, and call my mangy old sheep-killing cur 'Simon'—Simon Girty!"

"Ah, Kenton," said Girty, "such is your gratitude! I saved your life, and thus you thank me. Very good! I will be the wiser next time!"

Kenton was silent for several minutes. It was known that Girty had truly interposed and saved him from being tortured at the stake.

"I don't deny it, Girty," said he; "and I thank you for it. But I have twice spared your life since then, when you were within reach of my rifle; and I am bound in honour never to kill you, if I can help it. But I owe you nothing. You lead the savages in their attacks, and they slaughter our women and children,—your own people, and perhaps your own kin. I must defend them, and if you should fall by my hand it will be no fault of mine. Kentucky is my home, and it shall be my grave,* before I leave it at the bidding of you and your baby-murdering savages."

Kenton said no more, but sought the repose so much needed after the exciting scenes he had passed through.

Nevertheless, the eyelids of Charles and Julia were not oppressed by slumber. They eagerly broke open the let-

---

* Kenton, we believe, died in Ohio but a few years since.

ters from home brought by Skippie. The first one perused was from Mr. Schooley. It ran as follows:—"Esteemed Julia:—If this should reach thy hands, thee will be informed that thy guardian and friends have been sorely grieved at thy capture and at the supposed privations thou hast been exposed to in the wilderness; and thou wilt learn that it is not credited by thy guardian and others that the Indians were the authors of thy abduction; but we think it was the work of thy pretended friend, the rebel——"

"That must be me," said Charles.

"How could he be so much deceived?" said Julia, a flush of deep indignation overspreading her forehead.

"He is not deceived, Julia," replied Charles.

"What?"

"He is well convinced I had no agency in it."

"He certainly would be, if he knew all. But what does he say further? Yes," she continued, reading:—"Rebel, Charles Cameron. But I have sent £100 to Governor Hamilton for thy redemption. And if thee will say so to any of the Seneca or Mohawk chiefs, they will conduct thee to Canada, where thou wilt be ransomed; and I have requested them to send thee by a safe guard to New York, which thee should be rejoiced to learn is now held by the army of George, our liege lord and sovereign; and from thence thou wilt be permitted to pass with a flag through the rebel army to thy home, where thou wilt be received with affection. The £100 was truly thy money, upon which thou wert entitled to interest, and which, with other matters of business, we will adjust when thou returnest hither. Mary sends her loving greeting to thee; and she sends thee divers articles of apparel which thee will probably stand in need of. And now I will repeat to thee the great danger thou wilt incur by retaining thy partiality for the rebel youth. The British army is soon to possess all of New Cæsarea, (New Jersey,) New York, and Philadelphia; and thee must be aware that when the rebellion is put down its adherents will be subjected to forfeitures and other pains and penalties. So, if thee should commit thyself with the young man, it will be out of my power to serve thee. The whole of the fine estate left by thy father will be lost, and thou wilt be a beggar, mourning over the execution of thy unworthy lover."

"I shall read no further!" cried Julia, throwing the letter into the fire. Then, tearing open another, she read as follows:—"Esteemed Julia, I pine for thy return. I would have followed thee, and remonstrated with thy abductors, but it was necessary to secure the harvest which is to supply us with bread."

"Richard loves good eating as well as his sweetheart," said Charles.

"Oh, better!" said Julia. "And thou knowest, besides," she continued, reading, "it hath been decreed in the rebel legislature that all those who abandon their lands shall not possess them again. I would take no part in the awful conflict. I am a loyal subject; but I would not fly from my home. I am a non-combatant, and cannot abandon our society in conscience or for interest. I hope thee will return and attend the meetings. If thou wilt, I will agree to have our nuptials published——"

"That will do!" said Julia, laughing heartily, and likewise consigning the epistle to the flames.

Charles then read a brief letter from his father, charging him to take care of himself and to remain true to the cause of the tyrant's enemies. He said it was probable the armies and fleets of the usurper would seem to prevail at the commencement of the conflict, but that the cause of justice would triumph in the end. France was secretly favouring the Revolution, and would, before its termination, become an open ally of America. He charged his son to suffer no uneasiness on his account. There were men anxious to effect his capture, set on, he believed, by Mr. Schooley, for he was in correspondence with the British, and had already caused some beeves to be driven to them on Staten Island: but they would not succeed. His few Scots remaining with him were vigilant, and his little fortress impregnable. Besides, it was believed by many, since he escaped burning, that he bore a charmed life. His health was good, and his hours were pleasantly passed over the pages of Shakspeare and the productions of other sons of genius. Commanding him sacredly to guard the captive maiden from every harm, he concluded by imploring his Maker to spare his son for the comfort of his declining years.

Charles then, his eyes suffused with tears and his bosom

swelling with reverence and affection for his parent, would have prevailed on Julia to seek the refreshing repose he fancied she stood very much in need of. But he knew not the extent of the capacity of the sex for prolonged watching, and she merely smiled at his solicitude and declared that no slumber would visit her eyes if she were to lie down; but she would be silent while he slept, and guard his peaceful repose. This he objected to, and begged her to read the remaining letter,—an epistle from Kate Livingston, marked "Liberty Hall, near Elizabethtown Point." It began thus:—
"Oh, my dear Julia! I have just learned, by a letter from Mr. Cameron, brought to my father by the dumb but faithful Skippie, that you have been seized by the Indians and carried a captive into the wilderness! But the letter says a great Indian-fighter, named Hugh McSwine, and a band of Scots, are in pursuit, and will certainly overtake your captors. This is startling intelligence, indeed, and distressing, though relieved somewhat by the comfortable assurance—which is sanctioned by the prophetic looks and decisive gestures of Skippie—that you will soon be restored to your friends. And Skippie, in two words, has told me to write this letter, making me understand, I scarcely know how, that it will certainly be delivered into your hands. He sets out on his return in the morning, and I am resolved to write all night!"

"Do you hear that, Charles?" said Julia.

"Yes. Noble, generous Kate! Read on, Julia, and I will replenish the fire. She employed a whole night in its composition, and it should be read at such a time as this, in the profound depths of the forest."

"In the first place, then, dearest Julia," continued the letter, "let me beseech thee to be cheerful, and hope for a speedy deliverance, if thou art not already delivered whilst thy sweet eyes are tracing these scarcely-legible lines, blotted by my tears!"

"And she bids me be cheerful!" said Julia.

"Glorious Kate! Read on," said Charles.

"But, Julia,"—thus the letter ran,—"I, too, need the kind sympathy of friends. The British general has offered a large reward for the capture of my father, and it is said that assassins have been engaged to take his life! Several times we have been forced to fly, upon the landing of nocturnal expeditions. And it is averred the Quakers do not hesitate to sell them cattle, and deny having such property when applied to by the Americans, who are without gold."

"Once the enemy surrounded our house, calling upon the governor to surrender. Fortunately, my father was away. Yet they searched the house, but offered me no indignity; for they were accompanied by a gentlemanly young ensign, who pledged his word I should sustain no injury. Finding my father had escaped, they resolved to seize his papers, as he was known to be in correspondence with Washington. And, truly, many letters from Washington, and details of future plans deeply affecting the cause, as well as several secret resolutions of Congress, were at that moment in the house! But your wild Kate's wit did not forsake her. The papers were locked in the gig-box, then lying in the hall. The box was seized, and the point of a bayonet inserted in the lock, when I rushed forward, and—and what do you suppose? Oh, Julia, I told a deliberate falsehood, for which I can be forgiven. I declared the box contained portions of my private wardrobe, and appealed to the gallantry of the young officer to protect them from exposure; and if he would do so I promised to show them where my father's papers were kept. He placed a guard over the box and followed me into the library, where he seized the old musty law-papers, which I have often heard my father declare no mortal could ever unravel. He did not pause to examine the pleas, affidavits, declarations, (which, you have heard, are sometimes false and worthless,) but hastened away with his treasure to the barge, as if in fear of being intercepted. He bade me a very polite adieu, however, and hoped we should meet again. And I hope so, truly, after we shall have gained the victory; for I would thank him for his courtesy. A few hours after this happened, my father returned, and, upon learning what had taken place, he embraced your lying Kate and uttered some of his drollest flatteries

"Oh, Julia, I have seen General Washington! He dined at the Hall one day; and, although almost every one thinks his chances desperate, he seems cheerful. He is certainly the most amiable and unoffending man I ever saw. How he can be a general and kill his enemies is beyond my comprehension. He is good-looking too,—tall, straight, and his cheeks tinged with the healthful red. It has been maliciously hinted that his colour comes from the bottle, but, I dare say, without foundation. He has never indulged immoderately, and no one ever heard of his being intoxicated.

"And General Wayne was with him. He, you know, is called the 'Little Mad Anthony,' and swears like a trooper, sometimes. But his whole conversation was on religion; and, next to their pay and their rum, he said the soldiers required good chaplains. And then he told many anecdotes of the Rev. David Jones, a Baptist preacher, now among the Indians, whom he is extremely anxious to have with him. If you meet with this Mr. Jones, tell him his presence is desired in the camp of 'Mad Anthony.'

"What shall I do? I did intend to fly to you at the Jenny Jump, and live in Hope.* But, since you have been abducted, it cannot be a place of security. However, I presume the handsome Anglo-Indian chief is near you, which may serve to keep your spirits out of the depths of despair. I suppose I must remain where I am—between two armies, or, at least, subject to the visits of both. I would be happy if you were with me; and my father charges me to send you a special invitation to make our house your permanent abode when you return from your delightful tour in the wilderness. Keep a diary, Julia."

After filling several pages with the domestic affairs of the family, interesting only to Julia, Kate concluded abruptly, saying:—"The day is dawning, and we hear cannon at the Point. The people are running in every direction. I see old Molly Ketchup driving her cow past the orchard toward the woods. She limps, but does not appear to lag. What can the matter be? I've learned it! The British are landing! Lord Cornwallis is coming at the head of some 12,000 men. Pa has been in, and informed me that I must be prepared to leave in fifteen minutes. Farewell, Julia! There! A cannon-ball has knocked down one of the chimneys. God bless us! KATE.

"P. S.—I am now at a cabin in the hills, and Skippie will wait for me to add a few lines. They did not burn the Hall, as we supposed they would; and, as we are in sight of it, we begin to hope our eyes may not be shocked

---

* Hope is the name of a village near the Jenny Jump Mountain.

by smoke and flames issuing from the darling old homestead. I am sure that either General Howe or Lord Cornwallis must be occupying it. Just to think of such a thing:—eating at our table and sleeping in our beds, while we are fugitives, depending on the charity of Molly Ketchup's cow! But we are cheerful; and pa says the American army—rabble I call it, just now—is marching hitherward, and will interpose between us and the enemy. . . . . Did you know that they have bestowed on father the nickname of Flintface? He is called by that title all over the Colony, because, in his last message to the Legislature, he said, 'We must set our faces like flint against dissoluteness and corruption.' . . . . Another commotion! A foraging-party of the enemy! Oh, what screams at the hut in the valley! It is poor Molly Ketchup. They are driving away her cow! Adieu. KATE."

When Julia ceased reading, the dawn was apparent in the east. Charles heaped fresh wood on the fire, and prevailed on her to sleep until the breakfast should be prepared. He knew that the meat for her repast was then living and would have to be found and killed; so she would, in all probability, have ample time for refreshing slumber. He likewise sought repose himself at the side of the deeply-breathing Mr. Jones, who sometimes uttered prayers in his sleep, but more frequently sang snatches of the Psalms of David.

It was a calm, frosty morning, rosy with the deep red rays of an autumnal sun in what is termed the Indian summer. Boone and Kenton rose perfectly refreshed.

"I don't know how you feel, Mr. Boone," said Kenton, stretching back his broad shoulders, "but I am comfortable. I can breathe freely on the glorious soil of Kentucky; and the climate is a thousand times better than it is over the river yonder."

"The soil and climate are well enough, Simon," said Boone, sighing, "and there's plenty of game. But it makes me unhappy to see so many people coming to cut the trees and shoot the buffalo and deer. If you and I could only live here alone, I wouldn't ask a better paradise. No matter! When neighbours get too thick, Daniel Boone can go farther west."

"I like having enough neighbours to keep back the Indians and to sell horses to," said Kenton. They then disappeared in the cane-brake in quest of game for breakfast, and, before many minutes had elapsed, the sharp reports of their rifles were heard.

CHAPTER XV.

A "BAVER"—PADDY SHOT—A RATTLESNAKE—THE BLUE LICKS—SHOOTING BUFFALO—BOONE'S STATION—THE INDIAN KING'S OFFER DECLINED.

'It's a baver!" said Paddy, in reply to Van Wiggens, who, upon awaking from his troubled slumber, and hearing the report of a gun on the river-bank, had walked in that direction. Paddy, as he answered, was endeavouring to take a steady aim at the "varmint," which, most singularly for a beaver, did not sink beneath the surface, but persisted in its efforts to ascend the low embankment.

"Let me see!" said Van Wiggens, cocking his gun and peeping over. "Tam your Irish eyes!" he cried, a moment after; "if you shoot him I'll kill you! He's a dousand dimes better as you!"

"What! Isn't it a baver?" asked Paddy, upon hearing a low whine.

"Baver, de teiffel! It's my Vatch!" cried Van Wiggens, dropping his rifle and sliding down into the water, unmindful of the chilling bath, and hugging the poor shivering animal in his arms. "Poor Vatch!" he exclaimed, in broken tones of pity and affection; "you've been swimming all night to reach your master, who has nobody else to love since Mrs. Wan Viggens sold herself to der teiffel. And de savages nearly starved you, Vatch! See how little your pelly is! And de tammed fool Irishman," he continued, in tears, "has been shooting at you for a *baver*, as he calls it. Come, Vatch! you shall have blenty of my breakfast before te hot fire." Still holding the grateful dog in his arms, Van Wiggens ascended the embankment and strode toward the fire, while Paddy sat down on a log and gazed after him.

Paddy continued to sit there, enjoying the fumes of the broiling venison, and gradually yielding to the exhilarating influences of such a lovely morning in so genial a climate, when, lifting his head, he saw the smoke of a gun just discharged on the opposite side of the river

"What are the blackguards afther now?" said he, soliloquizing, as he beheld a dozen savages on the bank gazing at him. A moment after, and simultaneously with the report, a leaden ball struck the log on which he sat and just between his knees. He was not at first aware of the nature of the messenger, although he felt a stinging sensation from the particles of lead radiating on the hard surface of the wood. He gazed a moment at the blue spot between his legs, and, becoming conscious of having been made the target of the marksman across the river, fell down suddenly, and screamed "Murther!" so loudly and repeatedly that many of the men came running in that direction.

The Indians witnessing this scene yelled with delight, not doubting that one of their foes had fallen.

"Take care!" said Boone, standing over Paddy with an upraised club. "If you stir hand or foot, you'll be bitten!" And the next moment the club descended, and crushed an enormous rattlesnake within a few inches of Paddy's head.

"Murther! murther! murther!" cried Paddy, rolling away with great power and velocity.

"Stand up, mon! Ye're not dead yet, and ye were not born to be shot, droowned, or poisoned," said Hugh McSwine.

"Och, Mr. Bone," cried Paddy, "I thought these ugly bastes went into their howls when the frosts came!"

"So they do," said Boone. "This fellow was going to the cliff yonder, but stopped to sun himself on the warm side of the log."

"And sure I was doing that same thing meself! But it wasn't the baste that made me cry out."

"Why should you holler murder for a snake?" said Kenton. "Why not kill 'em and be done with it?"

"Och, it was the bullet!"

"Bullet?" repeated several.

"Yes, I'm shat! The baste made me forget it! Yes, I'm shat! See here!" and, unwrapping his leggins, Paddy exhibited several slight punctures and bruises. He then pointed to the blue marks on the log, and described the attitude in which he had been sitting.

The whole party, who had heard the rifle, laughed heartily at Paddy's expense.

"That was close grazing," said Kenton, "and it would have given a black eye. He must have aimed at the tops of the trees."

This incident over, the party, after a hearty repast, set out in the direction of Boone's station. They followed a broad buffalo-trail which led to the mineral springs afterward known as the Blue Licks.

The climate seemed to have a most extraordinary effect upon the spirits of all. Kenton was continually leaping up, hallooing, and letting off some hunter's joke that produced laughter. Boone's eyes had a bright, merry look. Several of the prisoners who had been captured in Kentucky, and among them a hale, hearty fellow named Chapman, had a propensity for crowing.

"Foo! Vat's dat schmells so?" exclaimed Van Wiggens, who rode a short distance in advance.

"The mineral springs," said Charles. "Our horses have been for some time pricking forward their ears and snuffing the breeze. And will we not find buffalo there?" he continued, addressing Boone.

"Certainly: Don't you see the fresh sign? And we must kill a supply for the winter."

A profound silence ensued as they proceeded, and all gazed in admiration at the most lovely country they had ever beheld. The climate was truly delightful, the soil fertile, and the surface pleasantly diversified with hill and valley, woodland and prairie. It teemed with game of every description; and hardly a minute passed that some one of the party did not behold buffalo, elk, bear, or deer.

Kenton led a number of men in advance of the rest to the Licks, and soon their guns were heard dealing death among the buffalo. Those huge animals had collected that autumn in vast multitudes. They had gone thither from all the adjacent countries for hundreds of miles round, meeting as if by concert at a common rendezvous; and it was feared they would soon be followed by the Indians, their natural proprietors. Therefore, Boone advised a speedy departure from the vicinity. A few hours would suffice for the slaughter of buffalo.

Boone remained with Charles and Julia, having no disposition to partake of the sport. His thoughts dwelt upon his family, who had been left at the settlement on the Kentucky River, and from whom he had been separated many months. He would soon see them if they still remained at the station. But who could tell, in a time of such vicissitudes, what might have happened?

"Mr. Bone! Mr. Bone!" cried Paddy, who, with the rest, drew rein and listened to a strange rumbling sound which appeared to shake the very earth, "what is that? Is it a harrycane?"

"Follow me!" cried Boone, with an excited countenance. And they had no sooner paused under the boughs of a dense grove of giant sugar-maples, several hundred paces west of the great trail, than an immense drove of the wild cattle came rushing past. It was a torrent which would have swept through an opposing army.

"Merciful heaven!" cried Julia, as the astounding apparition swept by.

"There is no danger here," said Charles, breathing freely. "Mr. Boone has saved us."

"And ye're quite sure we're saved?" asked Paddy. "Then, be the powers, I'll have a crack at 'em!" And, after a hasty aim, he fired at the moving mass of animals, the nearest of them being only some fifty paces distant. "Howly Vargin!" he cried, "I've kelt a dazen at layst. Saa how they tumble over!" He had, indeed, by a lucky shot, brought one of them down, and many of the rest fell over him. Several, untouched by Paddy's lead, were trampled under-foot and never rose again. And when the thundering mass had vanished, it was with great exultation that Paddy claimed them all as the extraordinary product of his fire.

Resuming the broad buffalo-trail, the travellers approached the Licks. In the immediate vicinity of the springs the earth seemed to have been scooped out or trodden down many feet in depth, for hundreds of paces in circumference; and this had been done by the animals resorting thither for ages.

The hunters had already collected a vast number of

tongues, and these, with the best of the skins, made quite as heavy a burden as the horses could bear.

About the middle of the afternoon of the second day after crossing the Ohio, the party paused on the summit of a high cliff on the northern bank of the Kentucky River. With a palpitating heart, Boone gazed in silence at the narrow tract of bottom-land on the opposite shore. Then, seeing the smoke curling up from the cabins, his face beaming with delight, and every nerve quivering with pleasurable excitement, he uttered a loud, clear halloo upon the still air, which was borne over the surface of the bright water. After a brief pause it was answered from the other side by a voice Boone seemed to recognise; and this was succeeded by a dozen others. Though long given up as dead, Boone's halloo was known. Whoops and cheers were soon uttered in quick succession, and the people were seen running about in great commotion.

"Thank heaven, I see women and children!" said Julia.

"But not mine! not mine!" said Boone, straining his eyes, with his hands on his forehead. "I see my brother, two sons, but no wife, no daughter! Gone! They would have known my voice better than the rest. Not there! no, they are not there!"

"You should not suppose they have fallen into the hands of the enemy," said Julia, witnessing his emotion with concern, "since the rest seem to have escaped."

"No," said he, recovering his self-possession, "I have no fear of that. I know what has happened. They supposed me dead, and returned to North Carolina. No matter. They have not taken the fort and the country with them, and I can bring them back."

Kenton, having assembled the horses and men in full view of the little settlement, gave a signal, and the air was rent with cheers. The people on the opposite side of the river seemed almost wild with joy, and sent over all the canoes they could command; and our party, following the winding path down to the water's edge, were met and rapturously greeted by the FIRST SETTLERS OF KENTUCKY. And it may be said that the example of extending a hearty welcome to a returning friend or a wandering stranger, practised by those adventurous pioneers, has never since been forgotten by their noble and generous descendants.

Julia and Charles, and all the weary fugitives, were now in a place of comparative security. Mr. Jones preached that night to a congregation of not less than sixty men, women, and children.

Among the women in the fort, or settlement,— for it hardly deserved the name of the former,— were Mrs. McGary, Mrs. Logan, Mrs. Todd, Mrs. Miller, Mrs. Hogan, Mrs. Harrod, Mrs. Bryant, Mrs. Trigg, Mrs. Bulger, Mrs. Harland, Mrs. Harrison, Mrs. Calloway, and others, from whom have descended some of the best specimens of humanity, whether in the field or in the forum, that have illustrated our history. Their husbands were absent building small forts or block-houses—called stations—in other portions of the country.

Nor was Boone quite correct in his conjecture. His wife, it was true, with some of the younger children, had returned to North Carolina. His favourite daughter remained, and had been prevented from coming forth on hearing his voice by an attack of the ague,—a disease which had periodically assailed her before leaving Carolina. But she was quite well the next day, and succeeded in cheering the heart of her affectionate father.

Skippie's bundle was now opened, and Julia overwhelmed him with thanks for the timely addition to her wardrobe.

The men made but little change in their dress, as all the hardy pioneers were habited in buckskin hunting-shirts; and, with the exception of their faces, which they washed occasionally, their resemblance to the Indians was not very remote. They wore moccasins, leggins, and, in cold weather, blankets, and each had his rifle, tomahawk, and knife. With the latter they carved their meat or scalped an enemy as occasion required.

After sojourning in the fort some days in perfect repose, those who had no intention of becoming citizens of the country began to make preparations for returning to their distant homes. But these preliminaries were cut short by the arrival of a prisoner who had escaped from the Indians, and who stated that the enemy were organizing an army for the purpose of exterminating the white intruders in

Kentucky, and that their arrival might be looked for in a few days.

This, according to Paddy's idea, which he strove in vain to impress upon others, was a conclusive reason why they should hasten to depart.

The fort was immediately repaired. It consisted merely of a quadrangular structure of some forty connecting log-cabins, the doors opening on the square within. The hardy pioneers relied more upon their own bravery and skill with the rifle for security than upon the usual artificial or scientific defences of civilized warfare.

At night, when they supposed the Indians were lurking in the vicinity, the cattle were driven within the enclosure, the gates fastened, and one or two sentinels placed on duty. And such was the reliance on the prowess of their defenders that some of the aged females, on one or two occasions, declined rising from their couches during a night attack, wherein the enemy quadrupled the little garrison in numerical force.

On the present occasion, when the history of Charles and Julia became known, and the sanguinary adventures of Hugh McSwine were related and the horse-stealing feats of Simon Kenton duly confessed, a belief prevailed that a more determined and desperate attempt to destroy the settlements would be made than any hitherto experienced; and preparations were made accordingly. Every man had a duty to perform, and Paddy was made to understand that any proposition to diminish the strength of the garrison at such a moment would be a pusillanimity deserving of summary punishment.

And during this period of apprehension and suspense the Rev. Mr. Jones reaped his harvest of souls. He preached and prayed with great effect. No less than five women and three men were plunged by him beneath the pellucid waters of the Kentucky River.

But still the savages delayed the assault, and, as the frosts were crisping the leaves, it was hoped the invasion would be postponed until the ensuing year, when the influx of emigrants would furnish men enough to meet the enemy in the field. Under this supposition some of the people grew incautious; and among them were Boone's daughter Mary, Miss Calloway, and Julia, who, becoming intimate associates as soon as they met, were afterward inseparable companions. They explored every hill and valley in the neighbourhood. They called the saucy squirrels that gazed at them from the low boughs their bonnies, and clapped their hands as the startled buck sprang up before them in the tangled brake. They gathered the wild plum, the haw, the persimmon, and the papaw. And at dusky eve, when the men ceased to garner the corn, and, guided by the sound of their bells, sought the cows and horses among the cane and drove them within the enclosure of the fort, the three girls loved to linger, striving, but in vain, to find the mysterious whippoorwill that filled the valley with its wailing.

And at night, when the weary labourer, his hunger satisfied, was steeped in profound slumber, the old women, not requiring recuperative repose, usually sat till a late hour before the broad hearths, the glowing embers of which illuminated the recesses of the quiet cabins. Then it was that Julia listened to the many thrilling narratives of "hair-breadth escapes" from the savages and fearful encounters with wild beasts and enormous serpents. Such was the staple material of the fireside conversation in the new settlements. And, although many a truthful tale thus narrated harrowed the feelings of the auditor, yet there was a fascination in the recital, a romance in the simple loves and distresses, which caused the most timid maiden still to linger and listen. And their dreams reproduced the most terrible scenes, to be followed, too often, alas, by the reality of suffering and death!

One evening, just at the first glimmer of twilight, when the owl came flapping down from the hills and the whippoorwill was uttering its first lamentation, the three girls were still lingering on the margin of the river.

"Come, Mary," said Sue Calloway, "don't you hear the bells? They are driving in the cows and horses, and will soon be looking for us."

"Don't fear it, Sue," said the daughter of Boone; "they will not miss us—I mean you and I. Julia, though, is always looked for and watched over by the handsome bird of prey."

"Bird of prey?" continued Sue, seeing Julia plunged in one of her spells of musing abstraction.

"Yes; don't you remember father says they called him White Eagle?"

"Oh, yes! I forgot. And we poor neglected creatures may wail with the whippoorwill," she added, with a sigh.

"Simon Kenton," whispered Mary, while the other blushed and turned aside her face, "says he loves the song of the dusky bird, and knows where it perches when singing."

"Eagle!" said Julia, roused suddenly from her reverie. "Did you not say something about the eagle?"

"Yes,—a *white* eagle," replied Mary.

"You mean Charles. You need not smile. You cannot annoy me by alluding to him."

"We would not annoy you if we could," said Mary. "We merely desired to rouse you. You seemed unconscious of the lateness of the hour."

"But see!" exclaimed Julia; "the hills opposite are tinged with the silver light of the moon before we can behold the disk of the orb. You know we cannot see it rise from the fort. Go in, if you will not stay with me, and I will follow presently."

The girls did as she requested, and left her standing under a hawthorn-tree. They had become accustomed to Julia's little eccentricities, which they attributed solely to the delightful influence of love.

Julia awaited the rising of the moon, which seemed to beam on her pale forehead as a light from her distant home; and she smiled as she gazed at the joyful messenger from the East. Then turning into the little path leading through the clustering vines and bushes toward the gate of the fort, she was startled by the rustling of dry leaves in her immediate vicinity, and paused to listen. To her dismay and horror, a tall Indian, of herculean frame, arose and stood before her. She did not cry out, but her heart throbbed audibly.

"Fear not. I am a friend," said the Indian, in very good English.

"Who are you? What do you want?" asked the trembling girl, quickly, and glancing hastily round, as if in quest of some avenue of escape. But there was none.

"I am one who will do you no ill. I want a few brief

words with you, and then you may go to your friends. You have heard the White Eagle say his brother Thayendanegea was incapable of lying. I am Thayendanegea."

Julia breathed more freely. She was aware that the savages often professed friendship when they meant harm; but it was not so with the great sachem of the Six Nations.

"Speak on; I am listening," said she.

"First," said the chief, making a stride toward the shrinking girl, and gently taking her unresisting hand, "promise that you will not make known my presence in this vicinity. On that condition you have my word that you shall return to your friends unharmed by me—if you desire it."

"If I desire it? But I promise. Now be quick!" said she.

"Yes, if you desire it. I am now a king. If you will go with me,—voluntarily, I mean,—you shall be my bride, my queen, and I will love you during the whole of my life. My sister loves the young companion of her infancy, and mourns over his desertion. Let him marry her. We will seek a retreat where the white man cannot come, and be happy. The tomahawk shall be buried. We will live in peace. Thousands of innocent lives will be spared. The Great Spirit you worship will smile on you——"

"Impossible!" said Julia, in tears.

"It is the last offer!" continued Brandt. "Another moon, and it will be too late. The tribes of every nation are rousing, and, when the hatchet is sharpened and the war-paths are trodden, neither orators nor sachems will be able to withhold the sinewy arms of the warriors. The Mohawks love their white brother, and their king loves the white maiden. Speak! But think of the benefits you may confer or the sufferings entail on your fellow-creatures."

"Oh, Brandt, it is impossible!"

"Go, then!"

"Oh, tell me," she said, pausing in her flight, "where your sister is, and if she reproaches us."

"She complains not — reproaches not — but loves on. She would die, if she were not a Christian and did not fear to offend her God."

"Bless her! Oh, Thayendanegea, tell her I love her dearly! But say her sister fears her, too — or else she would have her always near——"

"Brandt would slay her first! Say no more! Farewell. Breathe to no one what has passed this night. And yet, Julia," he continued, in faltering and softened tones, "you may reveal it to Charles, if he will promise not to seek me during the next twelve hours, in the event of rejecting my offer."

And before the girl could reply the chief had vanished; and, when she turned her face again in the direction of the fort, she saw Mary and Sue approaching with hurried steps.

"The moon is half an hour high," said Mary, "and yet you tarry."

"I've heard of people being moonstruck," said Sue. And then, seeing Julia pale and distressed, she took her hand tenderly and asked her forgiveness.

"There is nothing to forgive, Sue," said Julia, returning the caress. "You did not mean to offend me. That is sufficient."

"But why are you so cold and pale?" asked Mary.

"Am I?" was all the response Julia vouchsafed.

"Yes, truly. And I am sure you have seen something which has terrified you."

"Seen something?"

"A ghost, perhaps," said Sue. "It was not an Indian, or she would not have remained here alone; nor a lover, for he is in the fort seeking her."

A sad smile was all this sally produced. And then they entered the gate.

"You have been weeping," said Charles, late in the evening, observing Julia's abstraction while the rest were singing merry songs.

"And for what, pray?" replied she, with a faint smile.

"I know not, unless it be to return. But why should you seek to hide your grief? That is the mystery."

"It is a mystery and a secret," said the girl, her face assuming a deathlike paleness, "which I cannot reveal until you have first promised not to betray it to others."

"I cannot conceive the necessity. But I promise."

Then she related in a low tone what she had seen and listened to. Charles became very pale, and long remained silent.

"And you told him it was impossible?"

"Can you doubt it?"

"Certainly not, when you say so."

"I have said so. What else could I tell him? Why should he presume to make such an offer?"

"True. And he is ambitious. He could never love thee as I do. Pardon me. My mind reverted to the instances in ancient history of persons sacrificing themselves for their country—suffering death to save the lives of others. And Brandt has heard of them, and would be famous. But he is incapable of loving, and could make no one happy."

"Would the result be as he promised? Would peace ensue?"

"No! He is mistaken. He could not restrain them. He might detach some of the warriors from this section by leading them against others. But I doubt even that. The Shawnees of Chillicothe and the Wyandots on the Miami have sworn to drive the white people out of Kentucky. It would be a bootless sacrifice. You would be miserable, and I could never love the Brown Thrush but as a poor, simple, wild-wood sister."

"Nay, do not fear *I* shall become an advocate of the arrangement," said she. "The experience of poor Van Wiggens would alone deter me. But here is Skippie, who has been invisible for several days."

"Skippie," said Charles, gazing at the imperturbable features of the mysterious messenger, "how did you get in?"

"Over!" said he, his gestures indicating that he had entered over the roof without being seen by the sentinels.

"Well?"

"Going," said he, pointing eastward.

"When?"

"Morning."

"He will take any letters we may write, Julia," said Charles.

Skippie nodded assent.

"Then, like Kate, I will write all night," said Julia "Oh, I will freeze her blood with an account of the interview I have just had with the terrible Brandt!"

"You may injure your health, or at least your eyes, Julia, by writing so much. Permit me to work for you.

I will be your secretary. My letters can be despatched in an hour."

"Indeed! I will do my own writing. What! permit you to see my letters? You are very, very kind, sir! Where is Skippie? Gone! No matter. But in truth, Charles, I will not injure my eyes. My journal has been copied in anticipation of some such announcement from the faithful Skippie. And you know it is to be enveloped and sealed by Kate, and opened at some distant day when we shall not be living to blush at our silly confessions. I shall have plenty of time."

Charles returned to his room to prepare his letters, and Julia likewise hastened to perform her task. And it may be remarked that, as our narrative is partly founded on these documents, they were faithfully delivered by Skippie.

CHAPTER XVI.

HORSE-HUNTING ADVENTURE — KENTON AND PADDY — GROUND-HOG KILLED — THE GIRLS CAPTURED — THE PURSUIT — PETER AND HIS ASS — THE BATTLE, AND RECOVERY OF THE GIRLS.

AFTER the appearance of Brandt, Charles, accompanied by such of his party as were disposed to go with him, made several excursions round the fort, always ending at the river. But no traces of Indians were discovered, and he concluded his forest brother must have come alone, crossing and recrossing the river at the fort.

After this the vigilance of the people relaxed again, and the girls resumed their twilight rambles, forgetting that, although no savages might be within sixty miles of them at one noon, numbers could arrive before the next.

"Come, Paddy," said Simon Kenton, about this time, "let's go and see after the horses." It had been their custom to count them three times every day, and to collect the stragglers.

"'Faith, and I don't see the use of it," said the reluctant Paddy, who, although accustomed to taking care of horses in comfortable stables, never approached them in the cane without fear and trembling.

"The use of it? Don't we find some of them fast in the vines almost every day? There are no Indians about; but still they require looking after. I will go alone, if you prefer working in the field gathering corn."

But Paddy did not prefer any such labour, knowing that, if he should be suddenly assailed by the Indians while working in the field, he would be quite as liable to injury as when among the horses with a gun in his hand.

So the two sallied forth, and were soon counting the horses, which crowded around them for their accustomed salt.

"Hello!" cried Kenton, gazing about wildly, "where's Dan?" This was the name of his favourite steed.

"Sure enough, where is he?" said Paddy. "And I'd like ye to tell me who's here to answer a question the likes o' that? The dumb brutes can't talk in our language, and Paddy knows jist about as much as yerself, Mr. Kenton."

"All the rest are here," continued Kenton. "It's strange! Dan is generally the first to lick my hand."

"And who knows if a painter hasn't caught him? They say thim carniferous varmints always choose the best. If there's a tinder woman about, they'll niver gnaw the bones of a man. And it's dacent in 'em to spare us who are bound to go out in the wild woods and cane-brakes. And what is it ye're listening to, Misther Kenton?"

Simon had stepped apart and stooped down in a listening attitude.

"All right, Paddy!" said he, rising erect again, the dark cloud gone from his brow. "I hear Dan's bell. But it's a long ways off, down the river."

"And is he not a sinsible horse? He's promenading betwixt the stations, guarding and protecting the forts. He's a jewel of a baste, and good for his weight in goold. If we stay here a while he'll come to us, and so we naadn't budge afther him."

But this mode of reasoning did not satisfy Kenton. He insisted that something very unusual had caused the separation of his best and gentlest animal from the rest. Indeed, the whole drove were in the habit of following Dan's bell, and he must hasten to see what had happened. In reply to Paddy's objections to going with him, he merely said if any Indians were prowling about the greatest danger would be in the immediate vicinity of the fort. And, if Paddy's argument failed to convince Kenton, Kenton's hint was not thrown away on Paddy, and so they set out together down the river.

Their progress at first was very slow, as they traversed a dense cane-brake; and when they emerged from this they encountered tangled blackberry-bushes, often covered with grape-vines.

"Och, but I'm torn all to paices, Misther Kenton!" said Paddy. "Stop, if ye plase, till I cut meself loose."

"Tear through 'em, Paddy, as I do," said Kenton; "your buckskin shirt and leggins can stand it."

"If the skane of the dead buck can stand it, Misther Kenton," said Paddy, "divil the bit can the skin of a live Paddy! Me hands and face are full of prackles, and the blood of a thrue son of Erin is flowing in this nasty wildherness."

"Hush, Paddy!" said Kenton, again placing his ear near the ground. "I've lost the bell!"

"And what betther could ye expict in sich a place as this? And if you iver find it agin it'll not be worth the stooping for."

"There it is!" cried Kenton, smiling. "I hear it now. But we must get out of this. It is over yonder in the woods. Dan must have moved since we started."

"I'm much obleeged till him. And sure he's a sinsible horse to lade us out of these purgatorious brambles. But, upon me sowl, I haven't yit heard the first tankle of his bell!"

"You have not lived in the forest, Paddy," said Kenton, leading the way into the tall sumachs, where their progress would be less obstructed.

"That is thrue," said Paddy; "houses were made for men to live in, the wild woods for wild animals and blackguard savages. Yit, Misther Kenton, I have as many ears and as good ones as any person, and now I hear Dan's bell. I did not listen afore."

"We are getting nigher to him. But what the d——l

did he straggle out here for? And why didn't the rest go with him?"

"Will ye tell me one thing, Misther Kenton?"

"May-be so."

"Wasn't it wrong in him to come out?"

"Yes, hang me if it wasn't!"

"Hang me, then, if it wasn't right in the others not to go wid him! And so Mr. Dan must give up his bell to Misther Charles's horse."

"I don't believe he did it without a cause. His bell-band may be fast to a bush. Good-morning to your night-cap!" This was uttered when a large buck sprang up a few paces in front of them, and bounded away with his tail erect, the under or white portion of it, as usual, exposed to view.

"Be jabers, he's stopped to look at us!" said Paddy, throwing his gun up to his shoulder.

"Don't fire!" said Kenton.

"Don't fire? And what's your raison for that same?"

"I have a reason."

"And won't ye tell it before the deer's gone?"

"Oh, he's gone long ago. Don't you see him rushing over the ridge yonder, three hundreds yards off?"

Paddy, on turning his head again, caught a glimpse of the buck at the place indicated. He seemed much offended, and followed his companion several minutes in silence, and until Kenton paused abruptly, his lips slightly parted and his rifle half in readiness to fire.

"And what're ye frowning about now?" asked Paddy; "any child can hear the bell widout stooping down till the falthy ground."

"Hush!" said Kenton, in a low voice. "Sit down here with me, and don't speak above a whisper."

"Not spake above a whasper! For fear, I suppose, the horse'll hear us and run away?"

"Fool!"

"Did ye mane that for me, Misther Kenton?"

"Be quiet, if you don't want to lose your scalp!"

"Och, I beg yer pardon, misther! And there are Indians about, sure enough, thin?"

"I think so."

"And how could any one want to lose his sculp? You oughtn't to name any sich thing! I'll go back!"

"I wish you *were* in the fort! Could you find the way back yourself?"

"Niver! My head's been turned and twisted so I wouldn't know which way to start. Won't ye go wid me?"

"And lose *his* scalp? No, indeed! That fellow's hair shall be dangling from my belt when I go in, or my name's not Simon Kenton! Poor Dan's gone—that's certain!"

"Won't ye explain all this to me, Misther Kenton? I can't understhand a jot of it."

"The yaller rascal's stolen my horse, and thinks he is sure of my scalp in the bargain. Didn't you hear that?"

"The bell, ye mane? Of coorse?"

"Well, are there any flies at this season?"

"No, not that I knows of. But there's abundance of flaas in the garrison."

"That bell is not shaken by Dan. It is in the hand of an Indian!"

"Let's begone, Misther Kenton! Let's give the alarm to the paple. Run as fast as ye plase, and I'll kape up wid ye!"

"Hush! Be quiet! I will take that yaller rascal's scalp in with me, or Sue Calloway and Simon Kenton will never be man and wife! I place my hand on this log and swear to it!"

"And all for a single horse, which'll be bit by a rattlesnake next summer!"

"Paddy, you must do precisely what I tell you, or creep back to the fort alone!"

"Will ye tell me to do ony thing dangerous?"

"Dangerous? We don't know what that means. There's no such word in Kentucky. All that I want you to do is to hide under this log, and not let your own ears hear a rustle from you, or you may be tomahawked."

"I'll be still as a mice! And mayn't I cover meself wid the laves?"

"I don't care. When you hear my gun——"

"Och, Misther Kenton, how am I to tell yer gun from an Indian's? It may be the report of a blackguard savage's rifle shooting yerself!"

"Shooting your granny! I thought everybody could tell the crack of my rifle. I can tell Boone's, blindfolded Every man's voice is different, and so is his gun's."

"And Paddy's schoolmasther didn't tache him the language o' rifles!"

"No matter. The first gun you hear will be mine, and the yaller rascal shaking the bell will be sprawling on his face and the hot blood pouring out of his head. When you hear my gun, jump up and make a d——l of a noise. Fire off your gun—load and fire as fast as you can—beat the bushes, yell, talk Irish, and make 'em believe—that is, if any more of 'em are about—at least twenty men are coming. Now hide yourself!"

Paddy, knowing he could never find the way back to the station without a guide, was under the necessity of obeying. Then Kenton rose up and uttered a prolonged and not unmusical halloo, as he was in the habit of doing to attract the ear of his horse, which had, like most other horses, learned to know the voice of his master. Immediately after, the bell was shaken quite loudly, in imitation of the rattle made by a horse suddenly lifting his head.

Kenton smiled, and was just about to glide away in a different direction from that whence the sound of the bell proceeded, when he was called to softly by Paddy.

"Misther Kenton! Misther Kenton!" said he, "for the sake of the Howly Immaculate Mother, don't be afther calling 'em here, and laving me to be tomahawked be meself!"

"Lay still, you —— fool, and be silent, or I'll tomahawk you myself, and be rid of you!"

"Och, murther!" said Paddy, submissively sinking back under the leaves.

Kenton glided away stealthily, and made a wide circuit, so as to attain the opposite side of the locality of the bell. He knew every inch of the ground, and was aware that the Indian was posted in a dense grove of sugar-maples, some forty yards from the thicket of sumachs in the midst of which Paddy was ensconced, and precisely in front of the deer-path leading through it into the woods; and he was satisfied the face of the foe would be kept steadily in that direction. Hence his motive for the loud halloo before executing his project of circumvention.

No cat ever moved with less noise than Kenton in the execution of his well-conceived purpose. And so far was he from experiencing any trepidation, that more than once he was under the necessity of pausing to repress an inclination to laugh at the anticipated astonishment of the Indian and the ludicrous picture his fancy painted of a savage watching in readiness to shoot him as he emerged from the sumachs, when he should be aiming at the back of the Indian's head from the opposite direction.

And there was an instinctive prescience in his conception. For when he approached the designated point, without the crush of a leaf or the disturbance of a bough, he beheld the Indian, with the bell in his hand and a companion at his side, sitting on the fallen trunk of a tree which Kenton himself had cut down to capture a bear.

The Indians were laughing silently at the anticipated success of their stratagem, and expressing by mimicry the amazement they had no doubt their victim would exhibit when, instead of seeing his horse, he should find himself a prisoner or hear the whistling of their balls before he could present his own rifle.

Kenton paused and surveyed them when about forty paces distant. Their faces were steadily turned toward the place where the path entered the woods; and they were so near it they could have heard the approach of the horse-hunter before he came in view. Their position on that side was sufficiently obscured by the intervening trees to render any extraordinary precaution unnecessary.

But they were exposed on the other side; and Kenton was determined they should hear from him, if they did not see him, although he was a little embarrassed by the presence of one more than he had calculated upon. Shifting his position several times for the purpose of getting their heads in a line, so as to perforate them both, several minutes were fruitlessly expended; for, from the shape of the fallen trunk and the inequality in the height of the Indians, the project was impracticable.

He poured out a charge of powder in his buckhorn tube and placed it beside a bullet at the root of the tree behind which he was standing, so that he might be in readiness to repeat his fire before the surviving enemy could rush upon him. Then, taking a deliberate aim at the one with the bell, whom he recognised as the liberated chief, Ground-Hog, and the original owner of the horse Dan, he fired. The bell and Indian fell together. The other Indian sprang up astounded, and, after glancing hurriedly in every direction but the right one, prostrated himself beside his weltering companion, as if to elude the aim of an enemy.

Kenton, meanwhile, lost no time in recharging his rifle; and the surviving Indian, finding himself not assaulted, and not knowing where the foe might be concealed, hastened to make his escape. But, as is almost invariably the case, he determined to bear off his dead comrade. So, being a broad-shouldered, stalwart fellow, he rose with his neck between the dead one's legs, the feet in front and the body behind, back to back; and with his burden he ran through the woods, continually turning to shield himself from the aim of any foe that might be watching by interposing the dead Indian.

So skilful were his manœuvres that Kenton was finally under the necessity of firing *through* the dead body to reach the living Indian. And this he did effectually, for they both lay prostrate a moment after the discharge of his rifle. He ran up and scalped them, dispatching the last victim, who had been only desperately wounded, with his tomahawk.

No sooner was this bloody work accomplished than Dan was discovered a few paces distant, behind the roots of an immense fallen tree. Thither the savage was bearing his companion, and would have soon effected his escape. Kenton threw his arms round the neck of his snorting steed in a loving embrace, and then, mounting him, dashed into the sumach-thicket where Paddy lay concealed.

"Paddy! Paddy! Where are you?" cried Kenton, his horse standing with his neck arched over the log where Paddy had buried himself.

"And is it yerself who asks?" replied Paddy, in a tremulous voice, and at the same time springing up from the leaves,—an apparition which frightened Dan, and Kenton was near being thrown.

"Yes. Why didn't you answer me at first?"

"And how could I know it was yerself till ye towld me? Murther! murther! I see the nasty sculps hanging to yer belt!"

"Two of 'em, Paddy! So Sue Calloway and I may be man and wife after all, if she'll have me. But why didn't you fire and shout as I told you?"

"Now come, Misther Kenton, how could I tell they wasn't running this way, right over a body?"

"Well, suppose they had? Wouldn't you have 'em come where you could see 'em?"

"Och, murther! they might've kilt me, and Paddy, sure, would niver have enjoyed the smiles of any darlint wife."

"But there would have been no danger. Your firing and shouting would have frightened them away."

"D'ye say that? And, sure enough, there'd be no danger? Then here goes for a spicimen of the noise I can make in a case of needcissity!" And he sprang upon the log and fired his gun, and yelled, and howled, and beat and twisted the bushes, to such a furious extent that Kenton, half dead with laughter, was forced to alight from his amazed horse to keep from being thrown.

"Are you mad?" cried Kenton.

"Mad, is it? As blazes!" said Paddy, firing off his gun again. "Am I not fighting the Indians?"

"You are making a fool of yourself; and if there are any more in hearing they'll soon put a stop to your howling. That's not the noise a brave man makes, and I'll leave you!"

"Misther Kenton! Misther Kenton!" cried Paddy, instantly sobered, "ye are the bravest and the best man in the world, and I will tell iverybody of yer great dades this day. And sure, now, ye'll let me ride behint ye?"

Kenton could not resist the flattery; and, after some difficulty, Dan permitted Paddy to occupy a seat on his strong back; but there was no more Irish howling.

Kenton, when approaching the station, uttered the horse-halloo, a sort of whinnying yell used by the scouts to denote their success in the acquisition of horses. He listened in vain for a response. All seemed to be silent. Astonished and somewhat chagrined at this, he sounded the startling scalp-halloo. This never failed to produce a prodigious excitement among Indians or borderers. But on that occasion, and to the amazement of Kenton, only one or two responsive voices were heard; and when he dashed through the gate there was no enthusiastic crowd to receive him with plaudits.

Boone approached and examined the scalps in grave silence. McSwine sat apart with a dark cloud on his brow. Van Wiggens was still, staring at his dog, and "Vatch" himself stood like a marble quadruped, his blunt tail sticking up immovably. The voice of Mr. Jones was heard in the large cabin where he usually preached. He was praying fiercely. Maledictions were uttered and vengeance invoked.

"Oh, Mr. Kenton," exclaimed Mrs. Calloway, rushing out into the area, her long hair streaming loosely behind, "they've got her!"

"Got who? who's got? what's what?" cried Kenton, quickly, trembling from head to foot, and almost unnerved by the indefinable apprehensions which oppressed him, intensified by the singular change in the countenances of all and the disordered hair and tearful eyes of the woman.

"Sue! the Indians have got Sue!" she screamed; and then fell prostrate at the feet of the scout, whose breathing was quick and oppressive.

"Oh, —— them!" cried Kenton, in a shrill voice which rang throughout the building.

"Yes, tam dem!" said Van Wiggens.

"Vatch" barked fiercely.

"Come! come!" cried Charles, rushing into the area full-armed, and habited as an Indian. "We want ten men —the best in the station—all volunteers—to go in pursuit. Boone and I will lead."

Then Kenton, as if his sinews, which had been apparently paralyzed, were suddenly enfranchised from the spell that bound them, sprang up in the air, and, striking his feet together several times before descending, crowed vociferously, like a cock.

"I knew you'd be one, Simon," said Boone.

"*One?* and Sue gone?—I'll be SIX!" and, letting his rifle fall gently to the earth, he struck the palm of his left hand a violent blow with the fist of his right.

"Mary's gone too!" said Boone, in a husky voice.

"O Lord!" said Kenton; "and I was after Dan, and didn't know it! But we'll foller 'em to the other end of creation! They've roused a hornets' nest now! I feel as strong as a buffalo bull! I could bite off the head of a nail! I could—"

"And Julia!" said Charles—"they've taken her too!"

"That clips my tongue!" said Kenton, striding in front

of Charles and gazing steadfastly in his face. "I'm dumb now. I can't curse a bit. I feel like having the lock-jaw. My arms ache! I could bust a rock with my fist! I'd agree to strip and fight ten Indians at once. They might have their tomahawks; all I'd ask would be my knuckles and my teeth! Why are we standing here like scared turkeys that don't know which way to fly? Don't let us burn daylight, or moonlight either. Where's the volunteers? I'm six!"

The number designated, after such a speech from Kenton, were in instant readiness; and the most extraordinary thing was the persistence of Paddy in his resolution to accompany them. He said if the girls were not recovered he didn't care to keep his "sculp."

The three girls had been seized by a party of Indians near the spring, on the river-bank, just after Kenton and Paddy departed in quest of the horses. They had crossed the river in the night in a canoe, which they concealed in the bushes near the water, and then hid themselves in the vicinity. The seizure of the girls was followed so quickly by the pushing off of the canoe that, by the time their screams had roused the men in the fields, they had been conveyed to the opposite shore of the river. Their captors were only four in number; but on the northern bank they were joined by ten others. They hastened away toward the Ohio, but rather in a northwest course than in the line the fugitives had traversed from the Scioto

The girls were placed on Indian ponies, while most of their captors ran on foot. Kenton had diminished the number of horses in the Indian country.

Julia looked round, expecting to see Brandt; but he was not present; nor were any Mohawks among them. All were Senecas.

They had not proceeded far before they were met by Peter Shaver, on his jackass, whom the Indians abused for lagging behind. Peter had been a volunteer in the expedition, breathing vengeance against the whites, but determined, at the first opportunity, to desert to them; and it was to prevent such an occurrence, perhaps, that he was required to retain his ass, which could not be beaten out of his slow gait nor easily made to abandon the scenes and society to which it had so long been accustomed; and, be--

sides, the chief "Popcorn" afforded a fund of amusement which the Indians enjoyed most heartily, and no doubt Peter's life had been spared that he might continue to be the laughing-stock of the savage warriors.

"You know the jack can't keep up," said Peter, in deprecation of their reproaches.

"You be dern!" said the leader.

Just then the ass, snuffing the breeze which blew from the south, and upon which was borne the scent of the blood of the Indians slain by Kenton, began to bray.

"Dern! stop him!" cried the leader of the party, who drew his knife and threatened to cut the animal's throat.

"Wait till I get down!" said Peter, not at all reluctant to be rid of his ass. "Now cut away as soon as you please," said he, when dismounted.

This produced some laughter when the Indians comprehended the reason of Popcorn's willingness to sacrifice his long-eared steed; and therefore the animal's life was spared. But they choked him into silence, and, turning his head back, whipped him along the path in the rear of the ponies.

Then ensued an animated conversation among the Indians, in their own dialect, some portions of which Julia was enabled to understand. They were discussing the probable result of the pursuit they anticipated,—the number of pursuers, and how many would be left to defend the station. From this Julia inferred the object was to weaken the garrison.

Mary and Sue, though seemingly quiet and subdued, had not forgotten the lessons learned in the wilderness, repeated at many a glowing fireside. They broke off small boughs from the bushes, and strewed fragments of their handkerchiefs, and threads drawn from their clothing, in the path they were traversing.

This operation was seen and understood by the leading chief; and he did not forbid it until they reached the headwaters of the South Fork of Licking River, near where Mount Sterling stands. Here every effort was made to conceal their trail. The girls were threatened with the torture if they did not cease to scatter threads and twigs on the ground.

Daylight was fading, and the shimmering stars appeared

in the east; and, although the girls were both weary and hungry, their captors paid no attention to their alleged wants. On the contrary, they were forced to ride among the slippery rocks in the midst of the stream, then exceedingly low, as there had been a prolonged drought. The Indians, sure of foot and reckless of exposure, followed. The ass was sometimes urged forward by blows behind, or dragged along by the ears. In this manner they proceeded several miles, leaving, as they thought, no trace behind them. But the Indians were outwitted by the girls, as many wiser men had been before them. In the dusky shades of the clustering boughs, the Senecas could not prevent their captives from detaching some of their long silken hair and hanging it on the willows.

Their progress was now very slow, and it seemed they had no intention of flying far. The object was to confuse their pursuers. The girls were dismounted when the water became deeper. The ponies and the ass were taken to the opposite side and driven down the right-hand bank of the stream, while the captives were conducted along a path on the other side, which soon diverged from the river and led into the hills.

It was a well-beaten path, and quite dusty. The girls were ordered to keep in the centre of it and follow their leader in single file. Behind, an old Indian brought up the rear, obliterating the footprints with a bough of cedar, and leaving no traces but his own moccasin-tracks.

They travelled thus until, from the height of the moon, the girls supposed it to be near midnight, when they again struck the river, which had increased in width and volume. They descended the bluff and halted in a beech-bottom, near the mouth of a small rivulet that emptied into the larger stream. And here they were surprised to find the ponies, the ass, and the Indians who had separated from them several miles back.

The poor girls, supposing they would be compelled to mount again and pursue the journey all night, were ready to despair. They feared it would be impossible for their friends to follow. But no indignities were offered them, which, at least, was an assurance that their lives would be spared. The Indian never insults his female prisoner unless he means to kill her afterward. And Peter

Shaver had several times made encouraging winks and gestures.

The girls were not required to mount the ponies again that night. A fire was kindled under a rude shelter hastily constructed, and some buffalo-tongue, sliced and broiled, sufficed for their supper

Not fearing their captives would attempt an escape, the Indians returned upon their trail for the purpose of more effectually destroying it. Peter, known to be incapable of finding his way in any direction in the absence of a beaten path, was left to keep the fire replenished.

It was during this temporary withdrawal of the savages that Julia, learned from Peter that their seizure was to be attributed to Queen Esther, and that Brandt had nothing whatever to do with it. On the contrary, the great sachem had returned, silent and terrible in his gloom, from a solitary excursion, and, leading his people toward the East, announced his intention to strike his tomahawk into the heads of the white people living nearest to the Eastern lakes. His aunt, Gentle Moonlight, and sister, Brown Thrush, were still remaining at Chillicothe when Peter left the village; and Calvin likewise remained, and had been promised the hand of the beautiful Indian girl provided he would head the Delawares, who had just joined the confederacy of the Six Nations. To this, however, he objected; and Gentle Moonlight did not sanction the project. The forest maiden was silent, knowing her aunt could dispose of her as she pleased. But she sang continually of the White Eagle, and her thoughts and dreams were of the woods, and streams, and flowers, beyond the grave.

When their captors returned, the girls were ordered to occupy a small space in the crotch of a fallen tree near the fire. Leaves sufficed for a couch, and a buffalo robe for a shelter from the dew or frost. They kept themselves warm by clinging together under their weighty coverlet, and endeavoured to cheer each other with such prospects of a speedy rescue as the circumstances afforded. Their whispers were at last hushed in slumber, for the idea of escape, unassisted by their friends, never occurred to them. They dreamed of those they loved best, and that they had been delivered from the hands of the enemy; but in the morning they awoke to the sad consciousness that they were still in captivity.

After a slight repast the journey was resumed; and the Indians were merry with the conviction that they had effectually concealed their trail.

Their progress the second day was neither rapid nor in the most direct course for the Ohio River; and it became evident that the Indians looked for the arrival of friends who would be interposed between their captives and the stations of the white men. Being out of meat, several of the warriors diverged from the path in quest of deer, and their rifles were soon heard in various directions. This convinced Mary Boone that they no longer feared pursuit; but it did not quite extinguish her hope.

The first deer brought in, as usual, set Peter's ass to braying. Mary could not avoid laughing, and the Indians patted her on the head and said, "Brave Captain Boone's daughter—laugh at Popcorn's jack—good squaw!" And it was a singular characteristic of the Indian to praise, and spare, and love Boone, whom they dreaded more than any other foe.

In the evening they encamped at an early hour, having recrossed the Licking. The place where they rested was at the mouth of a creek emptying into the river, known since by the name of Indian Creek, about a mile from Cynthiana. It was a narrow bottom, overgrown with beech-trees, and a position well adapted for defence. And here the girls found a better shelter than that of the preceding night. It seemed to have been an ancient camping-ground, for old forks were found standing.

Leaving Peter with the girls, the Indians dispersed in various directions, to be satisfied, as usual, that no enemy lurked in the vicinity.

Peter amused himself firing at the ducks that pitched into the mouth of the creek, that being a famous place for them to collect of evenings; and, finding a canoe in the vicinity, he obtained his victims without difficulty. And Mary and Sue undertook to dress and roast them. This was done much to the satisfaction of the Indians, who partook heartily of the fowls, and praised the girls for their skill in cooking.

At night the repose of the captives was disturbed by the

howling of wolves. Those animals seemed to have collected in great numbers in the vicinity; and occasionally their glaring eyeballs, as they stood on the opposite side of the creek and gazed at the fire, were plainly discernible.

"I guess I can blot out one of their eyes," said Peter, raising his gun to his shoulder.

"Totem!—Seneca Totem!" cried the leader of the Indians, striking up the muzzle of the rifle; and the ball whistled over the tree-tops.

"I beg pardon," said Peter; "I forgot the wolves were your brothers, and that I was connected with the same respectable family."

The Indians comprehended his speech in part, but did not attach any importance to the jest. But they attached a superstitious signification to the presence of the wolves, or to their mode of howling on that particular night. They were even kind enough to throw the fragments of their feast to them, but this did not silence their cries.

"Mr. Shaver," said Julia, as she leaned upon Sue's friendly shoulder, watching the glowing embers, and unable to sleep, "how did you like the family into which you were adopted?"

"I guess you mean how I disliked it. There was no liking in the matter."

"I suppose Mr. Van Wiggens disliked it quite as much as any one, since he embraced the earliest opportunity to get away."

"I guess he did. He was my adopted mother's husband, you know. They had a row the first night. She was drunk, and wanted to make him drunk too. And I reckon he had no particular objection to being drunk, for I have seen him in that way; but it was the most abominable, outrageous liquor you ever tasted."

"I never tasted any, Peter."

"I beg pardon. Even Paddy, my new brother, couldn't swallow it, and he had a will to get drunk and forget his troubles."

"So none of you tasted it?"

"I guess we did, though! The scent of the stuff filled the wigwam. It druv out Paddy and his daddy. I fell asleep, or I'd'a gone too."

"What did Diving Duck say in the morning?"

"It'd've kept two or three interpreters busy to translate her words. She jabbled like a whole flock of parroquets. She was always a famous scold, and the Indians dislike scolding wives as much as white men do."

"Do they?"

"Darned if they don't! And some of the squaws have tarnation bitter tongues! But Didapper, seeing she had no husband to listen, soon stopped her Niagara Falls of words, and took up the frying-pan. The frying-pan is what she used to beat her old man with. She gave me a rap over the head, and it rings yet! And she told me if I didn't bring back my father she'd marry me! I guess she may, if she ever catches me."

"Hush!" said Mary, in a low voice.

"What do you hear?" asked Julia.

"Lie down, Peter!" whispered Mary; then, turning to Julia, said her eye had caught a signal from her father.

"I saw nothing," said Julia.

"There it is again!" said Mary, pointing at an acorn that fell near the fire and rolled to their feet.

"That is an acorn," said Julia.

"I know it," responded the other. "But we are not under an oak-tree."

"If it be your father, why cannot I see him?" asked Julia, rising softly and gazing round. "No," she continued, "there are no bushes here to hide any one. I fear you are mistaken."

"I am not! The signal is for us to lie down, so as not to be in the way of their bullets."

Julia involuntarily clung closer to her companions, and Peter himself seemed inclined to maintain a more intimate proximity to the girls than, under other circumstances, would have been permitted.

"How quietly the Indians sleep!" whispered Julia.

"They always do," said Mary; "and we must not move or speak above a whisper, whatever we may hear or see, until bidden by my father. The Indians will not have time to kill us, and we must not be afraid."

Soon after, their deliverers were seen to glide from behind the trees and stand with their guns pointing at the Indians. But the heads of the girls, as they peered over the crotch of the fallen tree, were between the rifles and the sleeping savages. Boone, by an emphatic gesture, commanded them to lie down and be still, which they obeyed instinctively. The next moment a deadly volley was fired into the midst of the unconscious savages, and such as escaped the fatal lead sprang up, yelling horribly, and disappeared in the forest.

The girls rushed into the arms of their deliverers; and Sue Calloway was embraced, and lifted up, and kissed, by Kenton.

"Sue!" said he, "I'd wade through fire forty foot deep to save you!" Sue said nothing, nor opened her eyes, her face reclining on her deliverer's shoulder.

And Julia clung to Charles, while Mary wept with joy on the breast of her father.

"Be me sowl, I'm hungry!" said Paddy; "and here the savage blackguards have been having a fayst to thimselves! And what do ye call that same noise?" he continued, arresting his hand as it was conveying the half of a roasted duck to his mouth.

It was the familiar sound of Peter Shaver's jackass, some forty paces distant, braying terrifically.

"Hello! Where's Popcorn?" said Paddy, upon recognising the voice of the beast.

"Here I am, Paddy Pence!" said Peter, rising up.

"Divil take me if I belave ye!" cried Paddy, aiming his empty gun at Peter's breast. "You're one of the savage Indians who saized the young ladies. Surrinder, or you're a dead man!"

"I rather guess I can soon convince you I am Peter Shaver, if you'll throw down the shooting-iron and stand up to a fair fist-fight," said Peter, deeply affronted.

"None of your nonsense!" said Boone to Paddy; "and do you go and stop that ass's mouth," he continued, addressing Peter, who obeyed reluctantly.

"And what's that same?" cried Paddy, dropping his duck into the fire. It was the warwhoop of the rallied Senecas, and a moment after their balls rattled like hail about the fire; but none of the party were killed, and only two were slightly wounded. Boone and Charles deposited the girls in the place of security, and ordered the men to post themselves behind the trees out of the light of the fire. This was done immediately, and a desultory conflict was kept up until early dawn, when the Indians retired into the wilderness beyond the creek.

When the gray morning appeared, Charles left his tree and approached the shelter which concealed the girls; and the first object that attracted his gaze was the form of Paddy. He was snoring lustily beside the silent though watchful girls. Charles roused him with a smart blow, and the Irishman sprang up and stared in amazement.

"I was dhraming, Misther Charles," said he.

"And what business had you here?"

"Och, I was proticting the ladies! But I was so hungry and tired, I fell aslape. I beg the swate craters' pardons!"

Boone discovered a slaughtered deer which the Indians had hung upon a tree beyond the reach of the wolves; and this sufficed for breakfast.

Without loss of time, the party set out on their return to the station. Kenton had found the ponies, which the Indians left behind. But neither Peter Shaver nor his ass could be seen; and it was supposed he had been recaptured by the Indians upon going out to silence the braying.

"Be the powers," said Paddy, "may-be it wasn't Pater afther all! And I was cheek by jowl with a savage inemy!"

Although the loss of Peter was naturally regretted, yet the party had been too successful to mourn a great deal over his fate, whatever it might be; and the joy of the enfranchised girls was a sufficient recompense for their fatigues and perils.

And Sue, although Kenton could not obtain the pledge he desired, acknowledged her deep indebtedness to her brave and generous deliverer.

Julia, in the exuberance of her recovered spirits, amused Charles and the rest with a recital of the information she had received from Peter regarding the inconsolable Didapper so cruelly deserted by her lord; and poor Van Wiggens was heartily congratulated upon his escape from the frying-pan.

"Tam dem! te vimmen!" said he. "And I shall pe in te fire, ven I gets back mit te oder Mrs. Wan Viggens!"

The hairs hung by Sue on the boughs pendant over the water, as she was assured by Kenton, had enabled them to follow the trail of the Indians. But Sue did not thank her beau for the compliment, for her hair was very red,—a colour never admired by its possessor.

Toward evening, and after a pretty good day's travel, the party were surprised to perceive signs of a large party of Indians, which had passed southward within the last twenty-four hours. This discovery was perhaps a fortunate one. They might but for it have encamped upon such ground as would have made their fire visible to the enemy; but now, instead of this, they resolved to push forward and cross the river without halting. This they effected before midnight; and their arrival at the station was the occasion of general rejoicing and of thanksgiving by the Rev. Mr. Jones.

CHAPTER XVII.

SIEGE OF BOONE'S STATION, AND BATTLES—BROWN THRUSH.

RUNNERS arrived the next day from Hoy's, Bryant's, Logan's, and Harrod's stations, with the startling intelligence that Indians had been seen in their respective vicinities. From the simultaneous appearance of the enemy in different places, it was inferred that all the forts were to be attacked at once, and, if possible, demolished at a blow.

Preparations were made to repel any assault, and to withstand a siege. The grain was gathered and all the stock confined within the hollow square of cabins.

Nor had these measures been taken a moment too soon; for, the day afterward, the enemy appeared in considerable force on the south side of the river, and surrounded the station. They consisted principally of Indians,—Wyandots, Shawnees, and Western Delawares; a small party of British from Canada, commanded by Duquesne; and some half a dozen renegade Americans, among whom were the Girtys.

Duquesne desired a parley, and professed to have been charged by Governor Hamilton to offer such terms as could be honourably accepted by the settlers. But their treacherous purpose was soon discovered.

From that moment the deadly strife began. On all sides the fort was assailed, for it was surrounded completely. But the fatal aim of Kenton, McSwine, and others, stretched so many of the savages on the plain that they were compelled, in despite of Duquesne's orders, to fall back and seek shelter behind the trees and under the protecting bank of the river.

At night the assault was renewed, and the besieged had to fire at the flash of the enemy's guns. The night was dark, the sky overcast with clouds; and the blazing arrows whizzing through the air, the continued fire of rifles without, in a crescent form, extending half-way round the fort, and, within, radiating outward to the enemy, formed a grand and terrific spectacle.

The females moulded bullets for their defenders and carried them food, so that they might not be under the necessity of abandoning their posts; and a certain number of the men, who were not expert with the rifle, or unpractised in shooting "at the flash," as it was called, were detailed for the purpose of watching the blazing arrows and extinguishing the roofs and sides of the cabins when ignited. Among these Paddy had been placed, much against his will, for he greatly preferred peering through a small loophole to exposing his person on the huts.

"And now, Mr. Bone," said he, leaping down, "I naadn't stay up there ony more, for all the water's spilt."

Boone long remained silent. His great error—indeed the only error he had committed in the location of his fort—was now painfully apparent. The spring was some distance above, and in possession of the enemy! The stock of water, as Paddy said, was exhausted!

"Fill your buckets with the damp earth!" the pioneer exclaimed; "and if that gives out you must roll upon the fire and smother it with your hands. If one cabin burns, all must go, and every one of us will be scalped!"

Paddy rushed back to his post, pale and desperate. He thought it better to be shot than burned; but he kept as much as possible in the lee of the apex of the roofs.

So far, only two of the garrison had fallen; but the enemy suffered severely, and the death-halloo was heard continually, as Boone, or Kenton, or McSwine, fired "at the flash,"—an achievement hitherto unattained by the Indians. At first they believed their warriors were accidentally stricken; but it could not long escape their observation that they always received the fatal wound in the head, and most generally in the eye, and when in the act of firing themselves. This discovery induced them to observe greater caution, and not to fire more than once or twice from the same position.

Toward morning a smart shower fell, much to the relief of the garrison, and apparently in answer to the petition of the Rev. Mr. Jones, who watched and prayed alternately. And about this time the besiegers ceased firing, and it was believed by some they had abandoned the attempt to reduce the fort. This illusion, however, was soon dispelled. For, early in the morning, Kenton, stuffing his buckskin coat with straw and surmounting it with his cap, pushed the effigy through an orifice in the roof. It represented one looking out boldly on a field supposed to be deserted by the enemy. In an instant several sharp reports were heard, and, Kenton making the man of straw fall back in imitation of one fatally wounded, a yell of savage exultation was uttered

"Look at that, Sue!" said Kenton, pointing to the perforations in his garment.

"I'll mend it for you, Simon," said she.

"Yes, you'll mend my coat, but you don't care for the wound under my vest."

"That was not done by a savage," said Mary, smiling composedly, being familiar with such scenes.

"A savage could not be more unfeeling," said Kenton. Then, listening to the reiterated shouts without, he continued, "The yellow d——ls know my coat, and are rejoicing over my death. You see, Sue, what a great man I am in their opinion. They count me six, and I *am* six in any common crowd! But won't I astonish 'em when they see me the next time?"

They were interrupted by the entrance of Boone and Charles, with excited countenances.

"Oh, what is the matter now?" asked Julia.

"Be not alarmed, Julia," said Charles, taking her cold hand. "We shall defeat them yet. Boone has conceived a plan which will frustrate the purpose of Duquesne and Girty."

"What purpose do you allude to?"

"Have you not seen how turbid the river has become?"

"Yes. It has been observed by all. Was it not caused by the rain?"

"Look at the stream above the spring."

Julia did so, and perceived it was clear, and then exclaimed, "They are mining! They will burst up the ground and appear in our midst!"

"No! be the powers, no!" cried Paddy, springing up. "And is it undermining us they're afther? Let Paddy alone for countermining 'em. He'll be in his ilement with the spade. Misther Bone, if ye'll give me a spade, I'll do the sarvice of three men. I'll give the yaller blackguards a lesson in the art o' digging!"

Boone smiled, and said if Paddy and a few others would work with expedition the danger would soon disappear. And Paddy performed wonders with the spade,—his natural implement. But again great distress was felt for the want of water, which, however, was never suspected by Duquesne, who doubted not a well had been dug in the fort.

Another shower fell during the day and revived the spirits of the besieged; and toward evening, from the accumulation of earth thrown up by Paddy and his co-labourers, the Scots, the enemy, perceiving their design had been counteracted, abandoned the attempt to effect a subterranean passage. They recommenced firing from several points, and manœuvering in such manner as seemed likely to produce a sally from the garrison. Once, for the purpose of inducing the whites to come forth, they affected to be panic-stricken and in full retreat on one side, while on the other all was silent and still, as if no foe lurked in the vicinity.

It was in vain. Boone and Charles understood their purpose, and succeeded for a long time in restraining the more impetuous and less experienced of their friends from pursuing the enemy.

There was one man, however, more intractable than the rest, named McGary, who swore that half the men were cowards; and, late in the day, when the foe made a final effort to draw them out on the east, McGary, in disregard of the urgent remonstrances of Boone, issued forth, followed by a few others, and charged the savages. Instantly, as had been apprehended, the main body of Indians sprang up from the place of their concealment on the west, and made desperate efforts both to storm the garrison and to intercept the sallying party. They reached the gate of the enclosure, which they hacked with their tomahawks. In several places they succeeded in setting fire to the cabins, while a detachment, led by Girty, got between McGary and the station.

Boiling rain-water and molten lead were contributed by the women to aid in repelling the attack; and the fire was extinguished and the assailants hurled back with loss. But the situation of McGary and his men became desperate.

Driven from the gate and the cabins, the main body of the enemy were soon concentrated near the spring, and kept up an incessant firing on the men who had inconsiderately left the defences and were now endeavouring to fight their way back to the friendly shelter.

McGary's men at length concealed themselves in a "sink-hole,"—a funnel-shaped depression in the earth often met with in Kentucky,—about ninety paces distant from the fort, but not more than forty from the spring. From this position they returned the fire of the enemy at the embankment of the river, but were liable at any moment to be assailed from an opposite direction by the decoying savages they had gone in pursuit of.

"There!" exclaimed Boone, listening intently, "they are doomed unless we save them! Girty is coming on the other side!"

"Let's plunge into 'em heels over head!" said Kenton.

"I don't believe any are now on the west of us," said Charles.

Boone darted a look of admiration at the young man.

"That's the idea!" said he. "They must not kill McGary. Take the Scots with you into the brake and make a circuit beyond the sink-hole. Give the attacking halloo as a signal. We will meet you at the spring."

Words were few and brief, and the order was executed without delay. The enemy retreated up the river, leaving a number of their dead on the ground, and McGary was rescued, but not without the loss of several of his men.

Charles and Kenton followed the foe until they made a stand in the thick woods, when Boone sent them word—

himself remaining at the spring, supplying the garrison with water—to desist from the pursuit.

The order was well timed; for the enemy, recovered from the surprise, were preparing to charge in turn. And when the whites were re-entering the garrison the bullets of the Indians were pattering around them.

The exasperated Indians exposed themselves more recklessly than ever, and challenged the white men to come forth again and have a fair fight in an open field. The garrison, being outnumbered three to one, of course declined the invitation.

In the course of the day the besiegers were reinforced by several straggling parties; and on each occasion the accession was announced by a particular halloo, well understood by Charles.

"That was the fierce howl of the Senecas," said Charles to Julia, whom he had briefly joined.

"The Senecas!" iterated Julia, in terror. "I hoped they were gone! Their presence here is proof that you or I, or both, have especial reason for painful forebodings."

"I think not," said Charles. "No doubt it is the party which captured you, and some of the servile instruments of the vengeful Esther. They fear to appear in her presence without being able to conduct one or both of us thither as prisoners."

"And what do you suppose would be our fate?" asked Julia.

"If the council of sachems did not interfere it would be a terrible one. The longer Esther hates, the more implacable she becomes; and we have thus far thwarted her designs."

"Yes, it is that party; I know it now," said Julia, listening to a familiar sound.

This was the braying of Peter Shaver's ass; and it was followed by the shouts and mirthful laughter of the Indians and British. No chief among them seemed to attract more attention than the renowned Popcorn.

Just then Paddy ran in.

"Och, Misther Charles," said he, with wide-staring eyes, "Misther Bone wants me to go out and help Misther Kenton, who's as crazy as a loon, to catch his horse. It got out of the gate and is playing round the fort, and the bloody savages are watching to kill the first man who lays hands on him."

"If it is Kenton's favourite steed," said Charles, it must be recovered, or its master will be lost."

"And Misther Bone says I ought to go out and expose me body as a target, because the horse knows me. I shall be careful in forming intimate acquantances with other paple's horses hereafther! I'll shoot, or I'll dig, but I won't go out horse-hunting wid the blackguard savages!"

When Charles accompanied Paddy to the gate, which was held partly open to admit of ready ingress if Simon should return with his steed, he beheld a spectacle which riveted him to the spot. The horse, having become impatient of his confinement, was now making amends by taking sufficient exercise. He ran round playfully, but would not permit Kenton to approach near enough to place his hand on his mane. He reared, kicked up behind, and then rapidly circled round his master.

The Indians, hoping to capture the spirited animal, came from behind the trees and embankments which had sheltered them, and gazed with interest at the scene. They hoped the horse would entice his master within their reach; and they forbore to fire, fearing, if the horse were killed, Kenton would elude their grasp.

Alternately, when the steed avoided a skilful attempt of his master to sieze him, or when Kenton by some manœuvre balked the horse in his purpose of passing him, shouts of applause and laughter came alike from the besieged and besiegers. At last, when all eyes were fixed upon the spectacle, and the deadly strife seemed suspended by mutual consent, they were startled by the renewed braying of Peter's ass, and the next instant that distinguished animal, perhaps recognising the horse as an old acquaintance, rushed forth from the tangled brake, with the frightened Peter on his back. Peter strove in vain to turn him aside, out of the range of the rifles of friend and foe, to which he was equally exposed.

Fearing the loss or desertion of "Popcorn," several of the Indians fired at the ass; but so greatly convulsed were they with laughter that their aim was wide of the mark, and Peter was resistlessly borne along toward the fort. The noble horse pricked forward his ears and stared at the approaching beast. Evidently he did not recognise his old acquaintance, whether from contempt of his meaner nature or because of the change in his aspect—for the Indians had painted the poor creature most fantastically—was not obvious; but, snorting loudly, the noble steed turned and ran toward the gate, followed by Kenton, and both were quickly admitted within the enclosure, amid the yells and huzzas of the spectators.

"Don't shoot me! Don't shoot me!" cried Peter, his braying ass still trotting directly toward the gate. "Don't shoot!" he continued, with his arms spread out, and his face turned now toward the fort and now in the direction of the besiegers. "I ain't an Indian! I ain't an Indian!" cried he; "and I guess I'm on your side!"

"Who are you?" demanded the man at the gate, who had never before seen Peter or his ass.

"I'm Peter Shaver! I'm Peter Shaver! Don't shoot! Let me in!"

Boone himself threw open the gate and admitted Peter. And when the jack met his numerous acquaintances, male and female, within the area, he ran about and brayed very rapturously.

There was much joy over the recovery of the long-lost Peter, and he was congratulated upon successfully running the gauntlet of two fires.

"Talking of fires," said Peter, "I reckon I can tell you some news that'll keep you from freezing this winter. The Indians have concluded to burn every mother's son of you! I saw 'em roast a poor fellow the other day! I guess I'll never have a pleasant dream again."

"Was it a drame?" asked Paddy.

"A dream! You'll see soon. They know you. They say they'll make splinters of the Irishman to kindle the others with."

"Och, murther! and will they split me up before they kill me, and burn me before I'm dead? Och, Paddy, Paddy! why did ye lave the cabbages of yer own native-born counthry!"

"That's a sensible remark," said Peter; "and if I ever set my toes in Harford streets once more, old Trumbull may hang me for a Tory before I go fighting the savages again."

"Every one to his post!" cried Charles. "They are coming from all directions!"

"Reserve your fire!" shouted Boone; "and when they're within twenty paces let each man aim at the one opposite him. After firing, out with your tomahawks and down with your rifles!"

The assailants were divided in four parties, approaching rapidly from the different points of the compass. They were in number fourfold the strength of the garrison. But there would have been a very material diminution of their force if Boone's directions had been followed.

Unfortunately, Paddy's agitation was so great that his gun went off a moment too soon. Many others, supposing this a signal, followed his example, but not before the assailants, as was doubtless concerted, had prostrated themselves, and thus escaped the fatal effects of the discharge.

'Be jabers, we've kilt ivery blackguard of 'em!" cried Paddy, in exultation. "Be me sowl, I was mistaken!" he added, the next moment, upon seeing them rise again; "they were only stunned."

The few who reserved their fire now selected their victims, and their fatal aim produced an astonishing effect on the savages, who vainly supposed all the rifles were discharged over their prostrate forms.

"We've stopped them! Now load and fire as fast as you can!" cried Boone, seeing the enemy reeling and hesitating, instead of attempting to surmount the picketing. This order was obeyed with alacrity and complete success on the sides where Boone and Charles and Kenton commanded. But on the other, where Girty led, the assaulting party succeeded in pulling down several of the palisades between the cabins.

They rushed in, tomahawk in hand, and were met by McSwine and his Scots in the centre of the area. A desperate conflict ensued, amid yells and shouts, the prancing of horses and the braying of the jackass. But the struggle was terminated by the fall of Girty himself, at whose side the Rev. Mr. Jones had taken a deliberate aim with his pistol. The Indians and the few British under the renegade's immediate command bore him out and retreated under cover of the river-bank. Several of the party, however, had been left within the enclosure, and these were immediately tomahawked and scalped.

It was just at this distracting moment, when the battle was won and the enemy were flying in all directions, that the ears of Charles were assailed by a familiar voice, and, looking in the direction whence it proceeded, he beheld, issuing from the cane on the west of the fort, the form of his forest sister.

She came, with arms uplifted, crying, "Kill me! kill me! kill me!"

"Don't fire, for your lives!" shouted Charles, seeing several of the men aiming at the advancing girl.

He threw open the gate and rushed forth to meet her, at the same time speaking in a loud voice, and in the Indian language, to the enemy, beseeching them to spare the sister of Thayendanegea.

Brown Thrush never lowered her uplifted hands, nor ceased to cry "Kill me!" until she fell upon the breast of Charles, who, turning, bore her through the gate into the fort, where they were instantly surrounded by eager spectators.

"Oh!" cried Julia, pale and tearful, "see the blood! Who could have done the cruel deed?"

The poor Indian girl was weltering in her gore, inanimate, but with her arms still clasped round the neck of Charles.

"Merciful heaven!" gasped Charles, on beholding the wound in the breast of the poor girl, "who could have done this? Some miscreant has killed her in my arms!"

Every one in the fort denied having perpetrated the act, and, as her history was known to most of the garrison, pity and indignation were felt and expressed by all.

"It was one of Queen Esther's instruments! It must have been!" said Charles, weeping over his forest sister.

"Bring her into the cabin," said the Rev. Mr. Jones, "and she may recover. She is not dead. I feel her heart beating."

"See! she revives!" said Julia. "Poor sister!" she continued; "I will be her nurse."

Charles followed the preacher with his burden, the arms of the wounded girl still clinging to his neck; and, when gently deposited on a couch, her consciousness returned, and, upon recognising the features of the one she loved, a sweet smile spread over her face.

DEATH OF THE BROWN THRUSH.—P. 247.

"My poor sister," said Charles, in broken accents, "why did you expose your tender breast to the aim of the Seneca dogs?"

"The Brown Thrush had sung her last song," said she, in her own musical language, which none but Charles and Mr. Jones could fully understand. "She longed to go to the happy land where the bright streams are dancing—where those who love can never be separated—and where the warm sunshine is never intercepted by clouds. Your wild-wood sister was afraid to take her own life, since the Great Spirit had forbidden it; but she thought he would not be angry if she had another to kill her. I was so unhappy! Oh, my brother, when will you come? And must I travel to the far land alone? How long shall I wait for thee?"

Charles was incapable of utterance, but wept like a child over his dying sister. Mr. Jones, perceiving the wound was mortal, and that the poor girl's life was rapidly ebbing away, strove to cheer her with such assurances as his mission authorized him to pronounce.

"Do not weep for me!" said she, seeing the tears of Charles and Julia. "We shall meet again where tears cannot come. Then the White Eagle shall love the Brown Thrush as dearly as the Antelope. I am happy now. My sight is growing dim, like the mist of the morning; but thou art near. My sister, give me your warm hand; let me place it on my cold breast. My brother, be happy; but don't forget her who charmed thee in the wild woods with her song. When we meet again in the spirit-land, open your arms as you did to-day, and clasp your sister to your heart. When you did so I was happy, though the wound came at the same moment. I will be more happy there, where no wounds can reach me. Dig a deep grave by the spring, and breathe a prayer over thy faded sister! Farewell!"

Her form sank back, and her spirit fled to its eternal abode. A profound silence ensued, and every head was bowed in sorrow. The preacher sank upon his knees, and, although his lips moved in prayer, no one heard his words but the Invisible Being who alone possessed the ability to grant his requests.

A flag was sent in the next day by Duquesne with a proposition for a suspension of hostilities until the dead could be buried; and, as his party had suffered the most severely, and he would derive the greatest benefit from a strict fulfilment of the terms, the request was granted. But the bearer of the flag was, to the astonishment of the garrison, the famous Simon Girty himself, whom they believed to be dead, and most of them had rejoiced in his supposed destruction. It appeared that a piece of leather in his pocket had saved his life. The ball of the pistol, however, had stunned him and brought him to the ground.

The body of the Indian girl, after being shown to the chiefs of the enemy at their special request, that they might know she had not been scalped, was enclosed in a bark coffin and deposited in a deep grave under the weeping-willow near the spring, as she had requested.

After lingering a few days in the hope of obtaining horses, but which was blasted by the vigilance of Kenton, the Indians departed for their homes on the Scioto and the Little Miami.

CHAPTER XVIII.

WINTER AT BOONE'S STATION IN KENTUCKY—CHARLES AND JULIA RETURN TO NEW JERSEY.

WHEN the savages withdrew from the vicinity of Boonesborough, it was observed by Paddy and Van Wiggens in their rambles that one of their rude bark shelters had not only been left standing, but several pieces of buffalo-meat remained on the roof, and smoke seemed to be still ascending from its centre. They drew near to gratify a very natural curiosity. Watch, the little mongrel cur, with his stump of a tail rigidly erect, preceded them; for dogs are quite as curious as men and women.

"Vat's dat?" cried Van Wiggens, seeing the dog retreating whining, and his tail down.

"Be my sowl, that's more than I can tell ye,' said Paddy, "unless ye step forrud and see what it is."

"Go see, den," said Van Wiggens.

"Who? I? And are ye afraid to do it yerself?"

"Afraid?"

"Yes. Are ye not frightened now, because yer dog is barking at a ground-hog, or polecat, or some other varmint, under there? I'm laughing in my slave at ye! Afraid of a skunk, when we kill 'em ivery week under the cabins!"

"Vat's dat you mean? Dunder! Me afraid? Der teiffel! Noting but Mrs. Wan Viggens can scare me!" and he strode forward toward the dark shelter, followed with reluctance by Watch, while Paddy remained at a respectful distance.

No sooner did the Dutchman enter the low habitation than his ears were assailed by a tempest of words which he was incapable of interpreting; and, before he could retreat, his leg was seized by some one half-buried in the leaves.

"Dunder! lev go my leg!" he shouted.

The dog barked furiously.

Paddy ran away, and never paused until he plunged into the area of the quadrangle, shouting "Indians! Indians!"

A crowd, of course, soon assembled, and Paddy was constrained, with some difficulty, to pilot the men back to the scene of the discovery.

Before they arrived in the vicinity, the bark of Watch was heard, as if baying some huge monster which he durst not approach. The next sound was the rattling voice of an old woman, whom Boone pronounced a scold, and a drunken one at that. Drawing near, they beheld poor Van Wiggens retreating slowly from the bark hut, dragging through the leaves by main force the body of Diving Duck, who still clung to his leg and called him her husband. In vain he strove to make Watch seize his tormentor. The dog had once been rudely handled by her, and could not be induced to venture within her reach.

"I was only jesting!" said Paddy. "I made ye belave I was frightened for the sake of the joke. Scared at a squaw!" Such were the replies he made to the sneers of the men who had come forth eager for "a fight."

"Tam it! von't nopody help me?" cried Van Wiggens, who, from his corpulence, soon became exhausted, and puffed and blowed prodigiously.

The old squaw, with dishevelled hair and bloated cheeks, turned her keen eyes upon the men and laughed. Even a dog can tell a man's humour by looking him in the eye; and Diving Duck perceived at once that she afforded amusement for the spectators, and was in no danger of being killed.

After the merriment had been sufficiently prolonged, Boone commanded the old squaw to release her lord; and the moment she did so Van Wiggens and his dog took to their heels and fled to the fort. The old woman ran about shaking hands with the men, fearless of injury, until she fixed her eyes on Paddy, whom she called her "pappoose." She tore a switch from a pendent bough, and seemed determined to administer chastisement for some previous offence, or to vindicate her authority, when Paddy, following the example of Van Wiggens, fled after him toward the fort. The old hag pursued; and when she approached the gate Van Wiggens would have fired upon her had he not been prevented by Charles. He then hid himself in one of the cabins, and the old squaw was permitted to rove about the huts without molestation.

Several weeks after the evacuation of Kentucky by the Indians, Boone, at the head of a party of twenty men, set out for the Licks to make salt,—that indispensable article having become exhausted in the settlements. In this expedition he was accompanied by his brother, and by all the men from the Jenny Jump settlement excepting Charles and Paddy. Van Wiggens led the van, gladly leaving Didapper behind.

During the absence of this detachment the fort was too much weakened to be abandoned by Charles; and his eagerness to return to the Delaware river had to be repressed. And Julia, pleading her promise to her dying father that she would not, during her minority, marry without the consent of her guardian, resisted the importunity of her lover to have their nuptials celebrated in the fort. She admired Mr. Jones very much, and could not entertain a doubt of his piety, or even question what seemed to be his divine mission; but, inasmuch as she had been baptized in the Church of England, by Dr. Odell, of Burlington, she had an irresistible desire to take the marriage-vow with the wedding-ring at St. Mary's holy altar; and in vain did Mr. Jones attempt to combat her prejudices, as he termed them. In vain did he propose to read the ceremony from her own prayer-book, and to manufacture, himself. aided by Van

Wiggens, (who was a blacksmith,) a ring from one of Charles's watch-seals. She begged him to desist, and announced that her decision was irreversible.

About this time, during one of the dark nights of winter, when the inmates of the garrison were assembled round the cheerful blaze on the broad hearth of the principal cabin,—the old women spinning flax and the young ones knitting or sewing, listening to narratives of adventures in the wild woods,—Charles was startled by hearing a pebble fall upon the roof and roll down to the ground. Used to such signals, he sprang to his feet and was approaching the door, when the gentle hand of Julia arrested him. Pale, and trembling very much, she begged him to desist.

"It is only the hail," said Mrs. Calloway, silencing the buzz of her wheel.

"The wind has been howling ever since dark," said Sue, "and it may be the large hail that sometimes falls at the beginning of a storm.

"I don't think any Indians could have passed my father at the Blue Licks," said Mary.

"Not unless they captured him first," said Julia, "which may have been the case!"

"And that's not onlikely," said Paddy, with staring eyes and fallen chin.

"Could you not get into the potato-hole, under the floor, and creep near the door?" asked Mrs. Calloway.

"Me?" said Paddy, in astonishment. "And sure I'd be smothered in a minute! I niver could draw me breath!—I mane, I niver could saa ony thing in the dark."

"It is not an Indian," said Mr. Jones.

"No," said Charles; "if they had captured Boone and his party they would have gone back to celebrate the event" (which was really the case) "before venturing farther into the country."

"But give me light, Mrs. Calloway," said Paddy, "and I don't fear the divil!" and he had made two strides toward the door when another pebble rattled down from the roof. He paused abruptly. "Och, it's only the hail!" said he, and resumed his seat. The next instant, however, hearing some one whistle, he sprang up again, very pale and trembling; but his trepidation was not observed. Both Charles and Julia recognised the signal, and, uttering together a joyous exclamation, the door was thrown open, and the imperturbable Skippie stood in their midst.

The faithful messenger was overwhelmed with hearty greetings, which he bore in silence, but with a proud expression of countenance. He brought, besides the packet of letters, (unsoiled, notwithstanding the inclemency of the season, and the long journey,) another accession to Julia's wardrobe. To the profusion of thanks showered upon him he made no reply, and, merely uttering the word "Virginia," the meaning of which was not comprehended, and pointing to the letters, as if to indicate that they would speak more explicitly, he withdrew to the kitchen, or rather the cabin where the savory viands were usually cooked.

Charles's letter was from his father, announcing his continued good health and the determination of France to make common cause with the Colonies. But this resolution had not yet transpired, and was still one of the secrets of the court of Versailles. The aspect of affairs, nevertheless, at that moment, was sufficiently gloomy. Washington, with a mere handful of men, was hard pressed, and retreating before Cornwallis; and a large portion of the people embraced the terms offered in the royal proclamations, returning to their allegiance. The Indians, too, led by Brandt and instigated by Johnston and the Butlers, were desolating the country on the northern frontier. Murphy, Charles's faithful sergeant, did all in his power to maintain the organization of the little band of patriots; but many difficulties were thrown in his way. In short, Charles was advised to return the first opportunity. Such was the purport of the letter he received from his father.

Julia, while reading her epistle from Kate, could not repress her joy upon learning that her old playmate was then residing with the Moravians, in the immediate vicinity of her guardian's house, whither she had flown as to a secure place of refuge during the perils of the invasion of the western portion of the State, then in possession of the enemy.

"He's well! He's well again!" cried Julia, holding the letter triumphantly aloft.

"He!" said Charles, gravely. "What he do you mean?"

"Solo! Kate says:—'When your monster of a friend,

from Newfoundland, first beheld me, I could with difficulty elude his rather familiar attempts to place a hand (paw) on each of my shoulders. Tears—whether of joy or grief, how could I tell?—trickled down, and I could not prevent him from placing his velvet tongue against my hand. How is this, Julia? Has the sagacious animal heard you speak of me, remembered your words, and recognised your friend? Rely upon it, Solo has my love, and will have my watchful care!' There, Mr. Eagle! Kate is in love with your rival!"

"Read on! God bless Kate! I shall love her for loving your dog."

"I believe you were once inclined to love her for herself, before she ever saw the dog. But I'll pardon that. Oh! here is something very sad and horrible! Read it for me, Charles."

It was an account of the death of Mrs. Caldwell, the wife of the Presbyterian minister. She had been shot by a brutal British soldier, through the window of her chamber, when in the act of prayer in the midst of her little children.

"This act," said Kate, "when known by the British officers, was denounced, but they had no time to seek the perpetrator. From the burning town they came to our house. Father was absent. My mother, my sisters, and myself, when we saw the British in the yard, retreated into the back chamber. The front door was soon burst open. Oh, it was a horrible night! A violent storm raging in the sky as well as upon the earth. The lightning flashed and the thunder rolled terrifically. But this was the voice of God, and the providential means of our salvation. It occurred to me that we might be less liable to outrage by meeting our foes boldly face to face. They were already striking their muskets rudely against the door. I stepped forward; in my loose white wrapper, for we had retired at an early hour, and threw open the door. At that instant the hall was illuminated by a vivid flash of lightning, and no doubt my face was as pale as the corpse they had seen. The soldiers, horror-stricken, fled away, declaring they had been confronted by the ghost of Mrs. Caldwell, murdered by them in the morning. In a moment the house was deserted by them. Julia, you know they used to say there was a resemblance between Mrs. Caldwell and myself. Who could have supposed it would produce such an effect?"

This portion of Kate's letter caused a profound sensation, and Mr. Jones no doubt would have gladly seized the opportunity to "improve the occasion," had his eye not fallen on his own name, in a familiar hand, on one of the letters brought by Skippie. It was from his friend Anthony Wayne, demanding his presence in Jersey, or, as he expressed it, "wherever the enemy may drive us, for we shall never get out of our difficulties without your aid, and I hope the cause is not past praying for."

There was likewise a letter from Mrs. Van Wiggens to her absent husband, but none present felt authorized to open it. But Kate, in her diary, mentioned her several times, and said she was succeeding very well with her tavern.

There were also letters from Thomas and Richard Schooley. The former intimated a purpose to have the lands jointly held by himself and Julia's father surveyed and divided, as he had no idea of any portion of his estate being involved in the confiscation. Charles Cameron had been excepted in the recent royal proclamation offering mercy and protection.

Richard announced his intention to seek the hand of Judith Carlisle, the daughter of Abraham, a staunch royalist. And he concluded with a proposition which startled Julia. "Thee must learn," said he, "that this farm, and all the improvements thereon, appeareth, upon an accurate survey, and the specifications in the deeds, to fall to thy lot. But, as the expenditures thereon were made by us, we do not doubt that thou wilt deal justly. The royal cause must triumph in the end, and it is greatly feared all thy estates will be forfeited. Now, as I have still a friendly regard for thee, I would gladly provide for thy maintenance. I learn that, with the consent of thy guardian, thou mayest execute a legal conveyance of thy lands; and, indeed, if thy father's Bible, found in one of the boxes, would be taken as evidence, it appeareth by certain writings therein thou art older than we supposed, and of an age to act without the concurrence of thy guardian. Therefore, if thee will name a moderate sum in ready money, as an apparent consideration for the lands, and execute a deed conveying them to me, I will pledge myself, after the bloody storm hath swept past, either to reconvey them to thee, or else to pay thee such additional sum or sums as three honest men may adjudge. And if thee will not agree to do this thee will be a pauper upon the county."

Julia's eyes flashed indignantly. Throwing the letter in the fire, she said, "Henceforth I am a rebel!"

"Amen!" cried Mr. Jones. "I'll tell Wayne, and he'll tell Washington! If I'm not mistaken, these Schooleys have more reason to apprehend a loss than yourself. But I must retire. At dawn I shall set out alone for head-quarters. Be not surprised, and do not attempt to interpose any objections. I shall find my way thither in safety. You cannot go till spring, and Skippie will remain till then. Let us unite in an earnest petition to the great Captain-General of the universe. If God be on our side, we shall prevail. Let us appeal to him and be of good cheer. He hurls the bolts of destruction, and the rolling thunders are the reverberations of his voice. Remember who said, when the tempest raged and the billows were lifted up, 'Fear not; it is I.' Yes, my brethren, if he be for us who shall prevail against us? And was not his will clearly manifested in the lightning's flash which struck terror to the murderers of Mrs. Caldwell?"

He then knelt down in their midst and prayed fervently and patriotically for about an hour.

The next morning, having provided himself with ammunition for his pistols, and taking with him a supply of dried buffalo-meat and a canteen of rum, the eccentric preacher set out alone on his journey, never for a moment doubting his ultimate arrival at the head-quarters of the American army.

Diving Duck became a source of great annoyance to Paddy, who regretted that he had not gone with the rest to the Licks. She could not comprehend why her adopted son should not yield obedience to her commands in the fort as well as in the wigwam on the Scioto; and all her orders aimed at the procurement of rum. She threatened, she stormed, she begged, in vain. Charles had forbidden it.

After lingering about the fort a few weeks, she announced

her purpose of returning to her own country, and demanded of Charles an order for Paddy to accompany her.

"Do you wish to go with your mother?" asked Charles, turning to Paddy.

"Me mother, is it? Howly mother forbid! And would ye be afther sariously calling sich a varmint as that me mother, Misther Charles? Plase don't do ony sich thing! Go wid 'er, did ye say? I'd rather go back and live wid the owld sow I kilt in the wild woods!"

"Shall I interpret your speech to her?" asked Charles.

"No! plase don't, or she'll be afther me wid the frying-pan. But I'll tell ye what I'll do, and if ye plase ye may turn it into the Indian brogue. I'll pack her up some jerked buffalo-bafe and start her off on Pater Shaver's jackass, provided she'll swear on the Howly Evangely niver to call Patrick Pence her son agin!"

"Oh, do!" said Julia. "The sound of that animal's voice is a terror to me!"

"And no wonder, Misthress Julia, as it reminds ye of blood. And besides, Misther Charles, only consider that Pater is anoder o' her sons, and she has a lagal right to the baste; and if Pater objicts to it afther the baste is gone, I'll give him me note for the vally of the crather."

"It shall be done," said Charles, quite anxious to get rid of the animal. And the old squaw was delighted with the arrangement. The only stipulation she added was a moderate dram, and when it was greedily swallowed she set forth on the ass.

As the winter passed away, the joy of the wanderers at the prospect of a speedy return to the Delaware was engloomed by the reception of melancholy tidings. A son of Mr. Calloway, about fifteen years of age, who had accompanied his father to the Licks, came in one day, pale, haggard, and half famished. He told his sister, who wept upon his neck, that their father and the entire party at the Licks had been surrounded and captured by an army of more than a hundred warriors. They had, however, pledged themselves to Boone that the lives of the prisoners should be spared, and that they should not be subjected to the humiliations and pains of the gauntlet.

The Indians, instead of assaulting the forts, which might have been carried when weakened by the loss of their best men, hurried away as usual to celebrate their success. And it may be here remarked that the stipulations agreed to by them were faithfully fulfilled.

The capture of the men at the Licks occurred late in January, and February had been appointed by Charles as the time of setting out. It was now feared some delay would ensue, as he could not in honour abandon the post assigned him when the opinion prevailed that the Indians would return after depositing their prisoners in a place of security; and the distribution of the emigrants recently arrived among some half dozen forts might not suffice for their defence if a single man were subtracted.

This apprehension was removed, however, by the unexpected arrival of another body of emigrants. It appeared that the glowing accounts of the salubrity of the climate and fertility of the soil, which had reached the East, had stimulated the people of whole neighbourhoods to emigrate; and every man brought a gun with him.

His design being thus facilitated, and having the repeated assurances of Julia that she would be able to perform the journey, (for she had learned many lessons in woodscraft during her sojourn in the wilderness,) Charles made preparations for an immediate departure. Their horses were selected and caparisoned. Buffalo-robes for their warmth and shelter were provided. Food was packed, and every needful arrangement for their comfort and safety completed. Then, taking leave of their Western friends, with many regrets for the loss of the comrades left behind them, Charles, Julia, Skippie, and Paddy, commenced the long and weary journey eastward.

CHAPTER XIX.

CHARLES AND JULIA IN BURLINGTON—THEY MEET THOMAS SCHOOLEY — DR. ODELL — THE HAUNTED KNOCKER — GOVERNOR FRANKLIN.

THE incidents of minor interest during the journey eastward, the scenery in the mountains, which were still covered with snow, the hunting adventures of Paddy, and the hearty though rude entertainment afforded by the few scattering cabins on the way, I cannot dwell upon in this place, although the diary of Julia is lying before me in unfaded calligraphy. Events of greater magnitude must occupy the remaining pages of my narrative.

Once more Julia and Charles and Paddy were in the ancient village of Burlington. And at that time it seemed to have greater pretensions to rivalry in the race of cities than at the present day. The idea that it would surpass Philadelphia in population had not, perhaps, been entirely relinquished; but the hope has faded since.

Julia, as soon as she was landed from the schooner at the foot of Main Street, proceeded without delay, followed by Paddy in the capacity of footman, to the residence of her guardian, which she supposed would be still found remaining in the occupancy of the old housekeeper. To her surprise, if not satisfaction, the first person she met, when passing the threshold, was Thomas Schooley himself.

"Why, Julia," exclaimed he, "do I behold thee again?"

"Plase yer honour," said Paddy, "I'll swear to her idintity, as they made me do wanst before the coroner, when Mary McShane made 'way wid herself.'"

"Swear not at all, Patrick," said Thomas.

"Not I, sir; but, plase yer honour, you have confissed to me, and called me be me own name."

"And am I so much changed, Thomas?" asked Julia, smiling. She had procured new apparel in Philadelphia, and there was no perceptible alteration in her appearance since their separation.

"No—Julia—no! Thee does not seem to have changed in aspect or inclination to follow the fashions in the style and colour of thy outward adornments. But I did not expect to meet thee here. Sit thee at the fire, and a breakfast shall be prepared for thee. How didst thou come, and from whence?"

"We have just landed from the schooner we embarked in at Wilmington. But, before leaving the fort in the western wilderness, Skippie had delivered thy letters."

"The letters!" said Thomas, with unwonted energy. "Hast thou preserved them?"

"No, Thomas," said the girl, with an angry look. "I consigned both thine and Richard's letters——"

"To whom? Speak, Julia!" he said, hurriedly, and in uncontrollable agitation.

"To the flames," she continued.

"Flames! I thank thee!" he added, breathing freely. "But it was not respectful; yet we will say nothing more about it."

"But we *must* have more to say in regard to those letters," said Julia. "Why didst thou write me in that manner? And why wert thou so greatly excited just now, Thomas?"

"Thee shall know all, Julia; only be patient. The times are perilous, and the world is ever changing. The offer was made by Richard in good faith. But since then George Washington has performed miracles. He has surprised and beaten the King's forces in several places, and recovered the greater portion of this Colony. But the next change will be in favour of the royal cause, and we who are opposed to strife will have rest and peace."

Julia listened attentively, without interrupting her circumspect guardian; and, when he had finished discussing the affairs of the Colony, she hastened to inform herself in relation to matters in the Jenny Jump settlement; but affairs there had experienced no material alteration since her last advices from Kate. She was gratified, however, to be informed that her guardian was only on a brief visit in Burlington, and, having despatched his business, would return immediately.

Charles and Skippie sat in the bar-room of the principal hotel at the junction of Main and Broad Streets. During the last year the establishment had experienced several changes of proprietors. When the British were overrunning the State, and Count Donop was encamped with four hundred Hessians on the Wetherill lot in view of the court-house, and the jail in the immediate vicinity was filled with rebel prisoners, the premises were quietly leased to a new landlord, who had, the next day, the sign of the British 'ion swinging before the door. But after the battles of Trenton and Princeton, the discharges of artillery on both occasions being distinctly audible at Burlington, the frowning lion lost his eyes, (the work of some boys in the night,) and was made to succumb to the impromptu representation of an eagle, and another transfer of the premises ensued.

The last landlord, whom we shall designate by the name of John Brown, to avoid identification, was familiarly known by the cognomen of Mr. *Allright*, John being peculiarly adapted to all parties and exigencies. Mr. Allright John Brown was a bustling, portly, talkative, accommodating host.

When Charles and Skippie entered the bar-room a party of Tories had just been drinking at the bar, and as they withdrew from the house they paused at the corner and cast curious glances back at the strangers.

"Don't notice 'em!" said the host. "They are idle characters," he added, in a low tone, "who do nothing but drink and pry into matters which don't concern them. I wonder they didn't question you as to which side you are on."

"And, pray, to which side do they belong?" asked Charles.

"Oh, they are for the King," said the host.

"And I am for the Congress!" said Charles.

"I thought so!" exclaimed Brown, smiling, and enthusiastically shaking the hand of his young guest. "*I* am all right," said he, with a significant wink. "But, my young friend, be cautious how you express yourself before strangers. One-half of 'em are rank Tories, and they swear every rebel here shall swing on Gallows Hill. By walking out into the middle of the street you can see the hill, and the scaffolding erected last Christmas eve. But that night Washington crossed the Delaware and played the d—l with their calculations. Walk into the next room. I smell the ham and eggs. And take my advice and hold your tongue when curious ears are about."

Charles and Skippie passed through the door to which the landlord pointed, and sat down to the savoury repast. And while they were appeasing their appetites, the door communicating with the bar-room being left ajar, they heard the following conversation between the host and a new visitor:—

"Thee must still see after my house, John," said the visitor, "and supply the servant with food."

"Certainly, friend Thomas," said the host; "you may depend on me. You have become my surety for the payment of the rent. As I was saying last night when General Cadwallader arrived and interrupted us, the 'Sons of Liberty' were once going to tear down your mansion, but I prevented it by saying you were as good a Whig as old Flint-face himself."

"Thee should not have said that, John. We are not permitted to lie. If they had torn down my house there would have been a reimbursement out of the forfeiture of their own estates."

"But suppose the rebellion should never be put down, friend Thomas: what then?"

"No matter; I tell thee I would not lie to save my house."

"I know thee wouldn't, friend Thomas; and thee didn't. Your conscience had nothing to do with it; I lied for you. *I* don't mind it."

"Thee must not do such things, John! I tell thee it will not answer. If thee don't mind lying, how am I to judge when thou speakest the truth? Thee says thy business is profitable. How am I to know it? Thee declares I run no risk in being thy surety for the rent; perhaps I shall have it to pay for thee! Besides," contined he, willing to change the subject, "I hear that thee professed great attachment to those officers of the rebel army who put up with thee when passing."

"Ha! ha! ha! Of course I did! Would you not have me be agreeable to my guests? And you'll hear the same thing of Lord Cornwallis and General Howe, when they come. *I'm* all right! You needn't fear."

Just as he uttered these words, Charles, who had finished eating, returned to the bar-room.

"Hem! I—just step into *that* room!" said the host to his young guest, pointing to another door. "There is a good hickory fire in it. Step in!"

"I have seen Julia," said Mr. Schooley, advancing and offering his hand, which Charles did not refuse, "and learned thou hadst returned. Thee looks well; and I am glad to see thee dressed after the habit of civilized men, albeit I do not approve the colour and fashion of thy garments."

"Hem! That's strange!" said Brown, aside. "Glad, and don't approve! And they know each other. I'm thinking friend Thomas knows more about lying than he pretends to."

"My garments suit myself," said Charles, "as thine do thee, friend Thomas. I do not object to thine."

"We will not quarrel about our clothes," said Mr. Schooley, smiling faintly. "I am a man of peace, as I would have all men to be; and I learn it is thy intention to return to the upper settlement. I am glad of it. I do not think thee will permit thy sergeant to annoy us any more by exacting money from Richard."

"Murphy must collect the fines prescribed by law," said Charles.

"Law! Well, thee may live to know what law is! But no more. We must not quarrel. To-morrow we will journey together. Farewell, till we meet again." Thomas withdrew, and hastened to collect the interest on various sums loaned to the thrifty members of the Quaker society composing a large proportion of the population of Burlington.

"Gad!" exclaimed Brown, approaching Charles, "you know him? I'm all right! Schooley's an old rascal,—a rank Tory! And he's going to cheat one of the prettiest girls in America out of her fortun'. He's as rich as Crashes now, but he wants more. It's a pity some handsome young fellow like yourself don't marry the poor girl, and save her fortun'. They say he had her taken off by the Indians, but they wouldn't kill her."

"That was a lie," said Charles. "I know her, and I know the tale is without foundation."

"I'm glad to hear it. There are always a great many lies in circulation. I hate a liar as I do a Tory. I'm all right! And I'm glad friend Schooley isn't so bad as represented. But he's as rich as Crashes, and you know such men always have enemies."

"Of course they do," said Charles. "But can you tell me what has become of Governor Franklin?"

"The governor? Certainly! He's in New York. The British exchanged a general for him. He's at the bottom, or rather at the head, of all the Tories in Jersey. He knows who's who in these times, and he knows *I*'m all right! Sometimes he is at Staten Island, and sometimes at Amboy; and they do whisper he has even been here, in disguise," continued Brown, in a low voice, knowing that Franklin was, at that moment, in his house!

"Who occupies his mansion on the bank?"

"None but one of the old women of the family. The celebrated doctor who, you know, is the governor's father, sent the woman up to see after his furniture and books, and the people haven't disturbed the place at all, on the doctor's account. But it's haunted!"

"Haunted?"

"Bless you, yes! I thought everybody knew that. Why, the old sycamore, belonging to the witches, is just before the door. They dance and sing and knock every night. It is said they have bought young Ben Sheppard from his father."

"And do the people believe such things?"

"Of course! And it's a good thing for the property."

"I suppose they are afraid to enter the mansion."

"They are, by gum!"

"Friend Charles," said Thomas Schooley, re-entering, his countenance betraying a mental struggle, "I have returned to have a sober talk with thee. Come into the next room. Now, my friend," resumed he, when they were seated in the snug chamber, since converted into a parlour, "why should we not explain ourselves and have a clear understanding of each other's purposes?"

"I do not know by what authority you may demand——"

"Tut! Pr'ythee, Charles, listen patiently to me. It may be well for thee and for us both. An accommodation may be effected, a compromise——"

"No, sir! I love Julia, and you are her guardian. You can withhold your consent to our nuptials until she arrives at a certain age, which, if the old Bible is to be believed——"

"Thee hast seen Richard's letter! Well, the figures are uncertain. Whether the date is 1755, or 1758, it would be hard to decide."

"No matter. I have no right to investigate the subject. You can withhold your sanction, and we can wait, till your authority ceases. That is all. I will not compromise my own or Julia's character by any sort of agreement or bargain——"

"Thee misunderstands me, and will not listen. Will thee answer one thing?"

"I don't know."

"I will ask the question, and thee can answer or not as thee pleases. Dost thou intend to wed my ward clandestinely, or openly against my wishes?"

"I will answer that, because it is not impertinent. You are her legal guardian——"

"I am glad thee acknowledges so much."

"And I am her ardent adorer."

"Thee speaks as if she were a divinity!"

"No matter. You do not comprehend such things. I intend, friend Thomas, to see Dr. Odell, and if he will marry us—Julia consenting—we will return man and wife to the Jenny Jump."

"Indeed! It is boldly spoken!"

"Yes, and——"

"Thee is disposed to swear. I will leave thee."

"It is an inclination I will repress:—a habit in civilized society, and particularly among the loyalists. I did not contract it among the Indians. They never swear. But, Thomas, I am quite sure—at least very fearful—that Julia will not comply with my request without your concurrence."

"I thank thee for thy frankness. Adieu, till we meet again at——"

"But, Thomas, why be in such haste? A word from thee will be sufficient to remove the obstacle, and then Julia will consent. I have been candid."

"Thee has, and I will be so too. Thee shall not wed my ward with my consent!"

"Very well! I shall not beg you to relent, nor attempt to entrap you into a compliance. But you may rely upon it that Julia will never marry your industrious son. So, if it be your expectation to obtain her fortune in that way, you will be disappointed."

"Thee may have learned, since our letters to our ward seem to have been subjected to thy perusal—albeit she said they were burned——"

"She said truly. She threw them contemptuously, as they deserved, into the fire."

"I am glad of the action, and care nothing for the contempt. Thee has no doubt heard of the purpose of Richard to marry Judith Carlisle. Thee has not heard of the misunderstanding since then—but no matter! Charles, thee thinks me a worshipper of mammon, an idolater of gold, without honour or religion. Thee does not know me. Fortune is desirable, and it is not sinful to seek it honestly. It is not wrong to marry a wife with riches. But I have a duty to perform. I made my friend, Julia's father, a pledge which I must fulfil. Her fortune shall not be imperilled while she continues under my control. That is the promise I made. If I were to consent to her marriage with thee, every thing would be lost when order is restored and the king's authority re-established."

"Oh, yes!—when the devil reigns, justice and virtue—but no matter! It will be seen who are the losers. You think the advices by the secret messengers from New York are cheering. So be it. I have advices too. Let the game be played. I win if you lose."

"Thee talks like a gamester. Farewell!" And Thomas withdrew.

Charles strolled out into the street, and, passing the Friends' burying-ground, where so many had been laid without monument or inscription, approached the Episcopal church, (St. Mary's.)

The door was partly open, and he thought he heard the last notes of sacred music dying on the air. He paused and looked in. The Rev. Dr. Odell stood before the altar, with cup and plate before him, while about a dozen females knelt around the chancel. On that unusual day, and at that singular hour, he was administering the sacrament to a small remnant of his flock. There was not a man among them. We trust the same disparity of sex may not exist in heaven!

Charles, yielding to the solemn impulse of the moment, strode forward and knelt among them. He, too, although so long a wanderer, belonged to the same flock. Tears were on the cheeks of the pious minister, and several of the women were sobbing.

When they arose, the eyes of Charles and Julia met. They had been kneeling together; and, when the rest withdrew, the lovers were beckoned aside by the priest.

"My dear children," said he, when they were seated, "God hath conducted thee to St. Mary's holy shrine on the day of separation."

"Separation!" said both Charles and Julia.

"Separation; and perhaps a final one," said the minister. "The earthly shepherd is driven away from his flock; but the heavenly Shepherd remains. Be of comfort. The spirits of the pious dead who lie around us are at peace. We must join them in time. They will inscribe our names on the marble over our dust, and we, too, will have our rest. It matters not where they may place us, or who chisels the monumental marble, or what inscription there may be upon it, so our names are written in the Book of Life. The faithful will meet again in heaven. Farewell, my dear children! I must go!"

"Go! Whither?"

"Whithersoever they may drive me. I must practise what I have preached. We are commanded to render unto Cæsar the things which are Cæsar's, and unto God the things which be God's:—to honour the king and obey his statutes. And for doing this my enemies have decreed that I must leave the Colonies. I will not attempt to pronounce judgment in this unhappy controversy. Neither will I violate my own conscience or shrink from my duty. It is the last time I shall see the faithful remnant of my beloved flock. Hence my tears. Farewell!"

"Doctor," said Charles, "Julia and myself are affianced lovers. Will you not unite us in lawful wedlock before you go?"

Julia's veil dropped down over her blushing face; but she trembled and withdrew her hand, which Charles had seized.

"It may not be, my son," said the minister. "I know all. Julia has told me all, and obtained my advice, which is disinterested. I could not sanction a violation of her solemn pledge to her father, nor could I approve of her linking her earthly destiny with one who might bring sorrow upon her gentle spirit. I know you would be incapable of inflicting pain upon the beloved of thy heart. Others would inflict it. When, as it is not improbable, like other mistaken enthusiasts, you shall be brought to the block for rebellion against the king——"

"Doctor!" exclaimed Julia, "it is not rebellion! it is revolution! And I am as staunch a patriot as Charles. Were I a man, I would rush into the battle-field and fight for liberty!"

"Poor thing!" said the doctor. "Well, my dear children, you must excuse me. I cannot and will not violate my sense of duty——"

"Forgive me, sir!" said Julia, quickly; "I do not desire you to perform the ceremony which Charles is so anxious to have consummated. But I do not condemn his patriotism, and I do not fear the cause he espouses will entail ruin on him. I will abide by my promise to my dying parent——"

"God bless you both!" ejaculated the minister, holding a hand of each. "Farewell! Postpone the solemnization of your nuptials until this hurly-burly be done. If God so wills it, the Colonies may be free—if separation be freedom; and if not—but time will prove all things, and you are both young enough to wait for the end. Adieu! And may heaven's choicest blessings be showered upon you!"

After lingering a few moments, Charles and Julia withdrew, and, as they strolled together toward the mansion of Thomas Schooley, they were met by that gentleman himself, very pale and anxious.

"I hope thee will tell me truly and without delay," said he.

"Tell thee what?" demanded Charles.

"Whether John hath spoken truly."

"What John? There are many of them."

"John Brown, the hotel-keeper. He says you have been married at the church."

"Friend Thomas," said Charles, "you know John has acquired the accomplishment of lying. And I am very sure you will be happy to learn he has been lying to thee this time."

"That may be very witty; but thou hast to learn that principles are immutable things. I shall be glad to learn thee has not been wedded, and regret that John lied about it."

"I am justly rebuked, Thomas, and ask thy pardon," said Charles.

"Thee has it. But thee has been to church?"

"Yes, sir. Dr. Odell believes, as you do, that we are rebels——"

"I know that."

"No doubt; but, unlike yourself, he intends to leave us."

"He leaves no estate behind."

"His treasure is above. He has been administering the Holy Communion to a remnant of his flock, who have taken a final leave of him at the altar."

"Mummery! Theatrical pageantry!" said Thomas.

"Mr. Schooley," said Charles, "if you discard the Holy Scriptures, your religion is that of the heathen; but if you be a Christian, how can you deride the commands of the Saviour?"

"Rebuked in turn!" said Julia, as she sprang into the hall of her guardian's house, which they had just reached.

"Charles," said Thomas, as the young man paused and was about to return to his hotel, "if thee will come and sup with us I will explain the principles of our religion."

"I will call during the evening," said Charles, "and listen to thee, provided, if we should be converted, thou wilt sanction our——"

"Pooh! nonsense!" said Thomas, entering the hall and closing the door behind him.

After tea, Charles strode out alone to see by the moonlight the changes which had taken place in the principal streets of the old village. Burlington had then been founded more than a hundred years.

As he slowly walked along the margin of the river, between Ben Shephard's tavern and the governor's house, he was overtaken by Paddy.

"Be jabers! and it's meself is glad to mate wid ye, Misther Charles," said he.

"The compliments of the evening to you, Paddy. I suppose, Paddy, you are a happy man, now; and nothing could induce you to quit the town again. There is no danger here."

"And there ye're out of it! The bloody Bratish, if they could catch me here, wud skin me alive, like an ail; and, as for sperrits, and witches, and hobgoblins, this ould village bates any of the round towers in Ireland. Misther Charles, do you belave the Quakers are rale flesh-and-blood paple?"

"Certainly!"

"Thin I don't! Look at their faces,—all tallow and no blood! If one dies, it don't disturb a tay-party in the same house They don't put stones over their graves, and a husband dont go in mourning for his wife. I don't belave they're rale flesh and blood. When one dies the rest know he's not gone far off; and I belave they can't be kept under ground. I've sane 'em set in the mating-house widout opening their mouths only jist to hoot and stare like owls. Sure they are convarsing with sperits when they're silent. Look at their hats and coats, and tell me if mortal men and women wud dress in that style?"

"They must be mortal, Paddy, for they love money."

"And don't witches and sperits love the falthy lucre? Why do the ghosts of murthered paple guard the puncheons of goold at the ould tannery in Wood Strate, hid under ground by the pirate Kadd? Why do the witches daunce and sing ivery night under the sycamore by the governor's house, if it ain't to watch the hidden treasure? I belave the Quakers are witches and sperits, and that the Yankees did right to burn 'em and drown 'em."

"Nevertheless, you are in the service of one, Paddy; but where are you going?"

"To the governor's house itself. Here's a paper sayled up which Mr. Schooley bade me deliver to an ould famale woman at the door."

"Very well, I won't detain you; but I'm afraid we won't have the pleasure of your society in the country."

"But ye will! Be the powers! I wuddn't stay here for—pause one moment, if ye plase, Misther Charles! Surely ye wuddn't be after going in that direction, right up Wood Strate, past the Pirates' Tra, when the stars and the moon are blanking, and wanking, and shammering, like the ghostly sunlight in one's drames!"

"Yes, I am. If dead men, or women either, walk the earth again, I'm not afraid of them."

"Thruc for you, Misther Charles; and Alexander, and Saizer, and Charles the Twelfth, didn't fear man or baste, but that didn't kape 'em out of danger. Let me go wid ye. The sperits wont appear before two o' us."

"I'm obliged for your offer of protection, Paddy; but you have the packet to deliver farther down the bank."

"And sure it's but a trifle of a little step, and you can jist come wid me, and thin I'll go home wid ye."

"Thank you, Paddy; but I'll take my chances and brave the anger of the dead pirates. Good-night!"

"Och, Misther Charles! now couldn't ye oblige me?—he's gone! And I'm in a cowld swate! And I'll have to tak' howld of that haunted knocker! And they say if the divil's the last one that entered, the brass'll scorch one's fangers! Och, murther! and there's no use in running from 'em! Onyhow, I'll pape round about first."

Such were Paddy's words as he drew near the stately mansion; while Charles paused at the tanyard in Wood Street, and gazed at the tree under whose roots, it was said, the pirates had buried their treasure.

"Who are you?" exclaimed our hero, his blood chilled, and his heart palpitating in spite of himself, upon seeing a figure rise up from one of the half-filled vats and approach him.

"Skippie," replied the other.

"And what are you doing here? acting the ghost? I have heard there was such humour in you."

"Knocker," said Skippie.

"Knocker! the haunted Knocker, I suppose?"

Skippie nodded affirmatively.

"Then I am to understand you are the one who knocks?"

Skippie again nodded.

"You need not have taken the precaution to inform me, Skippie."

"Horse-hair."

"Horse-hair? Now, you will have to make a speech of more than two syllables if you would be understood."

But he did no such thing, for the next instant he had vanished; and Charles, after gazing round a moment, resumed his brisk pace, and did not pause again until he was admitted into the presence of Julia and her guardian.

Paddy, after a somewhat prolonged reconnoissance, and during which he failed to discern the gliding form of Skippie, softly approached the door of the governor's mansion, and, raising the handle of the knocker, gave several timid raps.

But no sooner had he relinquished the handle, and was standing quite still, listening for a footstep within, than the handle seemed to lift up itself before his face and make three loud raps.

"Howly Vargin!" cried Paddy, sinking down on his knees.

The door opened, and a tall, gaunt, white-haired woman stood before him.

"What do you want?" she asked.

"Howly St. Pater presarve us!"

"What do you want? Did you not knock?"

"Plase yer hon—yer riv—I mane yer worshipful patticoats——"

"Did you knock?" again demanded the woman.

"I did; and, as sure as the sperits walk the earth, the divil rapped after me. I saw it wid me own eyes! And it's a blessing I arrived first, or me hand wud be scorched to the bone!"

"What do you want?"

"I'm sure I'm obliged to ye for thim words, or I shud niver've bane reminded of it! Here's a sayled paper Mr. Schooley has directed to somebody here, such as can rade the inscription; but, for me own part, I can't saa a scratch of writing on the back o' it."

The woman took the paper from his hand, and re-entered, closing the door behind her. Paddy, who had risen, stared after her, and then at the mysterious knocker; and, while he gazed, the handle was lifted up again, and three distinct raps sounded in his ears.

"That's another divil!" said he. "There's a whist club of 'em mateing here to-night. And they'll drink melted lead over their cards. Howly Vargin and St. Pater! kape Paddy Pence out of their stakes!"

The knocker was sounded again.

"Another divil! There's at layst a dizen in the club! Och, Patrick Pence! if there's ony sprangs in yer legs, let 'em do good sarvice now, or they'll niver be of any vally to ye aftherwards!" And, saying this, he sprang away, and ran with great speed up the river toward the Ferry-House. When he reached the corner of Main Street, he was met by young Ben Shephard, who accosted him.

"Are the witches after you, Paddy?" asked the youth.

"A whole club of divils! They're mating at the governor's house."

"If that's it, they can't be chasing you. Come in and take a glass of cideroil, and that will raise your spirits."

"Sperits, Misther Ben! Don't mintion 'em. But if you can let me have a glass of brandy or rum, I'll pay ye to-morrow afthernoon." Paddy drank the liquor, and then hastened back to his master's house, panting, but not so pale as he had been.

When he presented himself in the apartment where Julia, Charles, and Mr. Schooley were sitting, words rolled rapidly from his tongue. He said he had not only heard the devils, but he had seen them. The tips of their fingers were like the points of red-hot pokers, and their breath against the door made a black mark like burnt gunpowder.

"Thee has been drinking, I fear, Paddy," said Mr. Schooley.

"Bless yer honour's sowl, I've not tasted a dhrop the howl day, and I'll take me Bible-oath on it!"

"No oaths in my presence, Patrick, or thee must leave my service without a character. Answer me truly. Thee says thee has drunk nothing during the day. Has thee not been drinking to-night?"

"Only a dhrop I tasted to-night at owld Ben Shephard's—and that was afther I saw the divils and the witches. Your honour may belave me—it's thrue, ivery word!"

Just then a rapping was heard at the door.

"Go, now, Patrick," said Mr. Schooley, "and see who comes hither at this hour."

"Plase yer honour," said Paddy, his knees knocking together, "it's one of the divils! I know his knock. And he's afther me for promising to pay Ben Shephard for the dhrink to-morrow afthernoon, whin I will be on the road to Jenny Jump! Misther Charles! Miss Julia! Wud ye not, one o' ye, oblage me wid the loan of a thrippence to pay it?"

"Yes, Paddy," said Charles, holding forth the coin.

"And wud ye not bind me to yerself foriver by paying it to him for me?"

"Who?"

"The divil."

"Nonsense, Patrick!" said Mr. Schooley. "Go to the door! Does thee not hear the rapping?"

"Hear it? It sounds like the last thrump which is to waken the dead! Howly Vargin presarve us!"

"Go to the door, I tell thee!"

Paddy spasmodically rushed into the hall, and, throwing open the street-door, concealed himself behind it. He stood there some moments, but no one entered. Presently Mr.

Schooley came into the hall with a light, and, seeing no one, endeavoured to close the door, which, however, was held back by Paddy.

"What is thee doing behind there?" asked the old gentleman. "And who knocked?"

"Who knocked? Sure it was the divil!"

"Pooh! Close the door. But some one did knock; and I suppose he got tired waiting for thee."

"And, plase yer honour, I hope he'll niver return," replied Paddy, shutting the door and bolting it. But this had hardly been completed before three distinct raps were heard again.

"Now open it," said Mr. Schooley.

"It's the divil, yer honour; and he don't git tired waiting; but he niver forgits to remember who he's afther!"

"Do thou hold the light, and I will open the door," said Mr. Schooley. It was done; but, no one appearing in view, up or down the pavement, or across the street, Mr. Schooley seemed very much surprised.

"Plase yer honour, he's vanished into thin air, and ye naadn't look for him." Mr. Schooley made no reply, and was proceeding to close the door, when three more knocks, the vibrations of which could be distinctly felt, were sounded while he still held the knob in his hand.

"The divil agin!" said Paddy. "The club's adjourned to our house!"

Mr. Schooley, adjusting his spectacles, peered once more into the street; and, stepping out to the curb, stood some moments in silence. And when he turned to re-enter, the handle of the knocker was lifted, by some invisible means, before his face, and rapped quite as startlingly as ever!

"Murther! I felt his breath on me chake!" cried Paddy, letting the candle fall, and rushing back into the room where Charles and Julia were sitting.

He was followed by Thomas, whose face was paler than usual, and whose eyes stared wildly through the glasses of his spectacles.

"No one is there," said he. "I don't understand it. Thee may go to bed, Patrick."

"Plase yer honour, I'm afraid," said Paddy.

Charles and Julia were quite composed, for they knew Skippie was the author of the contrivance.

"Thee may satisfy thyself," said Mr. Schooley to Charles, hearing the rapping again.

Charles went to the door, and, hearing a rustling among the branches of the large tree that stood at the curb, looked up and recognised Skippie.

"Ask him now!" whispered Skippie.

"Ask for what?" demanded Charles.

"Julia. Consent!"

"Come down, and go to your room at the hotel," said Charles. "No more of this nonsense. I want none of your aid." Then, after a brief examination of the knocker, he discovered a line of white hairs, from a horse's tail, reaching from the handle of the knocker to the tree. This he snapped asunder, and re-entered.

"It was an idle boy's trick," said he, in answer to the inquiring eyes of Mr. Schooley. "Adieu, Julia," he continued; "we will start early in the morning, and should be at rest now."

"Howld! Misther Charles, if ye plase!" said Paddy, following the young man through the hall, and endeavouring to detain him.

"Go to bed, Paddy," said Charles, "and be up early in the morning. There will be no more knocking to-night."

"And did ye saa him, and have ye his word for it?"

"No matter; you will not be troubled again. Go to bed, and think no more about it."

"But me drames, Misther Charles!—they'll come back in me drames, and——" Charles was gone.

About the same hour that Charles retired to rest, a muffled individual emerged from the tavern, and, turning westward, proceeded along what is now Broad Street; but at that time there were no houses west of Main Street excepting the church and parsonage. The solitary nocturnal pedestrian, passing the Quaker graveyard, entered Wood Street and directed his steps toward the river. When he reached the gate in the rear of the governor's mansion, he paused and reconnoitred the avenues in the vicinity.

Taking a key from his vest-pocket, Mr. Franklin—for it was the late royal governor, a fair, fat man of forty—entered the garden. Breathing freely, for he deemed himself now in a place of security, he lingered a moment gazing at the loveliness of the scene, which it was quite impossible for him to abandon without regret.

By means of another key he entered the rear-door of the mansion, and was embraced by the tall gray-haired woman in charge of the premises.

"My mother!"

"My son!"

These were the words uttered.

"You must go with me to New York, mother," said he.

"No, I shall remain. Such is the will of your father."

"But if his will be done, mother, what will become of me? However, it won't be done! The cause he is embarked in is a hopeless one, and, as your affection for him can never be eradicated, it might be in your power to serve him if you resided near the head-quarters of the royal army. Depend upon it, he will require our interposition to save him from destruction."

"No more of that, William," said she, with a sigh. "Your father knows best, and it is my duty to be governed by his direction."

"Then be it so, good mother! But the papers! the letters!" he continued, following his parent into the library.

"Here they are," said she, taking a large packet from a table on which a small lamp was dimly burning.

"Are all of them here? I have not time to examine them."

"All. But why not destroy your father's letters?"

"I shall have use for them, perhaps, in my efforts to save him. If not, mother, they shall never be used to his injury."

"I hope not, my son! And, if they be properly interpreted, they could not be. Whatever Lord Bute may allege to the contrary, I have the best reason to know he was always true to the cause of liberty."

"Liberty! Mother, do I not enjoy as much liberty as my father?"

"I think not. He never skulked about in the night to avoid identification."

"But if he were to venture within our lines he would do the same thing."

"He will never go to the British——

"Enough, mother. Time is precious, and I must be on the road before morning. Has Mr. Schooley come?"

"No; I hear the signal now. That is the low rap."

She glided, feeling her way, through the dark hall, and a moment after returned, leading in Friend Thomas, who was greeted in a very friendly manner by the ex-governor.

"I am glad to see thee looking so well, William, and in such high spirits. I trust thee is cheered by the prospects ahead."

"Certainly. During the year both Philadelphia and New York will be in possession of his Majesty's troops, and it will go hard if I am not restored to my office, New Jersey lying between those cities."

"It would seem so, indeed, friend William. But thee must rely upon the royal troops; thee cannot count upon efficient aid from the citizens."

"Then the citizens, as you call them, will have no special claims on me when I am restored."

"Dost thou mean, William, that thy restoration will be a cancellation of thy debts?"

"No. Ha! ha! ha! I owe thee a thousand pounds, Thomas, borrowed money, which I will repay."

"I never could doubt thy honesty, William; and I hope thee intends to pay me to-night."

"Not a stiver! I have no money, and will not have any until the war is over."

"What? Does thee say thee has no money? Why didst thou, then, write me to meet thee here?" Thomas was much surprised, and deeply disappointed.

"I desired information and assistance."

"Thee gets no more assistance from me!"

"I mean assistance for the king. I hope *you* will not deny his authority."

"Thee knows I am loyal; but I will not fight. I can do nothing for or against either party. All I desire is to be permitted to rest in peace."

"You can tell me how the influential men are affected, and what is the sentiment of the other classes."

"Thee knows as much as I do. The people are divided, and are required at home to keep each other in order."

"Good news that, Thomas! The rebels have no money, and cannot long maintain an army if the people are equally divided. But we must be fed. We want another hundred head of cattle. Can you fill the contract?"

"I shall have some beef-steers and fatted dry-cows for sale. They will be driven to the Hudson in the night to avoid the robbers roving by day. I shall ask so much per head in gold, and I will not inquire whether the purchaser be Whig or Tory."

"And you can add fifty per cent. to their value and consider one-half of my indebtedness liquidated."

"I must do no such thing, William. If my price is too much, no one is bound to make the purchase. But thee has something else to say."

"Yes. When we are again in possession of the Jerseys, you must come back and reside in the civilized portion of the State. All the settlements near the head-waters of the Delaware will be destroyed by the Indians. Brandt and the Butlers have been charged with that service. The Sachem is furious. He has learned that his sister was murdered by the men under the command of the young rebel who levies contributions from thee and other true loyalists near the Gap, and who, it is said, is to wed thy rich ward."

"William, it is all untrue—untrue from beginning to end, as I verily believe. My ward says it was a Seneca Indian, obeying the command of the old woman called Queen Esther, who fired the fatal shot. And Julia never lies."

"But we must not discredit the other story. We must say nothing on the subject. We are at war, you know."

"I am at peace with all men."

"Nonsense! If you be at peace with his Majesty's enemies, you make yourself his enemy. You will need his clemency and protection to retain your estates, after this ward of thine has married the young rebel officer:—and he, too, the son of Lochiel! Why has not Bonnel Moody seized him? Why have you, as a magistrate, not had him arrested? Thomas, these things will be against thee when peace is restored."

"I have resigned my commission, William."

"And that was right!" said the old lady.

"It was not accepted!" said her son.

"But that man has more friends than the King in our

neighbourhood. I don't know where they come from," continued Thomas, "but I tell thee the truth. He cannot be taken. Whenever he is assaulted, the Scots come from every quarter to defend him."

"Well, get thee out of the neighbourhood before the savages arrive! They will overwhelm every thing, like the lava from a volcano!"

"Thee knows our people have nothing to fear from the Indians," said Thomas, "and I shall remain in the country till peace be restored."

"That is right!" said the old lady. "And I don't think King George will ever reign over this people again."

"You don't know any thing about it, mother!" said her son, evincing the impatience and displeasure he felt.

"But thy father does. He was never mistaken in his predictions."

"I am sorry to hear thee say so," said Thomas, musing, for he attached great importance to the opinions of the elder Franklin, with whom he was well acquainted, and with whom he had held several discussions on the subject of negro emancipation, Thomas being the owner of valuable slaves.

"He says France will assist the Colonies, and advises all persons who have estates not to imperil them by joining a doomed party."

"Mother," cried her son, "no more of this! I am the President of the Associated Loyalists, and have better means of judging than my father in France. One-half the people in Jersey are loyal."

"They were, William, until you set Fenton and other freebooters to robbing and burning!"

"They merely retaliate on the rebels who have ravaged my farm on the Rancocas."

"That was after you had Richard Stockton seized and thrown into prison."

"All the enemies of the King should be seized. We'll have Stevens and Livingston next! But I must away! Friend Thomas, if you would partake of the fruits of our victory, you must contribute something to produce it. Confer with your people——"

"We can do nothing, William."

"Enough! The sword will decide every thing. Then

there will be a day of reckoning! But learn that within a month the royal armies in the Colonies will number at least forty thousand men. Washington has not ten thousand! Choose ye between them!"

"No! Thee cannot make me choose either. I prefer the reaping-hook to the sword. But, William, canst thou not pay me in part——"

"Not a stiver, now! I have not money enough to pay for a dinner, as your man at the hotel can bear witness."

"But has thee not some plate——"

"Yes, on Staten Island! If you will call there, you may take it."

"Ah, William! I fear——"

"Yes, fear and tremble, and thus work out your salvation."

"Farewell, William! When we next meet, I hope thee will be in a better humour."

"And in a better condition to pay the debt. Farewell; but do not desert the royal cause!"

"Thee need not fear that, even if I lose the thousand pounds."

"The hope of regaining the thousand pounds will, I think, contribute to keep you faithful to his Majesty."

"Thee may think what thee pleases! But I will not rebuke thee. Farewell."

And Thomas departed, while Franklin hummed the verses from Shakspeare's Macbeth, beginning, "When shall we three meet again?"

CHAPTER XX.

JENNY JUMP—RETURN OF THE PRISONERS—BATTLE AT THE INN.

LEAVING to the imagination of the reader the meeting of Kate and Julia and Solo—of Charles with his father, and Paddy with everybody—and the effect the narration of their adventures had upon the minds of the neighbours,—it will be necessary, without delay, to proceed to scenes of a different nature, and to use the utmost privilege of condensation to confine them within the limits prescribed.

One day, when Julia and Kate and Charles were sitting under the broad boughs of the old council-tree, in the quiet little valley where the lovers' vows had been exchanged the preceding year, they were startled by the sudden barking of Solo, who had been panting at their feet. But, upon observing the faithful sentinel wag his tail, they were satisfied no enemy lurked in the vicinity; and, a moment after, they beheld Calvin, the young Delaware chief, slowly and gloomily approaching. His form was wasted, and his eyes deep sunken in his head.

"My brother!" said Charles, stepping forth and tendering his hand to the young man. He grasped it in silence, and then saluted the ladies in the same melancholy manner. After this strange proceeding the young chief occupied the seat which had been offered him, and, sighing deeply, remained with his eyes fixed upon the ground. His affection for the lost Thrush being known and respected, no one desired to make allusion to the mournful catastrophe.

"You do not come as an enemy, I am sure," said Kate, "or else the faithful Solo would have resisted your approach."

"No," said the Delaware; "the Wilted Grass lies on the silent grave. It is no longer among the dewy buds. The spring and summer of its existence have passed away. The blossoms have fallen, and the sweetest flower of the forest hath faded! It can never again lift up its head. Speak to one another, laugh, and be happy. As for me, regard me as one perished from the earth!"

"No!" said Julia, "you must learn to forget the woes of the past; be strong of heart and cheerful of spirit."

"Among the men of our race," said Kate, "with whom you have lived and been educated, it is not usual to die of grief when a loved object vanishes."

"No," said Calvin, his head still drooping; "they are like the fowls of the barn-yard. But I am as the lonely dove of the forest, perched upon a blasted tree, waiting in vain for the mate whose breast has been pierced by some cruel sportsman."

"But you will meet in heaven," said Julia.

"Ay—and I would go thither without delay."

"We must submit without complaining to the will of God," said Charles. "But tell me, Calvin, is it true the Mohawks believe that I or one of my party winged the fatal messenger?"

"The Senecas say so, and Queen Esther asserts it. The Oneidas alone deny it. Gentle Moonlight, your foster-mother, is a raving maniac, ever calling upon you to save the Thrush from the arrows of Queen Esther!"

"I feared so!" said Charles, sadly. "But the Senecas, who perpetrated the deed, and their demoniac queen, who demanded the sacrifice, shall pay the penalty! Will you not go with me and my company into Tryon county?"

"No. I am going home to die. Or, if the Great Spirit will not permit me to perish in my youth, I will bury myself in the Cedar Swamp, where neither wars nor the rumours of wars can reach me."

"But the rest?—can you tell me what has become of my faithful Scots and Van Wiggens and Peter Shaver?"

"There!" said Calvin, pointing in the direction of the Delaware River. And, to the great joy of Charles, Wilted Grass informed him that the whole party had escaped from the Indian villages, with some twenty Oneidas, and were then approaching the settlement. He had left them in the morning at the river, and parted with them merely to announce their coming.

And, having performed his mission, the stricken youth rose up and vanished in the forest. He did not pause when they besought him to remain, nor answered a word to their entreaties.

The girls and Charles hastened away to announce the tidings. The news was received with stoical indifference at the house of Mr. Schooley, where Kate was now sojourning with Julia. Richard was the overseer, and neither Van Wiggens nor Peter Shaver ever managed the farm to a better purpose than he.

But the tidings of the return of Hugh McSwine and his little band of Caledonians afforded very great satisfaction to the "Gentle Lochiel," the recluse father of Charles. Nevertheless, his bleached locks seemed to assume a more silvery aspect and his face a more deathly pallor as he gazed upon his son's preparations to march away again in obedience to an order from Colonel Dayton to join him with his company at Fort Schuyler, in Tryon county, New York.

"Charles," said he, "beware of the warning! It was the same that appeared to me in Scotland. *Never agree to any capitulation with a faithless foe.* Such were the words."

"You do not seriously believe in such things, my father," said Charles; "and I am sure it was but a feverish dream."

"Wizards are spoken of in the Bible and in the writings of Shakspeare. I spurned the warning before the day of blood on the field of Culloden. If I did not die, I fell. We may doubt, but not deny. May God shield you! For myself, my time is nearly spent."

Charles did all he could to cheer his desponding parent, and, prevailing on him to recount some of the romantic adventures of Charles Edward when a fugitive, he beheld once more the flashing eyes of the Highland chieftain.

In the afternoon the news of the approach of the returning prisoners, accompanied by twenty Oneida Indians, having spread for miles round, the inhabitants of the entire neighbourhood assembled in front of Mrs. Van Wiggens's tavern, now a famous stopping-place, to witness their arrival.

Mrs. Van Wiggens was very nervous, sometimes apparently gay and lively, and at others musing and abstracted. She was doing well enough alone. She had mourned her husband's loss without weeping, and had quite recovered from the effects of the deprivation. But now the wound was opened afresh, and Van Wiggens himself, having survived amid incredible dangers, was approaching, alive and in good health.

Julia and Kate sat in the carriage before the door of the inn, where they had been joined by Charles. Paddy held the reins. The drum and fife and bagpipe were heard down in the hollow, where Murphy had marched the company of patriots to welcome the wanderers and conduct them to the place under a spreading oak, where an ox had been slaughtered for their benefit. This was the contribution of the Whigs of the vicinity.

The first individual of the returning party who made his appearance at the inn was the little stump-tailed dog,

Watch, who was recognised and received with a burst of laughter. He ran into the blacksmith-shop and smelt at the knee of his master's negro.

"Is dat you, Watch?" exclaimed Sambo, his eyes twinkling and his uplifted arm suspended over the anvil.

Watch bounded away, and was met on the steps of the rude porch in front of the inn by Mrs. Van Wiggens's large black tomcat, whose swollen tail and arched back indicated the nature of the reception the dog was to have within. But Watch had crushed the bones of too many coons and other animals in the woods, to be easily repulsed by a domesticated "varmint," and that, too, on the threshold of his own premises. So he accepted the proffered battle, and, springing upon his foe, which was nearly as large as himself, but not so experienced in desperate warfare, filled the air with canine and carnivorous sounds, while the fur flew in every direction.

"It's my cat! my poor Tom!" exclaimed Mrs. Van Wiggens, rushing forth, broomstick in hand, and striving in vain to part the combatants. As often as she lifted the stick to decide the conflict, Watch shifted his position; so that, when the instrument was about to descend, the black cat was either uppermost or occupying the place the dog had held the moment before.

"Mercy on us!" once cried the frightened hostess, when she had made a determined rush upon the struggling animals, and Watch, avoiding the broomstick, rolled over with the cat and continued the combat under the protecting shelter of the strong linsey-woolsey gown of his mistress. Mrs. Van Wiggens sprang aside, and, with a glowing face, aimed a random blow, which fell upon poor Tom's head and terminated the battle. He was stunned, but not killed; and Watch would have given him another shake, had he not been prevented by his master, who stepped forward and lifted him up in his arms.

"The nasty dog!" cried Mrs. Van Wiggens. "Do kill him for me, Mr. Indian."

"Tam'd if I do! Poor Vatch!"

"Why, whose voice is that?" cried Mrs. Van Wiggens, rushing forward, and gazing in the face of her husband. "Is this you, Mr. Van Wiggens, coming home painted and dressed like a savage? And to bring back the impudent dog which couldn't be killed, like yourself! Yes, it is you! But the paint hides your blush of shame. And what did you go off for? Why did you abandon your family——"

"Tam it, stop! Stop a minute! You said vamily—vamily!—vat vamily's you got? My vamily never vas!"

"Oh, you needn't fire up so! And you must bring back the nasty dog! You know how I hate him! He'll steal the meat off the gridiron! You know I hate a dog and a bear!"

Mrs. Van Wiggens had once been almost suffocated by a huge pet-bear, and ever afterward that animal was the most terrible of all others.

"Vell," said Van Wiggens, "I've brung you von nice bear. Lead him here, Peter."

Peter Shaver, likewise habited as an Indian, came forward, leading a half-grown bear, whose eyes seemed to glisten with delight on seeing the horror-stricken hostess. He stood up on his hind-feet, his arms asunder, as if desirous of embracing his mistress.

Mrs. Van Wiggens screamed, and trembled violently. She besought her lord, to whom she promised entire submission, to send the horrid beast away.

"Vell," said Van Wiggens, "I'll have him painted first on de sign—and de sign shall pe te bear and te anvil. And you mustn't take it down agin."

And subsequently this sign became famous among travellers in that region.

During this brief scene it may be supposed that the young ladies in the carriage were highly entertained, and readily espoused the side of the husband.

But the general joy was cut short by the arrival of runners from New York and Pennsylvania, with the information that the Butlers and Brandt, led by St. Leger, were approaching from Canada, and, if the forts on the frontier were not quickly manned and bravely defended, the whole region between the Susquehanna and the Delaware, and on both sides of those rivers, would be overrun and ravaged by the Indians and Tories.

No time was to be lost. Disgusted at his own reception, and the manner in which his dog had been welcomed back, Van Wiggens was the first of the returned party who offered to march with Charles. But, subsequently, nearly all who had been in the wild woods with our hero, as well as the small party of Oneidas, enrolled themselves in his company. And, as each announced his purpose, Tim Murphy had the occasion signalized by a grand roll of the drum.

"I am almost tempted to volunteer myself," said Kate; "and I believe, if I were not here to keep her company, Julia could not be prevented from going."

"She has been accustomed to see her defenders in the act of fighting," said Charles; "and no doubt her presence has given additional vigour to many a sinewy arm. We shall miss her. But she will—both if you will—think of us and utter prayers for our success. We shall be defending you still; and it is better to meet the enemy at the first outposts than to resist them here. The forts once fallen, this would cease to be a place of security. But we shall probably return very soon. There will be no long sieges."

We must now pass over many historical events in which some of our characters were conspicuous actors, but which are not embraced within the limited scope of this narrative. The fall of Herkimer, the timidity of Woolsey, the venial tardiness of Van Rensselaer, and the alternate successes and disasters in the North, the reader must be already sufficiently familiar with. Charles Cameron, Hugh McSwine, and Tim Murphy, performed their duty in all the conflicts in which they were engaged with the enemy in fort or field, and received the commendations of their superior officers. Nevertheless, the tide of invasion was not driven back. Although Sullivan destroyed the Indian villages and crops on the lakes, and although Burgoyne was under the necessity of surrendering to Gates, yet Philadelphia had fallen, and the enemy possessed the two principal cities in the Colonies and commanded all the harbours.

It was at such a time, when the more densely-populated districts were paralyzed by the presence of overwhelming numbers of the British and Hessians, that the dark stream of sanguinary savages poured down the Susquehanna and Delaware valleys, and ravaged all the Western borders.

And during the absence of the Jersey volunteers from the counties of Hunterdon, Warren, and Sussex, Bonnel Moody, with his band of robber Tories, committed many depredations on the unresisting inhabitants, consisting mostly of old men, women, and children.

But the young ladies continued for some time to enjoy an exemption from molestation at Thomas Schooley's house.

And Paddy, with spade in hand, was content to fight his battles in the garden; while Richard, tired of the delays dictated by Judith Carlisle, who loved him not, and whose father, it seemed, had other projects in view as his fortunes rose, again sought to win the hand of Julia, to the infinite diversion of Kate. The hum of Mary's wheel was incessant in the parlour, and the bang of the loom, propelled by a negro woman, vibrated from the adjoining shed without.

Nevertheless, the repose of Mr. Schooley's household was doomed to a sad interruption, as will be seen in the next chapter.

CHAPTER XXI.

THE SETTLEMENT INVADED BY THE INDIANS—ASTONISHING FEATS OF PADDY AND MRS. VAN WIGGENS.

THE Indians, if they did not make night-assaults, prowled about in the day, killing their enemies and destroying such property as they could not bear away. The Tories, desirous of escaping detection when the next turn of Fortune's wheel might dim the lustre of the cause they espoused, contrived to keep out of view as much as possible. But their depredations and cruelties after sunset were awful.

Skippie, who saw every thing if he spoke nothing, had been well advised of the approaching tempest, and gave his chief early information of Moody's contemplated attack. And the Gentle Lochiel had invited Julia and Kate to take shelter within his strong walls, until the company of patriots, commanded by his son, whose absence had been protracted, should return to the neighbourhood. The girls, under injunctions of secrecy, had been previously admitted within the hidden chambers; and therefore, when the summons came, accompanied by the intelligence that the Indians (a detachment that passed the forts and descended the rivers) had murdered Colonel Allen in his bed, and a whole family by the name of Wells, even tomahawking and scalping the infant children, they obeyed with alacrity. It was in vain that Mr. Schooley objected; and Mr. Green and others, who were ignorant of the nature of the asylum tendered them, besought them not to take refuge under the roof of a proscribed exile. The Moravians—those that remained, being few in number—offered such sanctuary as their structures afforded, and vainly supposed their precincts would be respected by the Tory as well as by the Indian.

Kate and Julia were hastening away with Skippie, when Mary Schooley's wheel ceased its humming sound, and the old lady made a last adjuration as follows:—

"Thee will be scandalized forever! Thee must pause and reflect. Thee should be aware that to be shut up in a lonely place with a man——"

"I will go, Mary!" said Julia, with decision and firmness. "Dr. Odell, if he were here, would sanction our temporary abode with that pure gray-haired old man. And it seems to me that the pure of heart could never imagine any ill proceeding from such a source. We may confide in our fathers, I think, with quite as much security as in the usual gossiping guardians of the public morality. Come, Kate!"

"But thee must not return——" began Mary, when she was checked by Thomas.

"Not return!" cried Julia, thoroughly aroused; "and why not? Is not this house, this estate, mine? Come, Solo!"

"If the King will suffer thee to have it," was the only reply that reached the ear of the offended girl, who uttered not another word, but hastened away, followed by Richard, who had become more desperately in love than ever. But she did not heed him. Kate, however, pretended to admire the slighted young man, and derived much amusement from his perplexities.

The girls had not been gone more than a few hours, before Paddy ran in from the garden.

"They're coming, yer honour, they're coming!" cried he; "and I know they're tomahawking and sculping the paple on the way, for they are the bloody Senecas!"

"How does thee know that?" demanded Mr. Schooley "Has thee seen them?"

"No, yer honour, but I heard the jackass!"

"The jackass!"

"Yes, Pater Shaver's jackass; Popcorn's jackass."

"Thee knows Peter is with the wicked men of blood in the Northern forts."

"But the Senecas, with Pater's ass, are here—*here*, I tell ye!—and yonder they come through the orchard! Och, murther! I'll hide! They may spare you, but I know they'd kill me!"

And Paddy ran out through the back door, and into the loom-house, and concealed himself in the loft, where a few planks were laid loosely over the joists.

When the foremost of the Indians leaped over the fence into the yard, the fat old Rose, who was to have attended her mistress, but contrived delays, as usual, was met by them as she emerged from the kitchen with her packs and bundles.

The leader of the Indians ordered her to put down her burden, and, being neither comprehended nor obeyed, he attempted to snatch the articles out of her herculean arms.

"No you don't, you nasty mulatto! Clar out, and mind your business, or Massa Charles'll be arter you!"

"Charles! He come back?" said the Indian, still grasping a bundle.

"None o' your business! Let go!" she continued, and, making a violent effort, hurled the savage some ten feet distant, his shoulder coming first in contact with the earth, to the infinite amusement of his party.

"Dern!" cried the infuriated Indian, using one of the expletives of the white man; and, springing up, aimed his tomahawk at Rose's head. It sank into one of the bundles of clothing without doing her any injury. But it damaged her mistress's wardrobe, and roused the fury of the faithful old servant. So, seizing the glittering instrument, she hurled it back at the leader of the savages. It flew wide of the mark, but penetrated the forehead of one of the dusky laughing spectators. He fell, pierced to the brain, amid the vengeful yells of his companions. In an instant poor Rose was perforated with half a dozen rifle-balls, and expired without a groan,—her large white eyes still open, and her brow contracted.

Thomas and Mary, having witnessed these bloody feats from the window, were painfully shocked, but still apprehended no danger themselves.

"How do?" said the chief, entering the house, and followed by most of his companions.

"I hope thee is well," said Thomas; "but thee should not have killed the old woman. Thee should have sought justice before the civil tribunals. Thee——"

"Stop them, Thomas! Dost thou not see them splitting the oak chest?" cried Mary, whose wheel hummed spasmodically, and the thread was broken.

"I am a friend of the King, as thee has no doubt heard," continued Thomas.

"Me no hear!" was the angry reply of the Indian.

"I tell thee I am loyal; and we have been preparing food for thee. Sit down and eat. Call back thy band; they are killing my woman in the loom-house! Thee must not permit such acts!"

"Me no come to eat. Me come for scalps!" said the Indian.

"But thee must not hurt thy friends."

"Friends' scalp too. You no scalp our enemies. You no friend. Me take your scalp."

"No, no; thee will do no such thing. Let us save the woman in the loom-house. Thee must not permit them to kill her!"

And Thomas, despite the threatening attitude of the Indian, led the way into the loom-house, where he was followed, and quickly surrounded by the savages.

The negro woman, who had been weaving, lay bleeding before him, tomahawked and scalped; and there Thomas himself, and Mary, pale and speechless with terror, were rudely seized.

"Thee will suffer for this deed!" said Thomas. "Do not tremble, Mary. They will not harm thee. They merely want our money."

"Money! where is it?" demanded the chief, whose arm had only been withheld until he could obtain such intelligence.

"It is not thine, and thee shall not have it!" said Thomas.

"Oh, let them have it!" said Mary, recovering her speech. "They will then spare us!"

"No!" was the savage reply; and the Indian wound his hand in her long gray hair.

"Thee will all suffer for this outrage!" said Thomas.

This threat only precipitated matters. Several tomahawks were uplifted to dispatch the victims; and Thomas, seeing no relenting symptoms in the countenances of his captors, cried, "Come down! come, Paddy, to the rescue!"

The savages looked up. Paddy, in petrified horror, had been gazing down. He was now incapable of stepping back out of view; but rather, in the terrible fascination of the moment, like the bird when falling into the jaws of the rattlesnake, tottered forward on the loose planks, which gave way, the ends opposite flying up, and he was precipitated, with a terrible crash, to the earth. The Indians yelled and ran out. They supposed a large party of the enemy were concealed in the loft, and believed Thomas had led them into an ambuscade; and Paddy's voice sufficed for the tongues of a dozen men. Seeing them run, he called on an incredible number of saints to save him. The Indians believed they were the names of persons really existing, and then present with rifles in their hands; and so they fled away and sought shelter in the woods.

"Thee has saved us!" said Mary, seizing the hand of Paddy, which still trembled.

"Howly Pater and Paul!" cried he, "I thank ye both! It was the blissed saints, yer honour," he continued, addressing Thomas, who stood staring at his weltering slave. "The howly church has saved us; and I hope yer honour will go to mass for it!"

"Thee knows not what thee says," was the response of Thomas. "It was not thy saints nor thy valour, but my presence of mind, which saved us."

"Och, murther! Be me sowl, I'll niver do a great action agin! Sich ingratitude and vanity! And did not Paddy himself put 'em to flight like King David did Goliah and his hosts?"

"Nonsense, Patrick! Don't stand there repeating those old fictions. Thee must be active. Go for Mr. Green——"

"Misther Grane? He's gone himself, sir!"

"Where?"

"Plase yer honour, you forgit what he said yisterday."

"Thee speaks the truth now; I did forget. He said he would go to some block-house, and I should have gone with him."

"As I was saying, yer honour, the howly saints took pity on us, and tilted up the planks——"

"Thee must not talk such nonsense, Patrick. Thee must help me to bury this woman. Dig a grave in the orchard."

"But I hope yer honour will niver deny that I saved you and Misthress Schooley from an awful death——"

"Patrick, thee is trembling yet!"

"Trembling, is it? No, yer honour, it's hate!"

"Hate? thee must not hate any one."

"Hate onybody? that isn't it. I mane hate o' the blood—choler—passion. Me blood is byling with hate! And did I not rush down in the middle and surround 'em? Plase answer me that, Mr. Schooley! And it'll be a tale to be towld in the chimbley-corners o' winter nights after Paddy's flesh is grass! And I'm only sorra I didn't kill more uv 'em!"

"Thee has been much with the Indians," said Mary, "and thee ought to know what that noise means."

"That," said Paddy, listening to the yells down the valley in the direction of Mrs. Van Wiggens's inn, "is the murthering-halloo; and they'll be back agin for our sculps! so, Mrs. Schooley, if ye'll take an ould Indian-fighter's advice, you'll get Mr. Schooley's money and be off to the bushes widout losing a minute. I'll pilot ye through the woods to the Moravian church——"

"No, thee shall do no such thing," said Thomas. "If the episcopal mummery of those people can save them, the higher spirits within our own bosoms must suffice for us, as they have already rescued us once."

"Divil the fear they have of ony sperits! It was Paddy's arm that made 'em run."

"Patrick, thee forgets thyself!" said Mr. Schooley, nevertheless hastening to save his money; and, when it was obtained, they set out toward the block-house.

The Indian accidentally killed by Rose was buried with great care by his comrades, so that his body might not be found and the scalp torn from his head. The greensward, after being cut smoothly round, was lifted aside, and replaced when the body was deposited in the earth, so that no one could have discovered the grave. Nevertheless, the slain savage did not appear to be a man of much importance among his fellows, for their mirth and laughter, when they recounted the events at Mr. Schooley's house, seemed very hearty. However, they made no unnecessary delay in their progress, and the next place they visited was Mrs. Van Wiggens's establishment. They appeared first before the blacksmith's shop. There was a Mr. Van Etten (and Mrs. Van Wiggens seemed to have a partiality for Dutchmen) employed to shoe horses and mend ploughs during Van Wiggens's absence; and this man saw the Indians when approaching, guided by the sound of the negro's hammer on the anvil.

"Indians! Stop dat *blaw-mock*," (bellows,) said he, hurriedly, addressing the negro. "Dey von't hurt you, Sambo; tam it, you stay here, viles I climb up de chimbley."

The negro, terror-stricken, seemed incapable of disobedience. The Indians came in and gazed round. They looked under the bench and behind the bellows, but did not see the one they were in quest of. Van Etten had been a famous Indian-fighter in the former war, and was well known to them.

"Where Van Etten?" demanded the leader, seizing the negro by the shoulder.

"Gone!" said Sambo, recollecting his orders; "dar's no sich man here; he's gone, I tell you, and dat's 'ficient."

The Indians, amused at the negro's manner, entertained themselves with an examination of the tools in the shop, retaining such as they might have use for. One of them, in imitation of the smith, thrust a bar of iron into the fire, and, seizing the handle of the bellows, blew vigorously. The negro, hearing Van Etten sneeze, slapped the Indian on the arm, and said, as his master had done a few minutes before, "Stop dat *blaw-mock!*"

The Indians, diverted at his seeming unconsciousness of danger, desisted from further annoyance, and, leaving him in the shop, directed their steps toward the house. The leader, aware there were no men within, entered first, and seeing in the small bar bottles of apple-brandy and Jamaica rum, could not resist his inclination to take a dram. It was when the bottle was at his mouth that Mrs. Van Wiggens entered from the dining-room. Supposing the brawny savage to be her lawfully-wedded husband, returned from the war, she said nothing; but, seizing the broom, and approaching on tiptoe, aimed a blow at his head with the straw end of it. The Indian, astonished, and slightly stunned, let the bottle fall, and then, gazing regretfully a moment at the wasted fluid inundating the floor, fell into a violent passion.

"Dern!" exclaimed he. "Me—you be dern! White squaw! Dern me you!"

"How dare you swear at me, Van Wiggens?" cried Mrs. Van Wiggens.

"Van Wiggens be dern!" cried the Indian. "Me have white squaw's scalp!" he continued, drawing forth his tomahawk.

But Mrs. Van Wiggens, perceiving her mistake, turned the other end of the broom handle, which was of hickory, and dealt him a blow on the head that brought him to his knees, and the tomahawk falling from his grasp, she picked it up. But he arose and rushed forth before she could use it. She followed him to the door, however, and hurled the instrument harmlessly after him.

The Indians laughed heartily to see their leader flying from a squaw; and that little incident induced them to spare the lives of the negro and his mistress, or at least to postpone the operation of taking their scalps, and to pursue the trail of the young girls without further delay.

CHAPTER XXII.

JULIA AND KATE TAKE REFUGE WITH THE EXILE—THE CAPTIVES—MOODY'S LAST INCURSION—THE QUAKER'S MONEY—PADDY'S CONVERSION.

"SEE the poor fawn!" said Julia, pointing to a bleeding young deer that lay in their path.

"Poor creature!" said Kate; "some cruel man has done this merely to test his skill!"

"It's fat," said Richard, feeling the ribs of the dying animal.

"And would you be so cruel as to eat the pretty thing?" asked Kate.

"It is better than a pig, and I'm very fond of them. Thee would like it, I'm sure."

"Never! I would not taste the flesh of that poor——"

"Richard," said Julia, gazing at the arrow which pierced the fawn, "leave it! Do you not see it is wounded by an arrow? It may not have run a mile since the shaft was winged at its side, and its bloody trail may be followed by the Indian that wounded it!"

Neither Kate nor Richard had thought of that; and, abandoning the fawn, the party lost no time in reaching Tower Rock—the name bestowed on the abode of the aged exile.

Richard, declining the invitation to tarry, bade the girls, and particularly Julia, a doleful farewell. And Kate, when she extended her hand in parting, archly imitated the desponding gestures of the sighing lover. Richard departed bewildered and bewitched; for the girls, when mischievously inclined, certainly do possess the power of enchanting inexperienced swains.

Poor Richard, ruminating as he retraced the solitary path, sad and deserted, since the tiny feet of the dear charmers had abandoned it, forgot the dying fawn and all other shafts but Cupid's.

Thus enraptured, he paused in the densest part of the

forest before a large beech-tree, on the rind of which he distinguished something among the many marks that resembled a J. Supposing it might be the initial of his ladylove, he stepped forward and kissed it. It had been meant, however, for a horseshoe, to indicate that some one, probably an Indian, had gone in a certain direction on horseback. And feeling, for the first time in his life, quite poetical, he drew forth his knife and carved some verses on the tree.

After finishing the inscription, and when turning mournfully away, he was confronted by the leader of the Senecas.

"How do?" said the Indian, advancing, and laying his hand on the shoulder of the astonished youth.

"Thee knows my father——" began Richard.

"No. Don't know him! What's that?" he demanded, pointing at the inscription. It was a famous writing or picture tree, which had been used by the savages for many generations. They could interpret the marks made by themselves, but those cut by Richard were wholly unintelligible.

"Thee cannot understand it," said Richard.

"Read—say!" continued the Indian.

Richard obeyed.

"Julia! Antelope!" said the Indian. "He love!" Then, uttering something aloud in his own language, the rest of the savages rose up from the tangled bushes, or emerged from behind the trees, and came forward laughing heartily at the interpretation of the inscription given by their leader.

"Thee knows my secret now," said Richard; "and thee will not take her away again."

"Antelope must go! Queen Esther calls her."

"I tell thee no. She shall not go."

"She nice squaw. Make me wife."

"Thee a wife!" said the indignant Richard. "If thee harms her, or takes her away again, Sir William Howe shall be informed of it, and he will have thee scourged."

The Indian sneered at the threat; still, he could not forget that Sir William was the King's great General. But he was far away, and dead men could tell no tales. And yet he felt some hesitation in putting to death those who professed loyalty to the King, and moreover the proverbially peaceful Quakers. Nevertheless, as he paused in doubt, his anxiety to procure scalps—for which the Indians received a certain price from the British—almost induced him to sink his tomahawk into the unoffending head of his sighing captive. But, recollecting the enterprise was to be mainly under the direction of Bonnel Moody, who, with his band of Tories, had appointed the beech-tree as the place of meeting, he reluctantly desisted. Richard's hands were bound behind him, and he had no assurance of escaping death at the stake.

A rustling was heard in the vicinity, and soon after voices were distinguished. The Indians concealed themselves, commanding Richard to be silent.

The stragglers drew near, following the narrow path.

"Thee must be lost, Patrick!" said Mr. Schooley, weary, and with torn garments, supporting his wife.

"Be me sowl, I shouldn't wondher!" said Paddy, leading the way, and now in full view of the hidden Indians.

"Thee don't *know* it, though," said Mary. "Thee has been to the fort twice, and thee should have learned the way better. I pray thee, Thomas, let me rest a few minutes on this fallen tree."

"Thee shall be gratified, Mary. Patrick," he continued, when Mrs. Schooley paused, "thee said thee was quite sure the path we started in was the right one."

"Yis, yer honour, I'll be sworn we started right."

"Swear not at all," said Mary. "Thee knows it is wrong."

"Yis, ma'am. But I could take me oath I thought it the right one."

"I hope thee was not mistaken, and that we may be still in the proper path," said Thomas.

"And we may soon be there," said Mary. "Lead on; I can walk a little farther."

"It's no use!" said Paddy. "I know we're lost, yer honour. I know it by the queer fayling I have in me head. And, be that same token, we shall be saised by the blackguard savages."

"Thee had best be silent, Patrick," said Mr. Schooley.

"I will, yer honour. But, as I was remarking a while ago, if the Indians should saise us, I hope it will be no harm for me to pass for a Quaker, if it be the manes of saving me life.'

"Use no deception, Patrick," said Mrs. Schooley, "even for the sake of saving thy life."

"But, thin, yer honour," continued Paddy, appealing to Mr. Schooley, "I'm about to be in arnest. If it will save me life, divil take me if Paddy himself don't be as thrue and sinsare a Quaker as iver drew the breath of life."

"Thee can neither deceive us nor God," said Mrs. Schooley.

"Desaving, is it? I wud scorn to desave onybody but a blackguard savage, and I hope there'd be no harm in that. But I'll go to yer matings, wear yer coats, and spake in thaas and thous, and be as vartuous as ony saint, if it'll kape the sculp on the top o' me crown."

"Thee has yet to learn that our religion is not meant to save our lives, but our souls," said Mr. Schooley.

"And is that same the thruth? Och! I thought you wuddn't fight for fear o' gitting kilt! But—murther! I saa an Indian! Remimber, I'm a Quaker, onyhow!"

The Seneca chief, rising up, advanced toward them, followed by the rest, who surrounded the weary fugitives. They made no resistance.

"Thee is the same person we saw this morning," said Thomas, gazing at the chief.

"Oh, father!" said Richard, stumbling forward, "is it thee and my mother I behold?"

"Yea, verily, Richard!" said Mrs. Schooley. "And why didst thou wander so far away from thy home and leave thy parents to shift for themselves?"

"So far, mother? It is not far. This is the path leading from our house to the Tower Rock. Thee is now almost in sight of thy home."

"Verily it is true!" said Thomas. "I know that tree. It is on my land. Thee has been leading us a strange wild-goose chase, Patrick——"

"Plase yer honour," said Paddy, "don't use me name in this company. Thee knows I have been lading meself as well as thee in the wrong way. Yea, verily! Heigh-ho! And you, Misther Indian, tell me thy first name, and I will call thee afther the manner of our paceable paple, who fear God and honour the King, and——"

"Cease! cease thy silly jargon, Patrick!"

"Plase yer honour, don't call me Patrick," whispered Paddy, "because the natives hate the Irish worse than the divil!"

"But, Richard," said his mother, "why have they bound thee?"

"Thee sees I am their prisoner, and will bear witness against them."

The chief uttered some commands to his followers, when Mr. and Mrs. Schooley, and the quaking Paddy, were all seized and bound.

"Divil a bit more will I be a Quaker," said Paddy, "for they saize thim as well as other folks! And now——"

"Peace, Patrick," said Thomas, "and learn resignation from us. They have bound and plundered us, and yet we do not complain. We are sustained by a supporting principle within, and thee——"

"Och, now, Misther Schooley, none of yer praiching to me. It's too late. They know me; for one of 'em was in the battle on the Scioto, and at the fort, and he can't forgit Paddy. It won't do to stay here. I must escape. They won't hurt you, when all yer money's gone. But whiles they're dividing yer goold I'll git off."

They were truly at that moment in a dispute about the treasure. The sum found on Thomas and Mary was unexpectedly large, and it had been the weight of the money which produced the exhaustion of the latter.

Paddy, therefore, bursting asunder the cords, slipped away unobserved.

"Be jabers, I'm fraa agin!" said he, pausing and listening, after creeping some distance and finding himself not pursued. "And I mane to stay fraa. Divil take the Quakers! I thought the blackguards wuddn't handle the nasty craters! But they've bound 'em like pigs for a fair. The blissed Catholic religion is the best afther all, both for this world and the nixt! When I confess agin, I'll promise niver, niver to desart the pope!" And Paddy fell down on his knees and repeated a prayer. "Och, murther!" cried he, springing up again. "And I've been knaling beside a big rattlesnake! Jist hear what a fuss he makes! And there he is, kyled up, wid his head and tail in the middle o' him. I'll kill the divil! No!" he continued, pausing, with a stone suspended in the air; "it may be the divil himself, come agin in the form of a sarpent. And kin Paddy kill the divil? Divil the bit! The praist'll say he was afther me for tarning Quaker. Och, howly Saint Pater, forgive me! Good-by, Misther Divil, I'll lave ye, and I hope your nasty riverence won't follow afther me. I don't desire yer company, and I'm sure ye'll have yer hands full o' the Quakers."

So Paddy left the huge rattlesnake, which, as is sometimes the case, neither advanced nor retreated from the ground it occupied. But the fugitive had become confused, and knew not whether to direct his steps, and trembled lest he should again fall into the hands of the Indians. He recollected with regret and dismay the many tales he had told of the terrible slaughter he had made in the numerous battles he had fought, and was frightened at the conviction that his fame had spread throughout the wilderness, like that of Boone and Kenton and McSwine.

Meantime the contention over the treasure rose to such a pitch that knives were unsheathed, tomahawks brandished, and no doubt the disputants would have proceeded to blows, (such being the evil consequence of a lust for wealth,) had not Moody and his band of Tories arrived upon the ground in time to prevent the catastrophe.

The Tories being more numerous than the Indians, and the latter having been directed by Queen Esther to obey the commands of the royalist, Moody cut short the disputation by seizing the money himself, promising, however, to make an equitable division at his cave.

"And now, friend Schooley," continued Moody, "why are your hands tied in that manner? Did Murphy's men do it?"

"Thee knows, Bonnel, that Timothy is away with his company, or else thee would not be here. It was *thy* men—these Indians, Bonnel! And thee need not pretend to be ignorant of it. Thee knows it is my money in thy leathern bag. Ah, Bonnel, Bonnel! This is the protection of George's friends by his officers! Thee knows very well we are loyal to the King."

"I beg your pardon, Mr. Schooley," said Moody, in tones of pretended earnestness. "But you shall see that

I am not to blame. It is necessary for me to act thus. I intended to be here before the Indians, and then these things would not have occurred. But now, if I were to give you back the money, the savages would leave me, and perhaps murder you."

"Thee knows how to plead for money, Bonnel," said Mrs. Schooley.

"But you shall lose nothing, madam," replied Moody. "Every penny shall be paid back. We will go at once to your house—if they did not burn it—and I hope they didn't——"

"No, they did not," said Mr. Schooley; "but thee knows the burning would not be so great a loss to me as the taking of my money."

"I'll convince you of my friendship," said Moody, cutting the cords that bound the captives. "These are our friends," he continued, winking to the Indian chief, who had only executed the Tory-robber's orders. "We will conduct them back to their home, and dine with them, as a token of our penitence for the mistake."

"If thee would convince us of that," said Thomas, "thee had better give me the money."

"That is filthy lucre, Thomas, and its restitution might cause a quarrel, and perhaps bloodshed, among the King's friends. No! You would not have such sins committed for the sake of the dross! But you shall lose nothing. I will give you a receipt for the whole sum, which will be the same thing as an order on the King's treasury, when peace is restored."

"Thee has the power, and thee can act as thee pleases," said Thomas; "and thee can include the value of my negro woman, which was two hundred pounds."

"I will! And it shall be taken out of the pay of the Indians. They should have known better! And I'll add twenty pounds, friend Thomas, for our dinner, and we'll call it forage."

"Bonnel, thee knows my loyalty, and I do not doubt that George's armies will resubjugate this rebellious people. Nevertheless, thee would please me better by giving me back my money and withholding thy order."

"It is impracticable, sir," said Moody, "and I am sorry for it. Come on; you are now free, and the Indians will do you no further injury unless you insist too much on having back the gold."

"And, be the powers," said Paddy, stepping forward, having wandered back in his endeavours to get away, "I am included in the same party! I'm one of 'em, Misther Mody, and I'm thruly glad we have fallen into the hands of sich a liberal and ginerous gintleman."

Paddy's return produced no particular commotion, since his absence had not been observed. One of the Indians, however, seeing his hands were loose, seized him by the hair, and called upon his comrades to bind him again, saying, in his own language, that Paddy was a furious warrior and had killed a great number of their people. But this, when interpreted by Moody, was flatly denied by Paddy. He said his boasting was all gammon, and that he had never hurt the hair of an Indian's head; and Thomas demanded his release as one of his household.

"And that's thrue, Misther Mody," said Paddy; "I'm one of his family, if ye plase."

"You no son of Quaker," said the Seneca chief. "You Irish—and Murphy Irish. We burn Murphy—we burn Paddy."

"I beg yer pardon, sir!" said Paddy. "Tim Murphy's a great fighter and has killed a dozen blag—Indians. Tim's a brave warrior, and Paddy's a coward!"

Paddy had no sooner made this admission than the Indian struck him a blow on the head with the handle of his tomahawk, which, although it produced no wound, felled him to the ground.

"You are a fool, Paddy," said Moody, interfering and preventing further punishment, "for confessing yourself a coward. That is the greatest crime of which you could be guilty."

"Divil take 'em!" said Paddy, rising. "There's no plasing 'em! But I'll do as you say. And I'd be extramely oblaged if ye'd let me go and wait upon the young ladies, who are wishing for me at the Tower Rock."

"Tower Rock! Yes, you shall go there with us, Paddy. We will visit them to-night. They will know your voice, and perhaps you can aid us in getting possession of the old refugee. You shall share the reward and have a portion of his treasure. I suppose, Paddy, since you are one of

Mr. Schooley's family, we can rely upon your loyalty. If you are a Whig, say so, and we'll have your scalp on the same string with the negro woman's, and save the hindquarter of a pig at dinner."

"Say so? And wud ye have me tell a lie, Misther Mody? I was born under the reign of King George, of glorious mimory! Misther Mody, if iver I live to git back to ould Ireland, the king shall hear from Paddy's lips what a thrue and valuable subjict he had in the wild wuds of the Jenny Jump Mountain! You are fit to be a gineral, Misther Mody, and his Majesty couldn't do a betther dade than to make ye a knight, and bestow on ye a noble ancestry. Try me, Misther Mody, and saa if Paddy don't drive the ould gray rat into yer hands. And as for the reward, Paddy has not the maneness of sowl to desire a pinny of it! No, Misther Mody, it shall be all yer own." And, as he cast up his eyes to impress Moody with an idea of his sincerity, he beheld Skippie in the tree over his head, winking and making mouths at him.

CHAPTER XXIII.

THE EXILE'S STRONGHOLD—PADDY'S DIPLOMATIC SKILL—
THE ALARM—THE ENTRANCE—CONDUCT OF THE DOG.

When the girls entered the hut the aged exile cordially greeted them, and, having the dark barrier removed in readiness for their ingress, they passed at once into the rock-bound chambers of the cliff.

"My dear children," said the exile, "you are safe here. They dinna ken the holes o' the old fox, but believe he is in league wi' the de'il. But they will come again in the gloom of midnight, or when the shimmering stars are still gemming the early morning. They suppose there is treasure hidden here, and for that they would delve into the infernal regions. I have treasure for my bonny laddie and his love, but not for the instruments of the usurper."

He then exhibited to the admiring girls several rich presents from Charles Edward and other Scottish monarchs to himself and his ancestors, and entertained them with recitals of the deeds which had been commemorated by the gifts.

But the glittering stones were but as pretty toys in comparison with the indestructible products of mind; and cnief among these, and ever to be unrivalled, was the immortal Shakspeare. "The artist and the lapidary might fashion a gem produced by nature," said he, "but the great poet was a creator of worlds in which one might live and breathe unconscious of the ills that flesh is heir to."

Thus for several hours were Kate and Julia entertained, when they were interrupted by the creaking of the massy door communicating with the hut. It was Skippie, who had come to inform his chief of the arrival of several of the clansmen from the mountain, (being all that remained,) and who, in accordance with the chief's directions, were then concealed among the brambles on the summit of the cliff, armed only with bows and arrows and spears, being too weak in number to make any open resistance to the assaults of Moody's party. He likewise informed his chief of the scene he had witnessed under the tree, and repeated to the girls (for he could speak when commanded by Lochiel) the verses inscribed on the beech's rind.

Skippie was commanded to admit Paddy when he arrived, and afterward to go in quest of Charles.

When the moon had dipped beneath the western horizon, and the silent scene was wrapped in the solemn gloom of darkness, the approach of Moody and his gang was announced by the loud and shrill whistle of Skippie, who lay concealed on the margin of the stream that meandered by the base of the precipitous cliff. As he anticipated, the signal was heard by the hostile party, which immediately halted.

"They have been informed of our approach," said Moody "That is their signal. I have heard it before, and every time we were foiled. It must not be so now. They cannot have a large force, unless the old wizard has the power of calling infernal spirits to his aid. Go, Paddy, and deliver this paper to the old man. If he is not a fool he will grant the demand, and save at least the lives of his defenders and the two maidens with him, as well as his own. You may say I have the positive assurance of an officer of high rank that if he surrenders himself into my hands, although they cannot withhold the reward from me, there is not the slightest probability of his execution. Go, Paddy, and bring me his reply to the summons. And beware that you do not deceive us! We are at least ten to one, and there could be no escape for you. And you may say that Brandt himself, with five hundred warriors, is by this time sweeping down the Wyoming Valley. The garrisons are all surrendering. The tomahawk and the firebrand are doing the work of extermination; and it is not probable the old fox's son, or any of his company, will survive to raise the siege, if we must be delayed awaiting the prize. Tell him we believe—no, say we have learned—that he has a cave under the hut, into which he usually retires in times of danger, but that it will not serve him now. If he refuses to yield himself, we will dig him out; and the more labour and trouble he causes us, the greater will be the exasperation of the Indians. Go! And if you neglect your duty, or 'fail to return within ten minutes, we will commence the assault, and you will be burnt at the stake!"

"Murther! And if they won't let me come to ye, am I still to be roasted alive wid the wooden spit stuck in me?"

"Yes, you, and every one with him."

"But they may kill me as I go till 'em, taking me for an inemy!"

"Then you won't feel the fire. But you shall be roasted for the wolves."

"Och, Mr. Mody, don't say that, if ye plase! It makes the cowld chills run up me back!"

"The flames will take them out again. No more words—but go!"

Paddy started forward desperately, making a great noise in the bushes. And when he was in sight of the hut he began to call aloud, so that his voice might be recognised. "Don't shoot!" cried he. "I'm Paddy, the Irishman, and not an inemy. I'm only a flag of truce, that all the nations howld sacred as the howly wafer! I haven't the speck of a gun; and sure ye wuddn't fire at an unarmed and defenceless man who has been wid ye——waah!" he screamed, as he was seized by the lurking Skippie.

"Silence!" said Skippie, pulling him toward the hut.

"Ye may well say that, afther ye have taken me breath!" said Paddy.

"Whisper!" said Skippie.

"I can't. Me mammy didn't tache me that. But I kin run!" and he sprang forward with such activity that he was soon sheltered within the hut, where he was surprised to find no one to whom his message could be delivered.

"Where's the owld man?" he asked. "If he's gone, I shall be kilt and roasted alive! Skippie, dear, I forgive all the pranks you've played me, and only beg you'd git me out of the scrape I'm fallen into! What shall I do?"

"Go in there!" said Skippie, pointing toward the fire.

"No!—ye don't mane it! Sure ye wuddn't see me burn meself to save me life! And the minutes are flying like the sparks up the chimbley! I had only a repraive of tin, and half of 'em's gone a'ready!"

"Go in!" said Skippie, seizing the iron bar. "I'm in a hurry."

"In the fire, is it? Divil a bit! If I'm to be burnt, I shall wait till the time's up. And what're ye doing now? Tak care! The back o' the wall's moving, and the house'll tumble down. But that wuddn't save us, as they don't mane to lave wan stone on anither! Be me sowl, it's a door! And there's a howl in the wall!" he continued, in joyful amazement. "And if it lades to the divil himself, I'll in!" And, leaping over the crackling billets, he entered the opening, and the massy rock was pushed back by Skippie, who uttered once more his shrill whistle as he plunged into the woods.

The chamber Paddy was ushered into was illuminated by a small lamp. He stood in the centre and gazed round in utter astonishment. The aged exile and the girls were silently observing him, themselves unseen.

"Be jabers, but this is a quare place! And if Skippie is the divil afther all, it's Paddy himself who is caged! I'm in it now! But I'll sarve him faithfully if there's no worse punishment than to stay in sich comfortable quarthers. Be me sowl, I don't know whether I'm draming or waking. Rouse up, Paddy, and open yer eyes! Where are ye, me boy? Be the howly St. Patrick, it's not a drame, or I couldn't fale me ear when I pinch it! And is it his infarnal majesty who kapes sich nice apartments? I wondher if he allows his paple to ate, too? I smeli mate. And so they ate—and dhrink too, I hope—in the nather ragions. But, Paddy, don't forget the ten minutes! Time's up, by this time. And kin the blackguards come here too? It's meself who hopes not! Wa-ah! Oo-oh!" cried he, starting back, as he perceived Julia and Kate emerging from the dark passage. "And is it yer blissed selves the divil's got? And ye're smiling, too! Or is it fairies me eyes behowld? Och, and wuddn't ye be kind enough, gintle sperits, to tell me whether Paddy's raally slaping or waking?"

"Your eyes are open, Paddy," said Kate; "but still you may be dreaming."

"That's yer voice, I know. And so Paddy's alive, and not roasting at the stake? And this is the rale house of owld Misther Cameron! It's a palace for a king! And there's his honour himself. Och, and I'll deliver me message, onyhow!"

And he did so. The aged exile read the note and listened to Paddy without stirring a muscle.

"Go," said he, "into the balcony, facing the stream, where our foes are awaiting my answer, and say, with your loudest voice, that the usurper's enemy, whom they seek, will hold no converse with them, and defies them!"

"And it must be thrue that we are safe, or sure you wuddn't bid me say sich a thing? The saints be thanked! And Paddy's the boy that'll answer 'em. Plase, now, swate darlints, show me the way to that same balcony, and go wid me, or I might stumble and fall through."

"It is a solid floor, Paddy," said Julia, smiling.

"And it's yerself who considers us safe in this house?"

"Quite safe, Paddy; even if they were to discover the entrance from the hut, one man with a brace of pistols could defend the passage."

"And Paddy's as snug as a bug in a rug!" said he, half singing and half dancing for joy. "And you don't think," said he, "that if the blackguards were to burn the house, I mane the wudden hut, the hate would reach us here?"

"Oh, no doubt their hate would reach us anywhere; but we can defy their malice."

"I don't mane that, but the hot hate of the burning tambers."

"No; they burnt the hut once, and no one suffered."

"Good! Paddy's a fraa man agin! and as lively as an aal. Now, plase, lade me to the balcony, and jist listen at the brave missage I'll spake till 'em!"

Julia and Kate led Paddy to a sort of masked balcony ingeniously carved in the rock, where there had been a fissure, overgrown with ivy and small cedars.

"Now, Misther Mody, where are ye?" he cried, in a loud voice.

"Here! What does he say, Paddy?" responded Moody.

"He ses he won't disgrace himself by howlding any conversation wid sich a set of blackguards as ye are."

"What? What's that?"

"He says ye may all pack off to the divil, and——"

"Why, Paddy," said Julia, "he said no such thing!"

"I know it, Miss Julia. It is an imbillishment of me own."

"And you use the devil for an embellishment," said Kate.

"Och, if the ladies turn agin me, poor Paddy must surrinder!"

"If that's his answer, Paddy, you may come back," said Moody.

"Many thanks to ye, Misther Mody. And could ye tell me what time o' the day it is?"

"Day, Paddy?" observed Kate.

"Double day, miss, since two suns are baming on me."

"There!" said Julia. "Whoever heard a more gallant speech?"

"What do you mean, Paddy?" asked Moody, who, guided by the voice of his messenger, seemed to have drawn nearer to the cliff.

"What do I mane?"

"Yes. I don't understand you. Come back, if my demands be not complied with."

"But, Misther Mody, me time's up long ago, and I'm not going back to be roasted alive. I'm comfortable here, taking care o' the ladies, and I shan't lave 'em as long as they nade a protictor."

"That's very kind in you, Paddy," said Kate. "But, bless me, they're firing at us!"

This was true. More than a score of guns were discharged at the hut and the cliff; and some of the balls, as if attracted by Paddy's voice, bespattered the face of the rock, sending dust and scales into his face, which stung him smartly.

"Who're ye shooting at, ye nasty blackguards?" cried Paddy. "Have ye no betther manners than to be pointing yer falthy irons toward the young ladies?"

"Come in, Paddy!" said Julia. "Don't you hear their feet approaching?"

"If you command it, I must obey," said Paddy, ducking his head at the flash of another volley, and rejoining the party in the large apartment, where the aged exile sat in undisturbed composure.

"They'll niver find us here," said Paddy; "and if it wasn't for the Tories the Indians wud soon lave us. They're great cowards."

"Cowards, Paddy?" said Kate.

"Yis, indade—cowards. I'll tell ye how I put a whole party to flight meself; but I mustn't tell ye——"

"What? Do, Paddy, give us a narrative of your adventures to-day," said Julia.

"I must lave out the bloody part. Yer sinsitive narves couldn't stand it."

"Very well—go on. But, first, tell me where Rose is."

"Rose! Rose, is it? Did ye say Rose, or Solo?"

"Solo is asleep on his couch of leaves. He is safe. But what has become of Rose?"

"I'll tell ye when I'm done. Forty of 'em came to the house, and were afther sculping all they could lay hands on, Misther and Misthress Schooley and——"

"Mercy! You don't mean——"

"No, I don't mane to say ony sich thing. But they intinded to kill 'em if I hadn't riscued 'em."

"And how did you accomplish that?"

"Ye saa, I was up in the loft of the waiving-room, whin——"

"Pray tell us how you happened to be there," said Kate.

"How? How, is it? But that's nayther here nor there. It was the luckiest thing in the world. For they brought in Misther and Misthress Schooley, after they had tomahawked Dinah before me eyes as she was waiving——"

"Oh, Paddy! why did you permit them?"

"Wait a moment, and ye shall hear. It wasn't good

policy to interfare. If I had stopped 'em, they'd've kilt the ould white folks. I waited in silence, looking down in revinge. But when the tomahawks were lifted against the vinerable heads of Misther and Misthress Schooley, I plunged down upon 'em, calling upon the saints to help me! I called so many, the yaller divils thought I had a whole ragiment at me back. They ran off, and I say they are a pack of cowards!"

"Now, Paddy, tell me about Rose."

"Could ye bear it? And are ye prepared to hear the worst?"

"Oh, yes! She *would* linger, to hunt some article of clothing! Poor Rose!"

"She killed an Indian as dead as a hammer!"

"Rose!"

"Her arm was as thick as a traa, and as strong as an elephant's trunk. They threw a tomahawk at her, which struck the bundle of clothes. They were spylt, but they saved her. So she tuk up the hatchet and chapped one of their heads in two."

"Paddy, is that so?"

"I'll take me oath on it!"

"And so Rose was saved!"

"I hope so. But I don't saa how it could be, aither, for she had no praist."

"Priest? Didn't you say she was saved?"

"From the tomahawk. But her clothes couldn't turn the rifle-bullets. They shot her, and she's defunct."

"Oh, poor Rose!"

"She died widout a sthruggle, as Misthress Schooley informed me; and, as she didn't scrame, we may belave she suffered no pain. Don't wape, Miss Julia. Consider what you'd've done if it had been yerself, and be thankful it was no worse."

"Oh, they are burning the house!" cried Kate, hearing the roaring of flames and the yells of the assailants.

The aged recluse, awakened from his reverie, turned his calm countenance toward the young ladies, and besought them not to be alarmed.

"You can now comprehend," said he, smiling, " why the exile did not build a better house in the valley. It was quite good enough to burn, and it was foreseen that such would be its fate."

"There!" cried Julia; "one of the Indians has been killed by somebody. I heard the death-halloo!"

"Probably a shaft from one of my brave Scots posted overhead. They cannot bear to see my poor house, worthless as it is, destroyed by my enemies."

"Mercy on us!" cried Kate; "and what is that?"

"Another familiar sound!" said Julia. "It is the awful signal of blood!"

"It seems to me like the braying of an ass," said the old man.

"And yer ears don't desave ye," said Paddy. "Wan of Quane Asther's guards, who follers us from wan end of creation to anither, rides on a jackass that brays like the divil ivery time he smells blood. I hope the blackguard the Scots have kilt is that same murthering Seneca wolf."

"And can they not mount to the summit of the cliff and slay the poor Scots?" asked Kate.

"They might gain the summit," said Mr. Cameron, "but it would then be deserted. My men have holes, like foxes, to hide in."

"Be me faith!" cried Paddy, "but they'll find 'em! The Indians know how to hunt the foxes. They'll mount up to the top of the house and come down on us. Thirty to one! And it was Paddy who forgot there was any top to the Tower Rock!"

"Your alarm is needless," said the old man. "It is a solid rock. Long before they can cut through my roof, nearly two hundred feet in depth, my son will be here."

"Thrue, yer honour," said Paddy, reassured. "And I'm sure I trust the walls are strong enough to support such a roof as that."

Another fatal shaft from the summit was announced by the furious yells and maledictions of the besiegers, and it was succeeded by a general discharge of their pieces at the precipitous face of the rock. The altitude from which Paddy had spoken to Moody betrayed the locality of the besieged, and the mystery of the means of escape from the smouldering tenement was, in part, explained. It was announced by Moody to his followers that the refugee had retired into a cave whose entrance had hitherto escaped discovery; but he doubted not they would soon find it, when the rich treasure, so often dwelt upon in his speeches, and which had excited the cupidity of his company, would be divided among them.

Fortunately the mass of glowing embers deposited by the consumed hut prevented an immediate approach to the only place of ingress. Nor was it likely that the besiegers would suspect an orifice had been cut in the solid base of the cliff. They would rather look for an excavation under the hut, supposing the diminutive habitation had been erected over the mouth of the cave. And, impelled by this idea, the greater portion of the Tories and Indians were soon engaged in removing the smouldering rubbish from the earth, but still failed to perceive the entrance at the fireplace. The rest were dispersed in various directions, seeking the foe who winged the fatal shafts.

Another terrific yell announced some new event. Kate and Julia clung tremblingly to the aged chief, while Paddy turned pale and glanced toward the darkest recesses of the room.

"Fear not, my children," said Lochiel; "there is no danger. There is but one avenue of approach, and that a child might successfully defend. There are caves also entering into these chambers, which I have recently opened. But they are dark, and seemingly interminable. I have explored them, and do not think they lead to the surface anywhere."

"I saw the dark howls," said Paddy. "And we can hide in 'em if they find us here."

"We must defend the passage," said the exile, "if they discover the door. Listen! I understand it now. Some one has discovered whence the shafts of my faithful Scots are launched. Hark! They are rushing up the valley to attain the summit. But my eagles will have flown when they reach their eyrie. There are innumerable crags, moss-covered fissures, brambles and cedars; and my trusty clansmen are familiar with the hiding-places. Be not alarmed, dear lassies; the old chief will answer for your safety. Go to your couch and rest in peace."

Julia and Kate, yielding to the desire of the aged chief, retired for the night. The old man, left alone, with profound indifference to the machinations of his foes, opened the volume before him, and dwelt in rapture on the pages of the inspired poet.

Paddy was endeavouring to sleep on a bed of rushes in a corner near the aperture of one of the recently-opened passages in the rock. Into this cave it was his determination to plunge if they should be surprised before morning.

His recent fatigues and excitements soon caused him to succumb to the approaches of slumber. But he made many fitful starts and exclamations in his dreams. And once he was roused upon feeling his cheek strangely fanned. He lifted his head and gazed round; and his heart palpitated audibly when he beheld, a short distance from him, two luminous globes, the staring eyes of some frightful visitant. He turned over and groped in a circle round the object of his terror. But the eyes turned too, still fixed steadily on him.

The aged chief continued to bend over the volume, while the lamp flickered dimly, and Paddy crept noiselessly to his side.

"Plase yer honour!" said Paddy.

"Weel!" said the chief, slowly lifting his head.

"Plase yer honour, look yonder! It's the divil!"

"Ye kenna what it is, mon! Why should the de'il come hither? Why should we fear him? Gae to bed. That is ane of my owls, hunting the mice. And if you see a lizard, do not be alarmed, nor seek to injure it. Such creatures are better companions than ungrateful men."

Paddy, reassured both by the words and looks of the chief, returned to his couch.

Without, a solitary Indian stood by the crystal stream near the base of the cliff. He peered through the darkness at the place whence Paddy's voice had proceeded, in height some twenty feet, and, through entangled bush and creeper, distinguished the rays of the lamp within as they shot feebly upward in empty space. Lochiel was too thoughtful to permit them to reach rock or tree so as to betray his locality; but the Indian had perceived them in the atmosphere. He stood with folded arms, gazing with direful intent. Near him, on the margin of the water and opposite the cliff, was a tall hickory-sapling. The dusky son of the forest, when he removed his eyes from the leafy aperture in the cliff, gazed steadfastly at the young tree. After measuring its height as well as possible in the obscurity, he divested himself of his rattling beads, wampum, and silver plates, and placed them beside his gun on the ground. A strong buffalo thong, taken from his leathern pouch, was wrapped loosely round his neck. He then climbed the tree, as a sailor would a mast. There were no branches near the ground, and his ascent was unimpeded until he reached a height equal to that of the aperture in the cliff.

After pausing a few moments and gazing fixedly at the dimly-illuminated fissure, during which neither sound nor motion could be distinguished within, he proceeded upward, even when the stem of the sapling was no greater in diameter than his arm, and swayed to and fro with his weight. Keeping his back on the side next the cliff, he continued to ascend, until, arching over the running stream, the topmost bough of the tree rested against the face of the cliff. The Indian made it fast to a point of rock which projected over the vine-masked balcony, and then, softly detaching himself, obtained a lodgment in the rift where Paddy had been standing. Perfectly motionless, he listened for many moments; but, neither sound of voice nor motion of feet being detected, he entered the chamber.

Guided by the light of the lamp, he approached the table where the white-haired exile still lingered over the entrancing pages of the poet. He gazed cautiously round, and, perceiving no one else in the apartment, glided noiselessly toward the table, his glittering tomahawk brandished in his hand. The old man, unconscious of his approach, was smiling sweetly. This the savage perceived, and paused. Why should he smile? Was it an ambuscade he had plunged into? Certainly not; for the Kacha Manito and not man had made the hickory-tree. But might not the exile be a magician or great prophet? Again he paused. No! If so, why seek security within the rock?

Raising his tomahawk once more, the Indian stepped forward and aimed the fatal blow; but his arm was arrested midway by the teeth of Solo, who had been lying in the dark shadow of the protector of his mistress. The weapon fell clanging upon the stone floor. Releasing the arm, and twice barking sharply, the faithful dog grappled the throat of the Indian and bore him to the earth. The girls, awakened by the sound, sprang up, screaming hysterically, for they believed the place to be in the possession of the enemy. But, seeing no one near, they ran toward the lamp, still flickering on the table in the adjoining apartment. There they beheld the aged exile rising slowly from his great chair, with a finger on the page, that the place might not be lost. At his feet stood Solo over the prostrate Indian, who breathed with difficulty under the pressure of the faithful animal's jaws.

"What is it? who is it?" exclaimed Julia.

"Bless my life!" said the old man, "it is an Indian! How did he find access?"

"It is, indeed!" said Julia, thrusting away the tomahawk with her foot, and ordering Solo to relax his hold. "It is one of the terrible Queen Esther's guards—one of my captors—and the chief who wounded Solo! It is a just retribution."

"The noble animal has saved my life, lassie," said the old man, reluctantly withdrawing his finger from the page. "It was not so much revenge for the injury he had sustained, as the generous impulse to rescue me from death. Noble dog! Cherish him, Julia, my bonnie daughter!"

"Oh, I shall certainly do so!" said Julia, bending over the Indian, whose breathing became easier under the relaxed pressure. "See how bloody!" she continued. "I would not have him die. He might recover. He is a Mingo or Minisink chief."

"Do you surrender?" asked the aged chief. The Indian, still speechless, nevertheless comprehended the meaning of his words, and lifted up his hands beseechingly.

"Where's the Irishman?" asked the old man. "Let him bind his hands."

"Paddy! Where are you, Paddy?" cried Julia and Kate, but no Paddy answered. They sought his couch, and found his bed of rushes, but Paddy himself had vanished; and so they returned to the old man and his captive, the latter being narrowly watched by Solo.

"Stand up," said Mr. Cameron, placing his foot against the savage, "and tell me how you got into my house."

The Indian was soon sufficiently recovered to give the information demanded. He could speak enough English

MR CAMERON AND THE MINGO CHIEF.—P. 314

to make himself imperfectly understood, and his gestures did the rest. The tree was remembered, but no one had ever thought it could be made the means of gaining access to the apartments; and the old man smiled at the ingenuity of the savage, and felt satisfied that his little fortress was well enough guarded at all other points, and was not likely to have many assailants from the quarter whence the Indian had found an entrance.

"Pronounce his doom, my bonnie lassies," said the aged chief, drawing forth a pistol from beneath his chair.

"Oh, do not kill him!" exclaimed the girls. "He may become a friend, if his life be spared."

"He has penetrated my secret. His eyes are even now glancing at my little wealth scattered about the room——"

"Still, it will be out of their power to reach us. They will retire to their own country, and you will not be molested again!" said Julia, pleading for the life of the captive.

"I have no pleasure in slaying my foes, my dear children," said the old man, replacing the pistol. "Lead him to the balcony, and tell him he is free."

The savage understood him, and offered his hand in token of gratitude. It was not refused by the exile, who, a moment after, resumed his seat, and was once more bending over the volume.

Julia motioned the savage to retire toward the balcony, while Kate and herself, preceded by Solo, followed his steps. He cast a wistful glance at his tomahawk lying near the feet of the exile, but did not stoop to pick it up, for the teeth of his vanquisher were still visible.

The enfranchised Indian, by his looks and gestures, expressed to the young ladies the thanks his tongue could not utter. And when he reached the aperture, through which the early gleams of day were now struggling, he extended his hand to each of them, and bade them a grateful adieu. The next moment he had vanished, having descended the tree without detaching its top from the rock.

Then it was, and just as Julia and Kate turned back to seek their couch in the dim obscurity, that the face of Paddy became visible.

"Who's that?" cried Kate.

"It is Paddy!" said Julia. "Where have you been? Why are you so pale?"

"Pale, is it? It's rage—it's hate—I'm furious, because you lit him go. I wud've sculped the blackguard!"

"Why were you not present, Paddy, when we were deciding his fate?"

"Och, and if I wasn't there, I couldn't help it. It was no fault of mine, Miss Julia. I sprung up when the dog barked, thinking the whole gang was on us. I was half aslape, and couldn't saa objects distinctly; and so I got into the dark hole, where I couldn't behowld me hand before me eyes. There I stood with me knife and gun, thinking the savages had got in that way, and detarmined to defind the passage to the last dhrop of me blood. And this explanation, I hope, ye will repate for me to the owld chafe."

And, saying this, Paddy likewise returned to his couch.

CHAPTER XXIV.

DESPERATE ATTEMPT—THE PANTHER AND THE EAGLE.

The rising of the sun, its crimson rays streaming over the misty summits of the mountains, was the signal for a renewal of the fierce shouts of the implacable enemy.

A portion of the besiegers had ascended to the summit of the cliff. But the small band of defenders posted there the preceding day had vanished. Yet Moody congratulated himself upon the occupancy of positions which were calculated to effect his diabolical purpose. The besieged could not escape without falling into his hands, nor could succour reach them without first entering his ambuscade.

The aged chief, unmindful of the machinations of his foes, again entertained the maidens with anecdotes of Charles Edward after the disaster at Culloden, and described particularly the conduct of Flora Macdonald, exhibiting her miniature executed in Paris; and the admiration of the girls was not diminished by the assurance that Flora, like Lochiel himself, was at that moment sojourning in America.

But Paddy's views could not be confined within the narrow limits of his rock-bound habitation. And so he wandered to the balcony, and peeped out from behind the ivy-vines and cedar-bushes.

A single glance sufficed to appal him. A dozen Tories and Indians were grouped around the slender sapling, the topmost bough of which still remained attached to the point of jutting rock, bound by the strong cord of buffalo-hide.

They stood in silent wonder or whispered consultation, heedless of the dangerous proximity of the besieged. But no shot had been fired at them in the night, and it was inferred the old man had no arms, or was, like the Moravians and Quakers, averse to shedding blood. It did not occur to them that one of their own number (the Indian who had ascended the tree being absent) had used the sapling to gain access to the masked opening in the cliff, which, from the location of Paddy in the night when declaring the decision of the aged chief, they were now convinced communicated with the cave that contained the victims they had doomed to destruction.

"Some one of their friends got in during the night," said Moody. "And if a white man can enter, why can't an Indian?"

This was succeeded by "ughs!" of approbation, and several of the Senecas volunteered to make the attempt. At that moment the Indian who had climbed the tree joined them; and, as he was a famous adventurer, and one of the bravest men of the party, Moody was surprised to see him sit down and muse in silence.

"Will you not go first?" he asked.

"No! Me no go!" was the abrupt response. And Moody turned away, and bestowed his praises on the intrepid chief already ascending.

"Misther Cameron! Misther Cameron!" cried Paddy, rushing into the presence of the old man.

"Weel? Speak, mon."

"Plase yer honour, I want a gun or a pisthol. They're standing down there by the straine, and in full view o' me, and I want to give 'em a broadside from the balcony."

"Pooh! And why? Why would you shed their blude? Ane or twa more or less will make na difference. Be merciful, mon, and save thy valour for the moment when fighting is necessary. You shall not disturb them."

And, turning to the girls, the old man resumed his narrative with perfect unconcern. But he had not proceeded far before Paddy returned, pale and trembling.

"Misther Cameron! They're coming! They'll be here in a minute! They're climbing in at the winder! We'll be murthered!"

"Don't be alarmed, my children," said the old man, rising. "The thong must be cut, and then they will desist."

"Let Paddy do it!" said Julia. "Do not go yourself, sir!"

"Plase yer honour," said Paddy, quickly, "me knife's too dull!"

"Take my dirk," said Mr. Cameron, offering the polished blade.

"And plase let me have the loan of yer pisthol, for fear wan of 'em may be in."

"And Solo shall accompany you," said Julia.

Paddy returned cautiously and reluctantly to the balcony, accompanied by the girls and followed by Solo. The Indian had not reached the face of the cliff, but was within a few feet of it, and making rapid progress in the perilous ascent. By a spasmodic effort, Paddy, after giving the pistol to Julia, succeeded in severing the cord. The elastic sapling sprang back to its original position, and hurled the adventurous climber some fifty feet into the brushwood, through which he plunged with great force, crashing among the boughs, and finally fell to the earth, amid the shouts and laughter of the spectators.

The Indian, unhurt, but greatly exasperated, emerged from the bushes, and threw his tomahawk in the direction of the half-concealed aperture.

"Dodge!" cried Paddy, falling down on his knees, while the girls, supposing a volley was about being fired at them, involuntarily followed his example; and the next instant the tomahawk, glancing from the side of the orifice, fell harmless at their feet.

Moody soon after announced to his followers that he had conceived a plan by which they could obtain an entrance. And when he explained his scheme the whoops of the savages were almost deafening. They were seen running in different directions and gathering materials for the fabrication of a rope of sufficient length and strength to convey the men from the summit of the cliff down to the opening that had been discovered in its side. This was speedily accomplished, for the Indians have nimble fingers; and their exultant halloo, the meaning of which Julia perfectly comprehended, burst upon the air and was reverberated in the valleys.

The great cable, composed of hempen strings, hair, and hides, was tied to a rock on the apex of the cliff and within a few feet of the edge of the precipice. Here the scene was wild in the extreme. A few cedars and thorns, dwarfed in their growth for the want of soil, from exposure to the chilling blasts of winter and the excessive heats of summer, comprised the sparse vegetation of the spot, which seemed a locality never designed for the presence of man, savage or civilized. But now, like demons of mischief, the fell Indians and Tories, their faces bathed in the red rays of the morning sun, flitted hither and thither on the dreary apex of the summit, making the solitary place more hideous by their whoops and grimaces.

The summit of the cliff jutted over its base, so that those above, who were to lower their companions, could not see the aperture. Therefore the party was divided, one half remaining below, and the air was filled with their loudly-shouted communications.

It was decided that the cable should reach down to the stream below, to be ascended or descended, as might be the most practicable and advantageous.

The first Indian who ventured over the precipice was furiously assailed by an enormous eagle, having its nest on one of the ledges or shelves inaccessible to all animals not possessing wings or incapable of suspending themselves in mid-air. The brave bird, seeing the dusky savage approaching its young, uttered a shrill scream and darted at him, and the Indian's head-dress of feathers and tinsel was scattered in fragments on the wind. Descending again like a bolt from a thundercloud, the eagle ripped open with his beak and talons the skin on the shaven crown of the invader of his domestic precincts. A cry of pain startled the spectators, and the next moment the suspended savage relaxed his grasp and fell headlong into the shallow stream beneath, upon whose bed of rocks his body was crushed like the flattened ball of a rifle against a flint-stone! A cry of horror escaped the lips of Julia and Kate, who witnessed the occurrence from the masked balcony, themselves unseen. The friends of the unlucky Indian rushed forward and dragged his mangled corpse from the water. A broken shaft of an arrow floating down the current attracted no attention, or was supposed to have belonged to the unfortunate adventurer. His body was covered with wounds, and no minute examination was instituted, as the fall alone had been sufficient to produce death.

A second Indian descended the cable, and,—although untouched by the eagle, which, however, did not cease to dart at his head, in defiance of the shots fired at him,—like the first, and precisely at the same place, uttered the death-shriek, and fell upon the same rock at the bottom of the shallow stream.

This time the shaft remained in the body, and a yell of rage succeeded the discovery. But from whence had it been fired? They did not suppose it possible for the Scots to go over the edge of the precipice and find a lodgment in its face. Nor was it possible. But there were hidden paths at the extremity of the cliff, leading along the shelves on its front. With these the Scots were familiar; and these narrow paths were soon discovered by the Indians, burning more furiously than ever for revenge. But it was a fearful place,—a dizzy height,—netted over in some places by creepers and stunted brambles, with ever and anon dwarf cedars growing out of the fissures whose only soil was the decomposed leaves blown thither.

A general search for the hidden foe ensued. All other enterprises were suspended. Like trained bloodhounds, the Indians sought and found the trail of the three or four clansmen, sole defenders of the chief who had, in his native land, commanded a thousand.

Shouts of demoniac joy announced the discovery. Two or three of the boldest Indians precipitately followed it, unheeding the advice of the more aged and experienced warriors, who would have had a consultation upon the best mode of dislodging the enemy.

On they rushed, leaping over rifts and holding by the tenacious cedars, when their progress was suddenly arrested by the ferocious growl of a panther, whose head protruded from a small cave in the rock beside the path and but a few paces before them!"

"Ugh! ugh!" each of the Indians uttered in turn, on beholding the glaring eyes of the beast. The growl had likewise been heard by those below, watching the progress of the young warriors. And when they beheld the head of the animal thrust from the rock, they fired and wounded him. He sprang forward with a cry of rage, and, seizing the foremost of the Indians in the narrow path, they fell together on the rocks beneath, both mangled and dead.

At this juncture a warwhoop was heard in a westerly direction. Moody and the Senecas listened with suspended breath for its repetition, not having immediately comprehended its import amid the confusion of sounds. They knew not whether to look for friends or enemies. They were aware that the remnant of the company of patriots from that vicinity which might survive the slaughter in the valleys of Pennsylvania would soon arrive to the succour of the besieged. They had been assured, however, by Queen Esther and Brandt and Walter Butler, that but few of that little band would escape; and, whatever might be the number of survivors, they would be quickly followed, and perhaps preceded, by Brandt himself and the implacable Queen of the Senecas.

But the warwhoop was not repeated. Moody and his men immediately posted themselves in the passes of the intersecting valleys to defend the approaches to the cliff.

This was hardly accomplished, when the aged chieftain, hastily closing the book from which he had been reading aloud to his fair auditors, while Paddy slumbered in oblivious security, announced the approach of Charles.

"Thank heaven!" exclaimed Julia; "but how have you learned it?"

"My bonnie lassie kens not the meaning of the air played on the horn by my brave clansman hidden in the cliff. The young chief advances! My boy survives, and I shall once more clasp him in my arms!"

"Thank heaven!" repeated Julia. "But, sir, are we not here surrounded by the enemy? And may he not fall before our eyes?"

"He will sweep them away like the mist of the morning! Our cage will be opened, and my pretty birds will bask again in their native air and flutter in the sunshine. Listen!" continued the old man, leading the way to the balcony. "That is the *Oolah* of the Senecas! They are already flying before my victorious Charlie!"

It was true; but they were retreating toward the cliff, resolved to prevent any communication with it by a desperate stand at the stream that swept round its base. With their backs toward the besieged, and sheltered in front by the embankment of the stream, the bushes and trees, Moody and his party awaited the approach of the rescuers.

"Be me sowl!" cried Paddy, gazing down at the backs of the Tories and Indians, "it sames to me it would be a bloody shame not to help our frinds who are going to fight for us! Plase, sir," he continued, "let us open a masked battery on 'em behint, and show 'em we have the courage to fight."

"Oh, sir," said Julia, "let me unite with Paddy in beseeching you to render whatever assistance may be in your power!"

"It shall be done, my lassie!" said the roused chief.

He then directed Paddy to bring forth some half a dozen brace of pistols. These he charged with powder only, saying it was not necessary to spill blood in repelling such a foe. No shot having been fired from the cliff, the enemy naturally supposed they were unprovided with weapons; and when the pistols should be discharged in quick succession, the panic would be complete, for the inference that succours had entered the garrison would be unavoidable. But this must be done at the proper time, and he give the signal. Soon, the close proximity of the rescuers was announced by a simultaneous discharge of rifles, both from the embankment and from the trees and bushes on the level space beyond. The floating clouds of smoke prevented the spectators in the fissure from having more than fitful glances of the conflict; but the fire, once begun, was continued without intermission, accompanied by shouts and yells and the death-shrieks of the fallen. The fiercest intensity of the struggle fluctuated from right to left, as the combatants strove to outflank each other. The awful braying of the ass, still retained by the Senecas, announced that blood was flowing; and the continued barking of the little brown dog, ever and anon flitting in view, was proof of Van Wiggens being among the survivors.

"Now let us surprise them!" said the old man. "There are four of us, and if we fire in quick succession they will suppose there are eight guns in their rear. Besides, I see my faithful men on the cliff are plying their arrows."

He was obeyed. And the demonstration was crowned with complete success. Moody, appalled, was the first to give way, and his Tories followed him. The Indians could not maintain the conflict alone, and soon fled after them. Crossing the shallow stream, and passing over the ruins of the burnt hut, they sought shelter in the ravine at the head of the range of cliffs. Here they made another stand, their rifles still partially commanding the position they had relinquished, but not including within their range the ground occupied by Charles.

Charles, convinced that his parent and Julia must be looking down from the aperture, with the location of which he was familiar, advanced into an open space, and waving his hat, was joyfully recognised by those whose prayers were unceasingly uttered for his preservation.

He was joined soon after by Murphy, Van Wiggens, and Peter Shaver, the latter leading the ass, which he had met within the woods, and which it seemed was destined to be ever crossing his path.

"Where's Hugh?" asked the old chief, from the rift in the rock.

"Fallen!" was the sad response.

The old man, pale and sorrowful, bowed his head upon his breast.

"Tam dem!" cried Van Wiggens, as a fresh volley was fired by the Indians, the only effect of which was a slight wound in the ear of Watch, who uttered a sharp cry and shook off the blood.

"Hide yourself, my son!" cried the old man, "or come hither immediately; else they will slay you before my eyes. It is my little treasure and your life they seek!"

"I cannot abandon my brave men, father," said Charles. "And the battle is not over yet. We have been followed by Brandt and a few of his bravest warriors, urged on by the bloodthirsty Esther! She murdered my men who became their prisoners with her own wrinkled hands! And

Brandt, whom I loved and called my brother, seeks to slay me, believing I killed his sister. Twice have I spared his life, hoping to make him hear my denial, but I was disappointed. When he listens to me, and believes me, as he must, he will retire. I hear him now! That is his terrible warwhoop! Spare him, my brave men! Spare him, for my sake, and for the sake of his poor murdered sister. Let me speak with him, and we shall be reconciled."

When he ceased speaking, the junction of Brandt with Moody and his Senecas was announced by the most deafening yells.

CHAPTER XXV.

MEETING OF THE FOREST BROTHERS.

THE battle was renewed. The enemy poured down the narrow ravine into the broader valley, led by Brandt, who called aloud upon White Eagle to come forward and decide the contest by single combat.

And when the Senecas, Mohawks, and Tories returned to the cliff in such overwhelming numbers that Charles was forced to retire over the stream under cover of the intertwining thicket, the old hag, Queen Esther, stood upon the desolate apex of the knoll at the summit, waving to and fro a staff she termed her sceptre, and mumbling one of her incantations which had great influence over the superstitious minds of the savages. She had a book, in which were kept the names of her victims. The number was then two hundred and ninety-eight, and she declared the White Eagle and his father would make an even three hundred.

It was when Charles was retiring before the impetuous charge of Brandt, that Julia, seized with inexpressible terror, swooned in the arms of Kate. She was borne to the couch where she had slept during the night; but restoratives administered by the old man soon revived her.

"I am not ill," said she, smiling faintly, though still as pallid as ever. "It was a picture of the imagination, perhaps, which flitted athwart my vision. I thought I beheld the bleeding form of Charles borne in the arms of Brandt, who seemed to mourn rather than exult over his fall! Oh, it was terrible! And why should such a scene rise before me in the light of day and in my waking hours? It may be a premonition of the reality! Oh, go, and assist him! He is borne down by superior numbers! Go, Paddy, and fight bravely, for my sake!"

"I will!" said Paddy, bustling about. "Be me sowl, I'll kill ivery divil of 'em that comes within me range. Give me all the pistols! Paddy'll show 'em fates of valour this blissed day!" And, saying this, he withdrew, but did not join the combatants.

Brandt led the way over the stream, being some twenty paces in advance of his party; and, although several of them fell, victims of the deadly aim of the concealed remnant of patriots, the great chief himself sustained no injury. And Charles, although exposed more than any of his party, likewise remained untouched. Brandt had ordered his men to spare him, not that his life might be saved, but that he might be reserved for his own hand.

And soon they met face to face in a small opening in the forest. Brandt was pursuing his intended victim, who, perceiving it, had purposely separated himself from his party.

"Three times have I spared my brother's life," said Charles, lowering his rifle, and stepping boldly out from behind a holly-tree.

"And you did so because you had already shed enough of the blood of Thayendanegea!" was Brandt's reply, as he paused abruptly, frowning fiercely, his tomahawk brandished in his right hand.

"No, my brother, it was not so. It was because I desired to convince you that never a drop of my poor sister's blood was shed by me."

"And can you do so? Does the White Eagle say he did not shed the blood of the Brown Thrush?"

"Listen, Thayendanegea. We were boys together. We bathed in the same streams by sunlight and by moonlight, or when naught but the feeble rays of the distant stars twinkled upon us through the broad leaves of the sycamore. Then we clung to each other in confidence, and the Kacha Manito smiled upon our affection. I have not changed."

"Not changed! We bathed in the limpid Wyalusing, beside the wigwam of my people. The smoke of the council-fire ascended the blue sky. The tassels of the corn bent under the weight of the bees, whose hum filled all the air with music. All was peace and happiness. Not changed! Who has made the home of my people desolate? The corn is trodden under foot, the wigwam is in ashes, and the Wyalusing encrimsoned with blood! And who wrought this destruction? Why, the army of Sullivan, sent thither by the great village-burner, Washington, whom you serve! Not changed!"

"My brother cannot have forgotten who were the first aggressors. But I speak not of war. I say my heart has not changed!"

"But you have not said you did not slay my sister,—she who loved you and sang by your couch when you slept."

"I do say it."

"White Eagle once was incapable of lying. If he had not changed, I could not avoid believing him. But the white man has the ingenuity to prove the guilty innocent and the innocent guilty,—to make solemn oaths to dire falsehoods, the word meaning one thing, the act another. False! false! Not changed!"

"No; not changed. I make no solemn oath. I merely tell thee that I am innocent of thy sister's blood. If I lie, strike me dead, and send me with the falsehood on my tongue before the Great Spirit who judges all things. Strike! There is my rifle on the ground. Thy brother will make no resistance, nor shrink from the blow!"

"Oh, my brother!" exclaimed Thayendanegea, dashing his tomahawk to the earth, "I see the truth in thy tears. Let us clasp hands. Though separated, we shall be brothers still. They made me believe thee guilty. And who lied to me? Esther! she, more cruel than the Senecas, and a pale-face! Oh, my brother, she hath written thy name in her roll of victims! I may not save you. But this hand shall be guiltless of my brother's blood, and I will do all in my power to shield you."

"And, Thayendanegea," said Charles, "I here declare that, if I survive, my voice shall be heard in behalf of my forest brothers and sisters. Go back to your people, my brother,—to the nations which acknowledge you as their king,—and tell them they have been deceived. America will be free. To Washington they must look for protection. The British armies will be beaten, and who then will be their friends?"

"Friends? And who are the friends of the Indians?—those who pay them for the scalps of the enemy, or those who take the land which the Great Spirit bestowed upon them?"

"You will be paid for the land."

"Paid? And when we must sell our inheritance against our will, who is it that shall name the price? Alas! it must be so. I see it. The Indian is doomed. But, in the land of spirits, in the great hunting-grounds beyond the grave, he will be at peace. Then those who despoiled him of his fair country will rend each other. The lords of the forest must give way to the corrupt hordes of civilized criminals. They vanish like shadows into the land of spirits, to be at peace forever. But behold their successors, religious, virtuous, with written laws. See their destiny prefigured in the more than savage cruelty of Esther, the white woman. Yes, they will slay one another,—their religion a source of incessant hatred and contention, their virtues mocked at by scaffolds and prisons, and the law but the sword of the majority wrought for the destruction of the rest. Farewell, my brother. I will return to the last abiding-place of the deer and the wolf."

"Hark! what sound was that?" exclaimed Charles, turning his face toward the cliff, whose summit alone he could see from his position, and where he beheld the frantic gesticulations of the old fury—who likewise heard the sound—summoning the Senecas around her.

"It is the drum and fife of the white man," said Brandt. "They are coming to drive back the poor Indian from the last of his beautiful valleys. They will hurl us hence as the storm-wind rolls the foaming serf on the burning sands; but they cannot restore the dead to life. And it was necessary to appease the Malcha Manito by offering a certain number of victims. But enough has been done. I see a white flag approaching, and I will assemble my followers around me."

He then uttered the rallying-halloo, and commanded a cessation of hostilities; and, that his brother might not be mistaken for a doomed prisoner, he laid his arm on his shoulder, and they advanced together to the sparkling stream, where friend and foe were soon mingling in conscious security, and Charles was hailed with joy by the inmates of the excavated rock.

A company of Wayne's men had arrived from the glorious field of Monmouth. The British had retired beaten from the bloody plains of New Jersey, and detachments were sent from the American army to repel the aggressions of the Tories and Indians on the borders.

The first one recognised by Charles was the Rev. David Jones, at whose solicitation the company from Wayne's brigade had been marched in that direction. He was welcomed, likewise, by Julia, whose voice he heard and knew, although he could scarcely see her through the clustering foliage; and the aged exile would not permit the girls to join their friends below until the last of his treacherous foes led by Moody should depart.

"What have you to propose?" demanded Brandt, still encircling the neck of Charles with his arm, as if he feared the doomed victim of Esther might fall in his presence. "What do you demand of us?" he continued, addressing the captain of the company of Continentals. "You are about fifty in number. We can count ninety."

"Including the Tories," observed the officer.

"No matter who is included, so they are well armed and ready for action. I am Brandt, of whom you may have heard much, and probably much that is untrue. But he is your enemy. Yet he did not come hither to wage war, but to slay the supposed murderer of his sister. He was innocent. He is still my brother. For the last time my arm is round the neck of my brother, and we shall soon part to meet no more. I will return to that remnant of the broad country which was once all our own. Shall I go in peace, or must I fight my way thither?"

"Go in peace. We shall not be the first to break it," said the officer.

Brandt then spoke in a loud voice to Esther and Moody, who were on the summit of the cliff, surrounded by their followers. He told them that his brother was innocent of his sister's blood, and that the one who injured him would be the foe of Thayendanegea. And he said he had agreed to a suspension of hostilities on the eastern side of the Delaware. Then, by the authority vested in him as Grand Sachem of the Six Nations, he commanded the Indians to return to the Delaware.

"And now, my brother," said he, embracing Charles, "we are reconciled, but we part. Let us never be foes again. Believe not the extravagant stories told of the Mohawk chief, and no one shall slander the White Eagle. Farewell!"

And then, averting his face, Brandt strode away toward the dense forest. But he had only proceeded a few steps when the report of a rifle rang in his ear. His first glance was toward the crest of the cliff, where the small cloud of smoke still lingered. His next was at Charles, who staggered forward, and would have fallen, if the great chief had not caught him in his arms.

A prolonged, thrilling shriek was heard at the cliff. Then the heavy door was swung back upon the blackened fireplace of the consumed hut, and Julia sprang forth and glided frantically toward her beloved. Neither rocks nor streams nor armed men impeded her course. Her white robe streaming in the air, her hair hanging down dishevelled, she rushed forward and threw her arms around her wounded lover's neck. Brandt relinquished his burden, and, hastily uttering a few words to the astounded officer, leaped across the stream like an enraged tiger after his prey. Before a gun was raised by the astonished soldiers, the great chief was seen again upon the dizzy height, with his hand grasping the throat of the murderer.

"He confesses the deed!" cried Brandt. "And he it was who killed my sister. Behold the vengeance of Thayendanegea!"

He plunged his knife into the breast of the guilty savage, who sank down at his feet without a struggle. And before the eyes of the spectators could be turned again in the direction of the fallen youth, the gigantic chief dragged the murderer forward and hurled him over the precipice!

"Cold! cold!" said Julia, sitting on the ground, with the head of the speechless and dying Charles resting against her bosom. "Cold! cold!" she continued, kissing his lips, "and very, very pale!" But the youth was no paler than herself as she gazed with unmoistened eyes upon his face. "No! no!" said she, when the white-headed father of Charles came forward, weeping bitterly, and would have snatched him from her arms. "He's mine!" said she. "You shall not tear him away! But the damp earth must receive him! I will bury him, and I will remain bending over his grave, like the willow. But I do not weep. I cannot weep. Why is it so, Kate?" she continued, seeing the tears of her companion. "*You* know I loved him, Kate. Then why do not the tears gush forth? Mr. Jones, cannot you tell me? Oh, you need not feel his pulse, my friend. He smiled sweetly—it was for me alone, and I understood it—and then like the sighing zephyr his spirit passed away. And, Kate, he died in my arms. And I do not weep. If I cannot shed tears, I will sing—sing the rest of my days. Singing is better than weeping. And yet every one around is shedding tears! Am I not a very strange girl, Kate? Do not despise me; I cannot help it."

"Skippie," cried the poor old man to his faithful servant, sobbing at his side, "we will go to France. Make all the arrangements. And when I, too, am dead, take my body to Scotland. Then come hither, and convey thence to the same grave the bones of my son."

"No! They are mine!" cried Julia. "Although I do not weep like the rest, we were plighted lovers. I was his and he was mine—mine forever. We were one. Before God and man our hearts were joined together. No throb in his but vibrated in mine. He weeps not now, and I do not weep. He is dead, and I, too, am dead to the world. But I will love you still, Kate. And you will help me to plant flowers over his grave. I cannot dew them with my tears; but my Maker will send refreshing showers, will he not, Mr. Jones?"

"Come, my poor child!" said the sighing Baptist, gently removing her from the body. "This is no place for you. Come with me to the house of your guardian."

"Will they bear him thither?" asked Julia, in a low whisper, clinging to the preacher's arm.

"Yes, if you desire it."

"Desire it?" said she, her brilliant orbs fixed upon the

soldiers and others surrounding the body. "I COMMAND it!" she cried, in a loud voice. "There is a willow," she added, "with a million drooping boughs, near the council-tree beside the brook, where our vows were plighted. There they shall bury him. Come, Kate; they will follow us. You must not leave me to-day. I know your father has sent for you, and for me too, but we will linger a while, won't we? What would he think of me if I appeared before him with no tear in my eye? But, Kate," she continued, in a sweet, sad voice, as her arm encircled the waist of her sobbing companion, "my heart is broken. There is a cold spot upon it. It can never be warm again. Pity me, Kate. I am very miserable. And see his poor father— an exile in a strange land, bending over his murdered son! It was the work of the cruel Esther. O God! vengeance belongs to thee! I would not crush the smallest worm in my path. Enough of that! I alone am talking, while the rest do nothing but weep; and I feel as one standing on some dreary rock between the living and the dead; and death has no terrors, for he smiled in death. Come! But Solo remains. See!" she continued, glancing back, "my poor Solo lies beside the body. Stay there, Solo, and see that they bring him to thy mistress."

Pale and tearless, the poor maiden was led away. The body was soon after borne along the same path, and the next day it was placed under the willow. But Julia never wept. She only chanted the incoherent ballad which her disordered mind seemed to be ever composing.

Lochiel, bowed with grief and the weight of years, departed soon after in one of the French ships, and died in Paris.

After lingering a few days over the grave of the murdered youth, Julia and Kate were conducted, by the Rev. Mr. Jones, to the residence of Governor Livingston, near which were again established the head-quarters of Washington.

CHAPTER XXVI.

CONCLUSION.

Mr. Schooley and his son Richard were plunged into the depths of misery. The cause of King George was now truly desperate, and no one really supposed the United States could ever be conquered. Already the civil authorities were confiscating the estates of those who had given aid to the enemy. And, as friend Thomas was aware that the fact of the sale of his droves of cattle to the British could not remain unknown, he was endeavouring to summon the fortitude to bear with Christian humility the loss of all he held most dear in the world. His only hope was in his ward. Her intellects were wandering, and, if she remained *non compos mentis*, his legal guardianship might be prolonged. Her estate could not be forfeited. But then she was a guest at "Liberty Hall," the residence of the governor, and Thomas could have no controversy with him.

Paddy remained on the farm, at the special request of Julia, who charged him to watch the grave of her loved one during her absence. And Peter Shaver was the overseer when Mr. Schooley returned to Burlington. Peter retained his ass till his death, which occurred some fifteen years subsequently. The poor animal, which had been so often shocked at the spilling of blood, was ever an object of curiosity to the neighbours.

Mr. Van Wiggens, although he could never reconcile "Vatch" to the black tomcat of his spouse, had the sagacity to keep Mrs. Van Wiggens herself in a proper state of conjugal subjection, by means of his pet bear, which he chained to one of the posts of the porch of the inn.

Solo was the constant companion of his mistress, whose restoration was despaired of by the best surgeons in the army.

The commander-in-chief, dining one day with Governor Livingston, and, having heard some of the particulars of

Julia's history, expressed a desire to see the poor demented maiden. Kate led the benign general into the apartment where Julia was wreathing flowers and forming crowns of laurel. She looked up, and smiled sweetly, but sadly. Her paleness remained, and the wild expression of her eyes seemed not diminished.

Her thoughts were with the dead. Whatever reply she made to the interrogatories of visitors, she invariably reverted to the wild woods and to her departed lover. And her responses were frequently snatches of improvised verses, which, when one beheld her and listened to her mournful but musical voice, seemed the appropriate language of heartbroken maidens.

"I know what you would hear," said she, as the pitying Washington gently pressed her hand. "You would have me repeat my ballad. Listen:—

> "On the gentle Wyalusing,
> In the sultry month of June;
> When the stars begemm'd the heavens,
> And earth was silver'd by the moon——

They say, sir, or I've dreamt it, that wandering among the wild roses by moonlight with him (you shall hear) injured my intellect. But, pray, don't believe them.

> Beside the leaping laughing water,
> When the dusky bats were flying,
> When the whippoorwill was sighing,
> And the katydid was crying,
> When the leaves were trembling o'er us,
> And purest blossoms bloom'd before us,
> Nestling 'gainst his noble——

But, sir, that may be a solemn secret, not to be divulged. Mr. Schooley, my good guardian, says I ought not to sing such things. He is a good man, but I don't think his heart was ever broken. He must have fallen in love in the town, and not in the wild woods. Please, sir, don't let them injure my good guardian. He was very kind to me, and permitted Charles to come whenever he wished.

> Together on the Wyalusing,
> Or the pebbly Pa-pa-kating,
> Or the spreading Susquehanna,
> Or the rushing Lackawanna,
> Or the whispering Kittaning,
> Or the green banks of Neshaming—

> Hand-in-hand we roamed together!
> He was true, and I adored him;
> But the cruel Queen destroy'd him——

I must stop there to breathe, and I'm sure you'll wait. Whenever I come to that part I am seized with a suffocating sensation, and that is the reason why I am panting. They say, if I could weep — but why should I? I know he's in heaven. And will I not go thither? You are a good man, I know, by your face. Say, do you not think I may meet him in heaven? Oh, pray, do not weep for *me!* I cannot weep for *him.*

> "It was 'neath the quiv'ring tree,
> At our feet the brawling brook,
> He declared his love for me
> And——

Mr. Schooley might chide me, if I recited the rest

> "But the earth is his cold pillow;
> He lies beneath the weeping willow.

And, oh! Julia cannot weep for him! Dear sir, I would weep if I could! Won't you believe me?"

"Yes, my dear child," said Washington, bending down and kissing her ivory forehead.

"I thought so! Yes, you may kiss me if you will. They call you the father of your country. I am an orphan. We are good. The good meet in heaven. But do not weep for me. I am not so unhappy as they think. I have my dreams and my fancies, and I know his spirit attends me. Farewell!"

Poor Julia, although undoubtedly impatient for death to relieve her, survived all her youthful acquaintances except Wilted Grass, the Delaware chief. She wandered from the grave of Charles to that of his forest sister on the Kentucky River, ever accompanied by Gentle Moonlight, the Thrush's foster-mother. The faithful Solo was their only protector, until age and infirmities rendered him incapable of following them. Then Julia remained at her farm, sitting daily beneath the weeping willow. And when her gentle companion died, her body was placed beside the lost boy she had nurtured. But Julia remained, probably unconscious of the lapse of time, for many weary years, a lonely dweller among successive generations; and, finally, when she had attained her eightieth year, departed without a groan or a disease, and joined her friends in heaven.

The family of Schooley, tradition avers, removed to England. It is said the politic landlord at Burlington, whom Thomas had established in business, persuaded his patron, after the confiscation of his lands, to seek indemnity for Moody's spoliation, and to pursue William Franklin for the £1000 he owed him. As for the amount due from himself to the Quaker, he (Brown) was "all right," and would reimburse him some day or other.

Bonnel Moody was arrested within the American lines near Morristown, and hung as a spy.

The Rev. David Jones survived to a good old age. And when the second war was waged with Great Britain he again left the pulpit for the field. Many particulars of his life may be found in the "Field-Book of the Revolution."

Kate Livingston, likewise, lived to an extreme old age, and was blessed with a happy family. The only sad moments of her life, after the fearful scenes she had witnessed in the conflict for liberty, were when she visited Julia at her abode near the Rock.

Wilted Grass died only a few years ago near the ocean, in New Jersey, and was buried in the grave of his fathers. The Legislature of the State, shortly before his decease, bestowed a sum of money on the aged chief and the small remnant of Delawares who dwelt with him, as compensation for the destruction of their game. The original grants from the Indians reserved the right of hunting.

Simon Kenton's subsequent career, and Girty's doom, have been portrayed by a skilful limner of Kentucky, in two volumes, one entitled "Simon Kenton," and the other "The Winter Lodge."

Of Boone, the hero of so many legends and romances, it is only necessary for us to say that he died in Missouri, following the buffalo and Indians as they fled before the tide of civilization. Some of the adventures of his old age are described in the first series of "Wild Western Scenes," which may have fallen into the hands of the reader of these pages.

THE END.

www.ingramcontent.com/pod-product-compliance
Lightning Source LLC
Chambersburg PA
CBHW032358230426
43672CB00007B/742